PRAISE FOR

SERGIO ESPOSITO AND

Passion on the Vine

"Without qualification, the best book about Italian wine today, if only because Sergio Esposito understands that its mysterious greatness is in its poetry—the earth, its diurnal magic, the ghosts of great-grandfathers. A beautiful, boldly sentimental memoir."

—*Bill Buford*

"A full-bodied read about one man's passion and the many delectable moments along his journey."

—*Publishers Weekly*

"*Passion on the Vine* is a spellbinding memoir; a vivid, funny, and, yes, passionate tale of family, food, and wine. The tour de force chapter on his childhood in Naples will make you wish you were Italian. Sergio Esposito is not only a great epicurean—he's also a great storyteller."

—*Jay McInerney*

"Full of cousins with deep passions and deeper cleavage, grandmothers preparing bounteous Italian feasts, and wines from every corner of Italy, it reads like a novel."

—*Miami Herald*

"Sergio Esposito's culinary memoir is as delicious as the wines and food he lovingly describes. Well, almost as delicious. His literary talents are already known to those of us who eagerly await his periodic newsletters on the latest Italian wines, but he surpasses himself in *Passion on the Vine*."

—*James B. Stewart*

"Do not read this book on an empty stomach: The author lovingly describes so many exquisite-sounding Italian meals that those without immediate access to fresh mozzarella and artichokes will feel very sorry for themselves . . . A charming tribute to food, drink, and homeland."

—*Kirkus Reviews*

"Esposito's glass is always half-full, when not filled to the brim, and always with something beautifully red and swirling and passionate, as are his words in this wine-adventure, story-memoir. His words are like the vines he so ardently writes about—earthy, deep-rooted; and the wines—perfect on the tongue, with a long finish."

—*Frances Mayes*

"The wine read of the summer."

—*San Francisco Chronicle*

Passion on the Vine

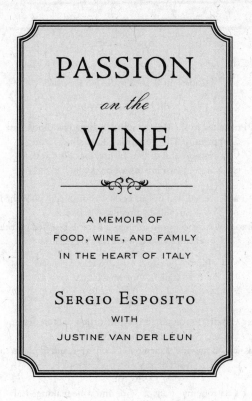

PASSION

on the

VINE

A MEMOIR OF
FOOD, WINE, AND FAMILY
IN THE HEART OF ITALY

Sergio Esposito

WITH

JUSTINE VAN DER LEUN

BROADWAY BOOKS | NEW YORK

LIBRARY OF CONGRESS CATALOGING-IN-PUBLICATION DATA
Esposito, Sergio.
Passion on the vine : a memoir of food, wine, and family in the
heart of Italy / Sergio Esposito.
p. cm.
1. Gastronomy—Italy. 2. Wine and wine making—Italy.
3. Italian Americans—Social life and customs—21st century.
4. Italy—Description and travel. I. Title.

TX641.E88 2008
641'.0130945—dc22
2007032009

ISBN 978-0-7679-2608-9

PRINTED IN THE UNITED STATES OF AMERICA

3 5 7 9 10 8 6 4 2

First Paperback Edition

For Alma Tschantret

CONTENTS

———✦———

CONTENTS

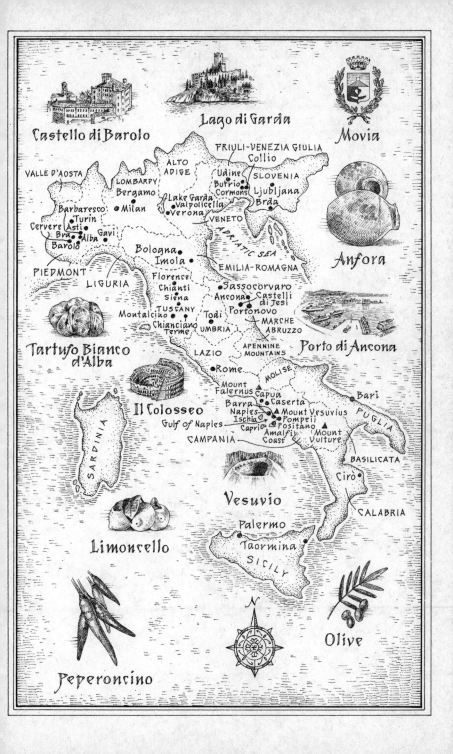

Castello di Barolo

Lago di Garda

Movia

Anfora

Porto di Ancona

Tartufo Bianco d'Alba

Il Colosseo

Vesuvio

Limoncello

Peperoncino

Olive

VALLE D'AOSTA

ALTO ADIGE

FRIULI-VENEZIA GIULIA
Collio

LOMBARDY
Bergamo

Udine
Butrio
Cormons

SLOVENIA

Ljubljana
Brda

Barbaresco
Turin
Cervere Asti
Bra
Barolo
Alba
Gavi

Milan

Lake Garda
Valpolicella
Verona

VENETO

ADRIATIC SEA

PIEDMONT

LIGURIA

Bologna
Imola

EMILIA-ROMAGNA

Florence
Chianti
Siena

Sassocorvaro
Ancona
Castelli
di Jesi

Montalcino

TUSCANY

Todi

Portonovo

MARCHE

Chianciano
Terme

UMBRIA

ABRUZZO

LAZIO

APENNINE
MOUNTAINS

Rome

MOLISE

Mount
Falernus

Capua
Caserta

Bari

Barra
Naples
Ischia
Capri

Mount Vesuvius
Pompeii
Positano
Amalfi
Coast

PUGLIA

Gulf of Naples

CAMPANIA

Mount
Vulture

BASILICATA

Ciro

SARDINIA

Palermo

CALABRIA

Taormina

SICILY

N

Passion on the Vine

Chapter 1

ROME

❦

WE'D LEFT BEHIND the south's sharp ocean inlets—its black volcanoes pasted against orange evening skies, its lemon groves and crumbling villages—for Rome. We followed the A1 Autostrada del Sole, the Highway of the Sun, which cuts through the country, straight from Naples to Milan. It was a two-hour drive, first through lush hills; then through flat farmlands, the standard horse vendors displaying their grazing wares for motorists; then past the withered vineyards, the smoky power plants, the stoic gray roadside corporations, the brightly colored Iperstores, the worker-free construction zones of crushed asphalt and detours, the elaborate Autogrills perched like bridges above the road, the Gypsy camps. We drove by it all and then through the concrete tunnels until we hit the capital, rising up around us in the form of shops and apartments, of ancient statues, baroque palaces, sweeping piazzas. My brother Sal and I had been on the road for days and *la città eterna* was to be our last hurrah before our return to the States.

Our roles in the rental car were always clearly defined: I was the driver, he the navigator. We were finishing up a whirlwind wine-buying trip, so we were pale and exhausted. I own a wine store in New York City and there wasn't a day that passed without some uninformed individual, a dreamy look on his face, telling me I had the world's most wonderful job. Such people thought it was glamorous, floating across the Italian peninsula, sipping wine poured from fine bottles, sleeping in villas on sweeping vineyard grounds. They couldn't be blamed for the misconception; God knows, I'd thought the same thing when I was a kid.

It may be a wonderful job, but it isn't always glamorous. I *had* slept in opulent villas and dined with royals, but usually it went like the most recent trip: in the last seven days, Sal and I had hit up almost sixty wineries and tasted countless bottles of wine. We'd woken up at six and gone to bed at four. We'd eaten at truck stops and at two-star restaurants, gobbled down *panini* in the car, and been forced by our producer-hosts into many long, multicourse, pasta-laden, oil-drenched meals—the kind of experience you'd savor if you did it twice a year, not twice a week. Sometimes it was kind of like working in the world's best cupcake bakery: no matter how much you love cupcakes, you don't want five a day, every day for a week. Sal and I had stayed in some moldy roadside hotels, a couple of simple rooms-for-rent, and one medieval castle; had tasted virtual vinegar and the most beautiful wines in the country. I'd spent time listening to a Russian scam artist who guided wine tours and I'd sat in the office of a wine producer whose family had at one time been commissioned by a king. We'd been social hostages, privileged to be included at the family table but also dragged to Italian discos filled primarily with men in tight pants. This was what a typical tasting trip was like, racing around the country, trying to find the best wines for my clients and for myself.

Sal didn't officially work with me, but he came along because he loved food, he loved wine, he loved the excitement. Round, rosy-cheeked Sal, his head topped with swiftly disappearing red hair, was the reason I was in this business in the first place. He was the one working as a chef, when he was only eighteen, in the little French restaurant in upstate New York, making beef bourguignon and duck à l'orange and chicken cordon bleu to pay for my clothes and my food and my bicycle. He was the one who hired me on as a dishwasher at that restaurant when I was twelve. I would stand on a stool and scrub plates after school, gazing at him with nearly religious devotion as he, baby-faced, clad in a crisp white collarless shirt, yelled at his staff to keep all the knives in place. He was the one who mocked a sous-chef who'd bungled the carving of a leg of veal.

"I bet you my little brother can do a better job than you can," Sal said to the defeated man. I looked up from my dishes and tried to suppress my joy. I was being given the opportunity of a lifetime, threefold: I could humiliate an adult, impress my brother, and cut meat. "Get over here, Sergio. Show them."

He was also the reason I had the thick scar on my left thumb, because as I expertly butchered the shank, I looked about the room proudly, lost track of what I was doing, and sliced my finger to the bone.

Despite the injury, I had gone on to make a career of wine and food, while Sal had branched off into business. Now, in addition to running a software consulting company out in the Arizona desert, he acted as my secretary on trips to Italy. He organized my schedule and kept me company in the car, and his payment was a series of excellent meals and lots of wine, both famous and obscure. Over the past fifteen years, we'd drunk wine from *botti* in Barbaresco, from cement tanks on the Amalfi coast, and from underground urns in freezing Friuli. We'd gambled until dawn at a Slovenian casino, watched an unimpressive show at a blue-collar strip joint in Turin, and spent loud nights with our extended family in the southern Italian ghetto from which we had emigrated long ago. And now we were on our way into Rome for a final meal before our departure for America, and for the most important tasting of the trip—and perhaps of our lives.

I'd had other plans. I wanted to take Sal out to a thank-you dinner at Don Alfonso 1890, a restaurant in Sant'Agata sui Due Golfi, near the coastal village of Sorrento, where we'd gone on vacation when we were kids living in Naples. Don Alfonso was a famous place owned by a well-regarded culinary family, the Iac-carinos. They had long been considered masters of the regional cuisine. A few years earlier, I'd eaten remarkable, refined versions of the area's most traditional dishes, all made from ingredients grown on the family farm.

I'd been talking it up to Sal and we were excited when we sat down in the sleek white dining room. We didn't even bother with the menu. I like to let culinary professionals do their thing: I told the waiter that we'd have whatever the chef recommended. We got a bottle of Mastroberardino Taurasi Riserva and waited. We were expecting lamb that had grazed nearby; spicy olive oil; spaghetti with tomato, basil, garlic; fish caught in the bay; local herbs. Then the first dish was set upon the table.

Sal and I looked at each other. Pineapple and foie gras? When the pasta arrived, it involved cheese foam, not basil. The main meat course was laced with curry. This was not the menu I re-membered. The food was excellent, but Naples is about eggplant, lemons, *mozzarella di bufala,* the flavors of my childhood, the pro-duce that grows on the hills. Foams and curries, fruits and pâtés—these were all fine and good, but they had nothing to do with the seaside zone. We could have been eating the same din-ner in Hong Kong or Paris.

The chef came out of the kitchen—a young, dark-haired man in a white jacket and rubber clogs. He was Ernesto Iaccarino, the newest generation to enter the business. He introduced himself and we began to talk.

"So, what did you think?" he asked. "Did you enjoy your meal?"

"To be honest," I said, "I brought Sal here for the traditional menu I had last time. Things have changed. What happened?"

Ernesto nodded. "We don't serve that anymore," he said. "It's too tough. Reviewers want you to have the food they're accus-tomed to, and they're usually accustomed to French stuff. They want modern touches. They want the foams, the unorthodox flavor combinations. We give them what they want so that we can survive."

It was the scourge of the Michelin star that I recognized. The same thing happened in the world of wine: producers, to keep selling, had taken to shaping their wares according to the tastes of major reviewers. I supposed it was the natural way of things, but it didn't sit well with me.

"But we still do the traditional stuff," Ernesto continued. "We've got a new place in Rome, called Baby. You're still around tomorrow, right? I'm going up there; why don't you let me cook you lunch?"

❧

THAT WAS HOW WE FOUND OURSELVES in Rome so early in the day, circling the Villa Borghese gardens, the former vineyard converted into gardens by a cardinal in the seventeenth century and currently the city's lush and extensive central park, around which cars, scooters, and buses raced. The restaurant Baby was in the majestic Hotel Aldrovandi Palace to one side of the whirling traffic, and I took a sharp right-hand turn to pull up to the grand doors.

The restaurant, situated downstairs from the extravagant lobby, was an ethereal series of rooms in gray and glass overlooking the hotel courtyard. Ernesto emerged, welcomed us, and then pushed back through the steel doors and began to work as the restaurant filled up. I ordered a bottle of Vestini Campagnano Pallagrello Bianco "Le Ortole," a southern white made from grapes picked late in the harvest, the sun having dried them just enough to concentrate their sugars. It smelled of apricots, white flowers, dried honey, and nuts, but to me the value was the images it always conjured up: I usually got the sensation that I was being seduced in a Pompeii brothel before the volcano erupted. Sal and I clinked glasses.

"*Al prossimo Giro d'Italia,*" I said. To the next tour of Italy.

Ernesto first sent out what technically could have been labeled "eggplant parmigiana," but was not in any way comparable to the heavy casserole most Americans understand the dish to be. It was, instead, a delicate piece of vegetable art: sweet local eggplant, sliced thin, layered with mozzarella made that morning and highly acidic tomatoes from the foot of Vesuvius, and drizzled with oil. Not only was it unlike the eggplant parm of American red-tablecloth joints, it was different from my mother's *parmigiana di melanzane*. But we weren't there for some good ol' home cooking. We were there to see how our good ol' home cooking was conceptualized at another level, how the same flavors upon which we were nurtured, the flavors that made us grow, the first, most common tastes for us, were made by the Iaccarino family.

"Now *this* is what you were talking about," Sal said.

Ernesto sent out a pasta next, *ravioli di caciotta al pomodorino e basilico,* pasta made with flour and olive oil—not with flour and eggs, as is typical in most of Italy. The pockets were the size of a quarter and filled with caciotta—a sheep's milk ricotta—seasoned with wild marjoram, prepared in small baskets and drained of their liquid, and then topped with little tomatoes, a play on the palate between the flavors of tangy cheese and sharp tomato.

"I could eat this every single day," I told the waiter. "For my entire life."

The meal reached its peak with the *arrosto di piccione con passato di ceci.* I couldn't figure out exactly how he roasted the squab to so perfectly caramelize the outer skin. But the true beauty of the thing was that the tiny breast was set atop a chickpea purée seasoned with cinnamon, and when I ate it—the bright young peas, the sparkling fresh spice, the crispy bird—I felt that I was somehow tasting liquid gold. Sal's expression told me that his experience was similar.

After some time, dessert came out: *pasticcio di melanzane con cioccolata,* squares of sponge cake topped with sweetened ricotta and studded with candied fruit and chocolate pieces. Slices of steamed eggplant—*dolce,* sweet, like only eggplants grown on Mediterranean soil can be—were placed on top of the mixture, and the whole creation was covered with a white chocolate sauce flavored with Marsala. Eggplant, it seems, was Ernesto's guest of honor that season.

Ernesto stopped by the table as we were drinking our espresso. "Traditional enough?" he asked. "Did you get what you were looking for?"

Ernesto had indeed done for us what a great chef does for his diner. He'd presented us with artistry—we'd consumed dishes that were the culmination of his vision, talent, history. Sure, you can standardize a great meal and serve it anywhere in the world, just as you might have watched Luciano Pavarotti perform in a great opera in Istanbul. But there was an added value to seeing Pavarotti sing an aria at La Scala in Milan; it was more illuminating to see the man in his element. The meal at Baby was a postcard from the south of Italy, made by a southerner with southern ingredients, with respect to tradition—to the long line of people before him who'd shaped the cuisine—and with respect to the land. Ernesto made us food of the region, the season, the place. You could make the meal all over again in Los Angeles, following a recipe with scientific precision, and it wouldn't be anything like it.

"I'd say we got what we came for," I answered. "Thank you."

But we had actually come to Rome for two things, and the second was far more significant. We'd come to drink some extremely rare wine, and by the time we'd finished up the lunch and I looked at my watch, we were late.

૭৵

I GRABBED SAL and rushed him to the street. I'd leave the car at the Aldrovandi because we didn't have time to find parking. I spotted a yellow cab smushed in the middle of the mass of Roman traffic, of two-seater cars and motorcycles, all weaving at an alarming speed through the narrow streets. The driver of the cab also saw me, and, with a calm expression on his worn face, he cut through the metallic throng. It parted, just barely, for him, and everyone honked aggressively.

"The St. Regis, please," I said. "You know it?"

"Of course I know it," the cabbie said. "Best hotel in Rome."

"Fast as you can," I said. I rubbed my temples.

"But Sergio, since when do you get nervous about being late to a tasting?" Sal asked. "I don't think I've ever seen you arrive on time."

Sal couldn't yet understand, but this was no regular tasting, not for me and not for him. I had bought these singular and particular wines a few months back, every case that existed in the world, and I was now having them all shipped to my New York wineshop. This was a gathering that involved a bunch of Italian journalists who wanted to taste the stuff before it left the country forever, but I didn't care about them. I was anxious, really, to see what Sal thought. He was my litmus test for sellable wines—a born Italian who was now essentially American, a noncollector and a nonprofessional with a good palate, somebody who didn't go for cookie-cutter drinks, for easy new styles. If Sal, who liked all things wild, strange, and beautiful, understood these wines, they had a real future in my store. If not, I'd be crushed.

"It's too complicated to explain right now," I told my brother. "I made a promise to a dying man. That was six months ago, when he was still alive, and these were his bottles."

Sal nodded, perplexed. "That does sound complicated," he said as we pulled up to the St. Regis. It was large and gothic, flags hanging from its elegantly carved stone doorway.

❧

THE HOTEL ITSELF was also known as the Grand Hotel, and it was essentially an immense artisanal work. The bottom of each step on the winding staircase was carved with faces and flowers, the banisters were composed of wrought-iron leaves, and the ceilings were painted with Renaissance-era murals. There was an imposing, gleaming ballroom, and the halls were punctuated with red and gold chairs. Inexplicably, amid all the stately opulence, there was, to the side of the lobby, a brightly lit glass box that contained a human-sized mannequin of a crow dressed in an expensive suit.

My friend and partner in Italy, Andrea Carelli, met us near the hotel restaurant, a low-lit modern establishment where the waiters and diners spoke in hushed tones and dressed in tailored designer wear.

"The Esposito brothers!" Andrea exclaimed, and kissed our cheeks. "A half hour behind, as always!"

We walked to the end of the restaurant and pushed our way through a gauzy silver curtain into the compact private dining room, a space called the Champagnerie. A dozen journalists and one former television host awaited us; they were seated in gray velour high-back chairs at the long, glossy table, twelve shining wine glasses in front of each of them. To the side, on a counter, sat twelve clear bottles of golden wine. I looked at the walls: two airbrushed amateur paintings of girls, one sleeping in blue flowers, and the other sitting with her head in her hands, surrounded by a wash of purple.

The former television host, acting as MC, rose to address the group. He gave a short lecture on the history of the wines, and then fanned his arm toward the counter. "And now, ladies and gentlemen," he said, "the great wines that have been awarded to Signor Andrea Carelli and Signor Sergio Esposito!" The journalists clapped softly and a sommelier began opening the bottles, pulling out the corks, pouring the drinks into the glasses in an elaborate ritual of rinsing and swirling. As people began tasting the wines, I focused my attention on Sal, sitting a few seats away. The journalists were scribbling notes. Andrea and the former TV host were next to each other, encased in silence and nostalgia— they had drunk these wines together before, many months ago.

Sal, I noted, had been trying and retrying each vintage in an almost fevered state, as though attempting to piece together a puzzle. He put his nose in the glass, pulled up the perfume, and wrinkled his forehead. Then he did it again. His expression telegraphed the question: What the hell is this?

After ten minutes I walked over to him. "So, what do you think?" I asked, leaning down.

"These may be the weirdest wines I've ever tasted in my entire life." He went back to the glass, swirling the liquid, looking at it. He took another sip and frowned. Then his face opened up and he smiled widely. "But I'm pretty sure they're also the best."

I took my own sip, and remembered the day I first tried the wine, in a village in the middle of the mountains, sitting across from a new friend. That friend was no longer with us, yet his memory remained, somehow, within the wine.

Sal leaned in toward me. "So, Sergio, who is this mystery man?" he asked. "And what, exactly, did you promise him?"

Chapter 2

BARRA

꿈꿈

TO GET FROM THE TABLE in Rome to the place where I took
my first sip of wine, you must travel south 150 miles and back
thirty years. Take the A1, follow the Tangenziale di Napoli, exit at
San Giovanni a Teduccio, turn left onto the street with the bakery on the corner, make your way through the winding roads,
packed tight in between buildings, lined with teenage boys selling strawberries and asparagus. Park between the miniature
cars smushed together, wheels up on the sidewalks, and enter
the flat white cement building on the corner. There, in a two-
bedroom apartment on the fourth floor, I sat at the heavy
wooden kitchen table, my feet hanging off the chair, sipping
a mixture of bubbly water and rustic red wine and eating
spaghetti mixed with olive oil, black pepper, and caciocavallo
cheese. My mother was in the background, maybe talking on
the phone or bent over a steaming pot or pan. I couldn't have
been more than four. This was how we did things in Barra.

The last suburb within the Naples city limits, Barra stands
right before a string of impoverished villages that surround the
foot of Mount Vesuvius called the Paesi Vesuviani. The town consists primarily of government-subsidized housing projects—
clumps of tall communist-era buildings made of marred stucco
and Tarmac, rising up around courtyards planted with short,
plump palm trees. Each window is covered by a green or rust-

colored metal shade; from each balcony, a dull rainbow of pants and shirts, underpants and dishcloths, towels and sheets blows in the breeze.

For most of the 1980s and '90s, Barra was a black hole of crime—mob-run, broken-down, full of drugs and violence. But when I was growing up there, in the early 1970s, the neighborhood was still relatively innocent. Or perhaps that's only how I imagined it to be; to me, then, Barra felt like the safest place on earth, swathed as I was in the soft blanket of my loud, large family, of the predictable, delicious rituals that made up our days.

❧

EVERY DAY, AT THE CRACK OF DAWN, vendors' shouts would pierce the silence of the sleeping town: " 'O mellone!" "Pane frisco!" "Muzzarella!" The farmers, hauling behind them carts piled high with striped beige melons or steaming bread or still-warm mozzarella, let everyone know what they were selling. One by one, women threw on their housecoats, opened their windows, and started to barter. With her arms draped over the balcony railing ten flights up, a middle-aged brunette in slippers would ask how much the cherries cost.

"Two thousand lire for a kilo, Signora."

"Oh, give me a break—too much!"

"Signora, I'm just trying to make a living!"

"How about this: I give you three thousand and you give me two kilos."

"But Signora! Be sensible! These are the best cherries in the world, guaranteed!"

"I'll be the judge of that. Now give me a taste."

And she'd slowly lower a small basket into which the vendor would place several choice fruits so that the *signora* could decide if, indeed, the cherries were *le migliori in assoluto*. I lay in the bed I shared with my brother Stefano and listened to the early-morning commerce, the loud, boisterous haggling bouncing off buildings, each woman's voice rising above the next. And I heard my mother shuffle out to our tiny terrace and start to piece together an answer to the most pressing question of our days, our weeks, our lives: What to eat?

Once the morning had begun, I was dressed in my Mussolini-era smock and bow tie and sent off to school—a big, impersonal building about which I remember almost nothing. But that place isn't important anyway; I did my real learning as soon as the bell rang and I was swept up into my mother's family. She and her sisters and all of us children who were not off in a field somewhere catching lizards, or playing soccer with a duct-taped ball, or stealing figs off a tree, went to town, which had morphed, in the hours since dawn, into a bustling market.

I wandered, nestled within the loud brood, through the packed cobblestone streets. Every few minutes, a Vespa—driven by a cigarette-smoking man with a toddler hanging on each leg, one baby balanced on his lap, and another sandwiched in between him and his wife, who was eating a *panino* on the back—honked its way through, and the crowds backed themselves up against a wall to make way. Italians are famously insane drivers, but Neapolitans, who live their lives in the shadow of a live volcano, are the most fearless of all—and the most faithful. The unspoken philosophy of traffic seemed to be: Worry not; God will take care of us! At that time in Naples proper, there were approximately five traffic lights, and upon seeing one of them lit up red, everybody knew to floor the Fiat and speed through as fast as possible; logically, this lessened the window of time in which you might be hit by someone speeding through the yield sign on the other side.

The market of my childhood was appropriately wild, a sea of people weaving from side to side. I watched my aunts and mother pick through mounds of bright vegetables, carefully inspect fish cooling on dripping stacks of ice, tenderly roll huge lemons in their hands. The ancient Romans called the southern soil surrounding Naples *campania felix,* "joyous land," because there the combination of intense Mediterranean sun and rich volcanic soil results in bright, abundant produce—massive black eggplants, fluffy zucchini blossoms, tiny jewel-like apples, shiny yellow persimmons, beans, tomatoes, oversized lemons, purple artichokes, white hazelnuts. The stands at the market were full of life and death: bursting tomatoes and overflowing bushels of greens sat next to wooden carts upon which were nailed boiled pig snouts; one stand offered crates of juicy blackberries, the next, whole skinned baby lambs, their bloody eyes staring mournfully from coolers.

The snacks that we begged for every day were unique to the south: cups of the savory broth used to cook octopus—a muddy purple liquid boiled with garlic and pepper; *frittura,* or mounds of fried vegetables, meats, and fishes—oily, salty, and coated in a delicate batter; slices of tripe, those intensely textured innards that taste like the depths of the cow's body; airy, spicy slabs of headcheese. Every day, my curvy little mother in her bright cotton dress swerved about absently as she talked and sipped a cup of lemonade. Sometimes she would treat me to a fruit gelato made of fresh peaches, or a coffee gelato made with ground espresso beans. On special days, I was allowed my favorite sweet: fresh-from-the-oven *sfogliatella,* a ricotta-and-orange-peel-filled pastry that I would crack open and watch the steam spiral out of.

Everything was at its peak of flavor and freshness. You couldn't find a tomato that was overripe or underripe, or day-old mozzarella. There wasn't a competitive economy, so all the food was of the highest quality and none of it cost much. Every woman in the area knew where the finest, most fragrant spices were sold. You didn't buy eggs off the shelf, you knew the man who raised the chickens. He might say to you, as you cradled the delicate brown orbs in your hands, "Maybe you'd like a bird, too?" And if you said yes, he scooped from a cart one of his doomed, scrawny chickens, sliced its head off, plucked it, wrapped it in wax paper, and handed it to you.

"We'll figure out how to make this delicious," my mother would say on those occasions, giving me the package to carry.

My mother, Alma Tschantret, was a typical Neapolitan woman—rowdy, warm, sensual—and, as such, she had mastered the kitchen so completely that when she was cooking an elaborate meal, it almost seemed as though she was doing nothing more than standing absently at the counter. She bought what looked best and prepared it intuitively. Some days, we returned from the market with a bunch of tomatoes and a box of pasta; other days, we might come back with a live eel, pearl onions, lemons, zucchini, potatoes, and arugula.

I doubt that my mother has ever followed a recipe in her life. The kitchen was her cocoon and her kingdom. She had been raised in it, and she spent her days there, surrounded, often, by several of her ten brothers and sisters, a few of her four children, or a bunch of her twenty nieces and nephews. They smoked and drank and cooked and talked in the kitchen.

The foods my mother and her sisters spent their time searing, braising, and baking were the center of our lives, and we all often gathered in one minuscule apartment or another to consume them. My father's family lived in the middle of the city of Naples, so they did not often join us at the table, but my mother's clan, the Tschantrets, lived, for the most part, within seventy steps of our dining room.

༄

"*SIAMO FIGLI DI SIGNORI*" was the Tschantret mantra. We are the children of gentlemen.

They were the children of a muscular half-Swiss police marshal and his soft southern wife; in a different life, my grandfather Luigi had owned a sprawling home in the ritzy Vomero neighborhood of Naples. He and my grandmother Anna collected heavy, expensive furniture and read literature and raised their children to stand up very straight and speak in proper Italian, not in the curious Neapolitan dialect that nobody north of Campania can quite comprehend. The house had a view of the dark, majestic bay, the castles on its shores lit up bright in the night. But my grandfather was a dedicated fascist, which meant that after World War II, he was put under house arrest and promptly lost his fortune. The family was forced, in 1945, to move to Barra, where all twelve members shared a three-bedroom apartment. Over time, my grandparents passed away and the siblings had scattered from the apartment, and with the exception of *zia* Vera, who lived in the countryside, and *zio* Aldo, who lived in America, the Tschantrets had remained in Barra—stuck, somehow, to each other and this ghetto that all of them, with their rich roots, professed to disdain just a little.

"Tschantrets don't own *delicatessens*," Zio Franco said if a well-meaning neighbor suggested a business plan that might help the family out of poverty.

Then, dressed in a meticulous suit and just-shined shoes and holding the umbrella he carried from October to May, Zio Franco sauntered off to one of his many jobs—he was the singer in a traveling band, a post office employee, a flash photographer (or: a fellow with an empty camera whom starlets hired to show up at the clubs and repeatedly hit the flash button so that hordes of people would gather together and whisper, "Who *is* she?"). In his free time, he sat outside with his binoculars, hoping, inexplicably, to spot a UFO.

Zia Liliana was the only one with money—though none of us ever knew how much. We did know that she took over as matriarch after my grandparents died, that she had been the lone survivor of a terrible car crash as a teenager and had received what we speculated was a vast sum that was as yet untouched. She was a stunning redhead with a pair of seductive cat eyes and a bee-hive hairdo that required two hours of dedicated sculpting each morning. She spoke seven languages fluently (including self-taught Japanese), worked at an international jewelry manufacturer as an interpreter, ate an apple with a knife and fork, and lived for her entire life in the family's first Barra apartment with elegant Zio Franco and red-lipsticked Zia Maria. Back then, none of them were married, though Liliana had been proposed to, according to family lore, upwards of two dozen times, and Franco had a son somewhere in Sweden (the obvious result of being the lead singer in a traveling Italian band). Eventually, at the age of fifty, Maria married the only man she ever loved and moved to New York (he died seven years later). Strict and overpowering Zio Oscar and his no-nonsense wife, Maria (whom we referred to as Zia Maria Tarallo to avoid confusion), lived with their eight children in a two-bedroom on the next block, and sweet Zio Boris and his shy wife, Rita, were another block away, stuffed in their own two-bedroom with their six kids.

In Barra, you were never alone, even when you slept. And nothing you owned was simply yours. Were you missing your lipstick? Check next door. Where was the sugar? Probably down the street. What about your favorite blue sweater? Cousin Margherita was wearing that at the movies yesterday. It wasn't claustrophobic to me, though; I was very young, and sitting on a lap in a car, wedged among eight other children, was a luxury. Even when we were not together, it was easy to change that; to go from home to home, we would all—adults included—crawl through a hole in the cracked brick wall that separated our two complexes.

The shortcut was best utilized on Sunday, the day to the chief aspects of the Italian religion: churc it was spring, after we'd worshipped, we might meal with rich *mozzarella di bufala,* still so salt, sliced thick. And moist fresh ricor falling-apart mounds that we spoone spread on our brown, crusty bread, rip from platters of prosciutto sliced so thin you could see through it, from plates of baby octopus broiled, with olives, in red wine and tomatoes. We had linguini with little clams still in the shell and sweet baby tomatoes mixed in, drenched in garlic and oil. The main course was a massive *branzino,* or sea bass, roasted whole and seasoned only with rosemary. Then we ate a salad made of lettuce and arugula plucked from the farmer's field that morning. And then plump oranges and pears, followed by liqueurs, syrupy and homemade, walnut and strawberry and creamy lemon, that would burn your throat and coat your belly. The kids snuck the dregs that the adults left in their glasses. Then one of my *zie* would come out with a dessert tray—a massive pile of profiteroles, puff pastries filled with homemade custard and drizzled with melted dark chocolate. We finished with espresso, black and bitter.

Of course we drank wine. Italian wine, like Italian food, is simultaneously no big deal and the biggest deal possible. Eating a sun-ripened, bright red tomato is at once unremarkable for the many times one does it and equally remarkable each time for its deliciousness, for the miracle that is a perfect tomato. Cooking a gorgeous meal is a daily endeavor, and expected—and insomuch as eating well happens all the time, it is not exceptional, though it's never less than fulfilling. Like the love of your family: you don't usually think of it as a special treat, but you need it and thrive because of it all the same.

Wine is like bread and salt: without it, dinner is incomplete. I remember one evening when we ran out of wine. My mother had planned to prepare lamb roasted with peas, onions, and potatoes. When she told my father that we didn't have a backup bottle, he looked grief-stricken; if you didn't know any better, you'd think he'd just been informed of a loved one's premature passing. And in a way he had—his dinner, he realized, wasn't going to happen.

"There's nothing to be done," he said, looking defeated. "We might as well have soup."

In other words: If you didn't have wine, you didn't have a meal.

&

ONCE EVERY TWO MONTHS, my father would say, "Time to drive to the country and get ourselves some good wine." He'd look almost . . . excited.

Personality-wise, my father, Ciro, was the opposite of my mother: impossibly proper, silent, introverted. He wore cuff links every day and I've still never seen him in a sweatshirt. He had grown up in a cracking tenement a block away from the Garibaldi train station in Naples; his family, headed by his bank teller father, consisted of six people, and one of his sisters was, as the result of a childhood illness, severely developmentally disabled. During World War II, their city had been trashed. Legend had it that once a ship at the port was hit so directly that its pieces landed throughout the city, and when workers went to clean up the roof of the train station, they found a human head. Perhaps due to the many humiliations they—and all impoverished Italians—suffered, the Espositos held fiercely to all the dignity they could muster. My father was terrified of people becoming too comfortable with him. It would have disgraced him. He addressed his own father as *Voi*—then the formal version of *tu*, or you, and the Italian equivalent of calling one's parent "sir."

In contrast, my mother liked to tease people. "What's the matter with you—are you a bunch of corpses?" she'd say to a room full of staid adults. She was tiny and hippy, with a long line of readily apparent cleavage—"If you got 'em, flaunt 'em," she liked to say—and a mass of light brown curls. Within minutes of her entrance, she'd be belting out a regional anthem in her beautiful voice or telling an inappropriate joke, and partygoers would be gathered around, laughing raucously. My drawn, skinny father always stood next to her, straightening his silk tie and hissing, "Alma, Alma, *calma, calma*!" (My mother had developed some sort of situational deafness early on, and his pleas seemed not to register.)

In short, my father was a WASP in an Italian's body. He should have been born into an aristocratic British family somewhere in the Norfolk countryside. Naples was entirely too alive, too open, too sexual for his tastes, and he spent a good portion of time wracked with embarrassment and exhausted by the effort it took to hide his shame from the rest of the world.

"My husband is one hundred percent man," my mother would say loudly to her girlfriends at a dinner party. "I tell you, if it were up to him, we'd spend our life in the bedroom!"

This was typical Neapolitan dinner-table talk. My mother's friends giggled, and then tried to one-up her:

"My husband is hard twenty-four hours a day."

"My man, I have to keep an eye on him because as soon as he sees a woman, he's off and running."

Though my father appeared to be staring out of the living room window, his internal organs were probably melting.

My mother was, in addition to being an expert storyteller and a charming partygoer, a child-magnet. She could soothe a child just by whispering. She'd clean up mucus and tickle and cuddle and hush. My father's mantra, when it came to children, was *"Nun me tucca'."* Don't touch me.

But there was one thing my father loved openly, passionately, and shamelessly—wine. When he took a sip, he exhaled and his face relaxed a little. It wasn't because of the alcohol; it was because he was delighted.

My father wasn't interested in the intellectual aspects or the intricacies of the drink—what its undertones were, how it finished, the oakiness, or how long it was aged. He didn't break the bank to buy wine or build up a cellar of valuable gems. He just loved good wine—no more and no less. He used to take hunks of bread and dip them in wine and slowly savor them.

For our trips to get a few months' worth of wine, we loaded a dozen or so empty, grape-stained clay and green glass jugs into the back of the car (my father was, oddly, the only man in Barra with an oversized American sedan) and took off for the countryside.

We drove for an hour, along the side roads, past the persimmon and olive groves, until we reached the vineyard. The entire crop stretched for acres. There were two rows of poplar trees, twenty feet apart. The vines were trained to grow from one tree to the other, and in the center they wrapped together in a web of branches, thick with green leaves and bunches of freckled yellow orbs. Thirty feet above the ground, the tops of the vines had been wound around trellises.

We turned down a dusty road and drove by the crops, my brothers and I with our heads out the window, breathing in the country air like little dogs. At the end of the lane, a tanned farmer carried our jugs over to concrete vats that had small brass spouts on their sides. He placed the lip of the container beneath the spout and turned the spigot, and we watched the empty green glass fill with purple juice. My father waited patiently, yet excitedly. He let us children free, to run through the vineyards, looking up to see not sky, but leaves and fruit.

Mostly, we went to the *cantina sociale*, a cooperative of area growers. Each year, the members pooled their grapes together; the bulk was separated by color, pressed, fermented, and released onto market under the *cantina*'s name: Cantina Sociale di Solopaca Rosso or Cantina del Talburno Bianco. The *cantina* itself was an impersonal stone factory building surrounded by dry shrubbery. It was a self-serve establishment; you put the jug under a spout coming from the side wall and paid the well-fed woman who sat smoking a cigarette at the payment window.

The wine we drank was not distinguished by mysterious letter codes like IGT or DOC or even by the name of the grape. An Italian would not say, "I prefer Barbera d'Alba." He would say, "I like my wine strong." Or he would say, "I like my wine not-so-strong." Or, "I like my wine light." That was as complicated as it got.

It didn't mean that he didn't understand the drink at a deep level. But Italians understand wine the way they understand people, art, accomplishment—intuitively, emotionally, without pretension or overanalysis. A good wine is good because it tastes good. *Basta.* That's enough.

And that is the Italian approach to all that is right:

Why is the Mona Lisa great? *Perché è così*—because it's like that.

Why is the Ferrari so amazing? *Perché è così.*

Why is Capri so gorgeous? *Perché è così.*

Why is fresh mozzarella the best mozzarella? *Perché è così.*

In Italy, many an argument is won by the person who says *"perché è così"* first.

The drinks that were good *because it's like that* were rustic and pure and a pale red-violet or a rosy pink. They were usually low in alcohol. We drank them constantly and casually—for the children, just a drop was mixed with fizzy water, or a tiny glassful was placed beside the plate. Some kids, when choosing between a cup of water and a glass of wine, reached for the water. I reached for the wine. It quenched my thirst.

In the summertime, we would slice mature peaches and macerate them in white or red wine. The next day, the flesh of the fruit had sucked in the wine's flavor, and the drink had become sweet. We drank the wine and we served the peaches topped with a dollop of fresh whipped cream.

Wine didn't get us drunk. It brought out the flavors in our food. It cut the spice, cooled down the heat, heightened the sensations. We needed it as we needed one another: it made every taste, every moment complete.

As a bonus, not only was the wine for pleasure, it was for health—though in the Italian psyche, the two are eternally linked. The root of all evil is blocked digestion, and wine is believed to improve the internal flow of things. When I was coming off a cold, my mother would give me a sip of strong red to clear out my system. When I looked pale or when I had a stomachache, my aunts would huddle around me.

"Put a little wine in him to help him digest," they would say, pressing the backs of their hands on my hot forehead, pushing back my hair. They smelled like garlic, lilac water, soap. They looked down on me with their brows furrowed.

"He's hot, the poor thing. See, feel his head, it's all congested for sure."

"He looks run-down. Honey, you need to have some liquid."

"Alma, give this kid a little glass of wine to put some color in his cheeks."

My mother poured an inch into a cup and brought it to me.

"*Ti fa bene*," she said as she handed it to me. It will do you good.

We did ourselves good every night—at celebrations, on Sundays, on holidays. On Christmas Eve, we had a fish feast of vermicelli with anchovies, fried eel, baked lobster, fish *caponata* stuffed in a loaf of bread; afterward, there were tiny frosted sugar cookies, dried fruits, and *la collana del prete*, "the priest's necklace"—chestnuts all strung together. We drank cold white wine. For Carnevale, we had rich ricotta lasagna and saffron fritters with deep red wine. On Pasquetta, the day after Easter, we packed a picnic of *casatiello*—fresh bread stuffed with chopped cold cuts—and tender sautéed zucchini and day-old pasta, cooked with eggs, herbs, and *parmigiano-reggiano* into a spaghetti frittata. We brought along *pastiera,* a traditional pie made of ricotta, orange peel, and *grano,* pearled durum wheat. We packed bottles of seltzer and jugs of white, and drove to the top of Mount Vesuvius. The only snow in all of Naples powdered the ground at the volcano's peak, and in between courses, we built snowmen on the hoods of our parents' cars. We stuck a zucchini in as a nose. Then we went back to the spread-out blanket, where the adults were deep in conversation, and asked for seconds.

In the summertime we traveled the country, all together as always in the backseat of somebody's car. We did not travel as a single nuclear family—we were more a double-digit clan. Sometimes, we stayed with Zia Vera at her working farm in Camaldoli. I killed my first chicken there when I was four—swung the ax as a farmer held the bird down—and the family celebrated by eating my chicken *alla cacciatore,* hunter's style—braised in white wine and covered in mushrooms, onions, fresh tomatoes, herbs, and red pepper flakes. In the mornings, my cousins and brothers and I brought the warm red eggs inside. My mother would separate the white from the scarlet yolk, beat it, add sugar and espresso, and serve the treat as an airy dessert. During the day, we ran through the pastures and into nearby farms, foraging for wild berries and picking chestnuts. We warded off the foxes that stalked my *zia*'s chicken coops. At night, we sometimes joined the locals in their search for mushrooms. Folklore had it that mushrooms picked under a full moon kept better.

During some summers, we traveled to Ischia, a small green island rising up from the Naples bay. We drove through all the grandeur and squalor of Naples—past mangy dogs running in packs around palaces—and boarded the ferry. Then we stood on the deck, feeling the salt spray on our faces and watching our city grow miniature before our eyes, until it was as perfect and color-ful as a cartoon, the pink, white, and yellow buildings climbing up the dark cliff under the cerulean sky.

Ischia arose from the sea as a result of volcanic activity. Its hills are spotted with hot springs and mud baths, which the an-cient Romans enjoyed. The island's turquoise water laps the white, sandy shores, and its cliffs are carpeted with jasmine and wisteria. There, all the Tschantrets that could fit stayed together in an apartment by a private beach. In the morning, when the tide was low, you could open some of the bedroom windows and jump right onto the damp sand. The apartment's kitchen was open to the sea air, and when it rained, we children all sat with the adults and played cards and ate.

Sometimes we meandered to the docks, where the perma-nently sunburnt commercial fishermen had their blue wooden boats. We hopped on, helped them with their catch, and re-turned home by noon with a fresh *orata,* gilthead bream, as our day's wage; our mothers sautéed the fish with olive oil and pars-ley and set it out, surrounded by tomatoes and capers, on the table for lunch. We drank crisp white wine mixed with soda wa-ter and stared out at the flat sea. And then we were free again, to run in our gang out to the pier and splash around and then dry ourselves on the gray rocks jutting out, like seals soaking up the sun. When night came, we were back at the house, back around the table, for chickpeas with mussels and fennel seeds, cod with potatoes, pasta with walnuts, white beans, and *alici,* Mediter-ranean anchovies. And, of course, wine.

We always ate with gusto: we didn't ask for the bread to be passed or sit up straight with our utensils primly poised. It would have offended the cook if we had nibbled or picked, and no sane person with taste buds intact would ever find reason to do so. Our mothers and *zie* didn't inquire as to the states of our bellies; they just put the food on our plates.

"You only ask sick people if they're hungry," my mother said. "Everyone else must eat, eat!"

But when Italians say *"Mangia! Mangia!"* they're not just talking about food. They're trying to get you to stay with them, to sit by them at the table for as long as possible. The meals that my family ate together—the many courses, the time in between at the table or on the mountain or by the sea, the six hours spent talking loudly and passionately and unyieldingly and laughing hysterically the way Neapolitans do—were designed to prolong our time together; the food was, of course, meant to nourish us, but it was also meant to satisfy, in some deeper way, our endless hunger for one another. And at home, when we had wiped our lips for the last time, my parents, my brothers, my sister, and I climbed through the hole in the wall, waddled up to our beds, and promptly fell asleep.

❧

THIS IS ALL, OF COURSE, a child's perception. I saw the resplendence and pride of Naples, the lingering memory of its millennium as a European cultural nexus. It had been, two hundred years earlier, one of the richest cities on the continent, home to an advanced university and some of the world's greatest artists and thinkers. As I sat, content, on the ferry on my way to Ischia, I saw the Castel dell'Ovo rising majestically above the bay. I didn't see how fragile the rest of that city was, and how imperiled.

In the late 1800s, the Mafia had taken control of the area, and by the end of World War II, Naples was in shambles: impoverished, gripped by a heroin epidemic, and rife with violent crime. Once the cultural center of the Western hemisphere, Naples smelled burnt, and the streets were sticky, covered with trash. Families of a dozen or more people lived in single, windowless rooms; packs of stray dogs roamed the streets; a cholera outbreak swept the city; the militant leftist Red Brigade was bombing public buses.

But more disturbing to us than all of that: my father couldn't get a job. In Italy, nepotism rules. Families begin businesses just so that their young children will someday have a way to make a living—you must create the job, because it probably doesn't exist otherwise. When a job does open up—when someone becomes sick, dies, or retires—it is often offered first to the child of the person who previously held it. Most people in Italy don't follow their dreams; they take what they can get.

My paternal grandfather worked for a bank all his life. My father, like any poor Neapolitan of his generation, went straight from high school to vocational school, where he got a degree in accounting. But there wasn't much of a market for accountants in Naples, so he had to scrounge around for work. He helped a friend sell construction equipment, helped a cousin fix car engines, and traveled the country selling fancy lace tablecloths. But there simply wasn't any demand for anything—how could poor people invest in construction or collect pretty linens? The economy itself was trashed; few men could support a family of six. So we were officially broke; all of our vacations, the few we had, it turned out, had been partially subsidized by my mother's unmarried siblings, by my father's sister and her husband. When my father's one-man tablecloth company went bankrupt, my parents had to make a decision. The family simply didn't have the funds to bail them out again.

My parents were consumed by stress, and the drawers in our tenement apartment were stuffed with unpaid bills. At night, they yelled at each other, desperately trying to argue their way into a more comfortable financial situation. Maybe if we borrowed a little more money? Maybe if we asked the neighbor to ask her son about yet another job? Finally, when I was six, they came up with a plan. My mother's older brother Aldo lived in Albany, New York; we could go there for a year, make some money, get back on our feet, and return to Barra. It was agreed that we would try to go. Aldo entered us in the green card lottery. To our surprise, we won.

But our victory wasn't exactly cause for celebration. None of us had ever known anything but Naples. My brother Sal was an awkward fourteen-year-old with a puff of bright red hair and a face full of pimples; he was ruined by the thought of leaving his lifelong friends, his cousins, boys who were like brothers to him. Eight-year-old Stefano stayed quiet, uncomprehending. My twelve-year-old sister, Anna, chubby, with long black hair, attempted politely and unsuccessfully to argue my parents out of the move. My father maintained his usual poker face. My mother, as always, did the opposite. She sat at our kitchen table, surrounded by her sisters and brothers, tears streaming down her face.

"I'm so scared," she said, day after day. "I can't believe my life has come to this."

"Look on the bright side," Zio Franco said.

"At least you won the lottery," added Zia Liliana.

"America won't be so bad," Zia Maria chimed in. "My friend's brother's cousin opened a pizzeria there, and they like it."

"Gianni's brother's cousin?" Zia Maria Tarallo asked. "Yes, I heard they're making lots of money! Tons of money! A truckful of money."

"America is supposed to be great, very pretty," Zio Boris said. "It'll be good to see the world."

"How come my husband couldn't just find a good job?" my mother pleaded, weeping. "How can I leave you all? How can the children?"

"Oh, Alma," Zio Franco said, "I wish I could help you."

"Perhaps if I got another job . . . ," Zio Boris said. "You can take what I have. You can take everything."

My mother shook her head and they all sat in silence.

"You'll be back before you know it," Zia Maria offered.

"You'll be back before you even notice you're gone," Zio Boris said.

☙

IN THE PHOTOGRAPHS of our last day in Italy, October 24, 1974, my family is seated on the concrete steps outside the Rome airport. Everyone wears a muted, mournful expression—except for me, unaware of time and space, standing in front, grinning, positioned in a flamboyant bow. I figured we were going on a trip, and just as Zio Boris had said, we'd be back before we even noticed we were gone.

Chapter 3

ALBANY

———⚜———

ZIO ALDO MET US at the airport. I'd never seen him before, not even in a photo. He was a compact little bull of a man who resembled a dour, fedora-wearing Popeye. His arms were muscular from years of masonry, his hands as tough and solid as baseball mitts. He stood in the bleak beige waiting area at John F. Kennedy International Airport and waved at us solemnly. I was never quite sure if Aldo had been so serious before he moved to Albany, or if Albany had sucked the Italian joy right out of the man.

After the requisite greeting kisses, we nervously followed Aldo to his car, where his teenage son Carmen loaded all of our worldly belongings onto the roof. Carmen, though a strong, friendly fellow, was no intellectual. We stood together as he tried to secure our suitcases with a rope. My mother, father, and Aldo were discussing our journey.

"What is he doing?" Stefano whispered from the corner of his mouth.

Carmen had broken into a sweat and was muttering in English.

"Yeah, I don't know," said Sal. Carmen had inadvertently begun to wrap the rope around himself.

"Tell him," Anna said. "He's gonna get himself stuck."

"Yeah? Well, how exactly do you suggest I communicate with him?" Sal asked. Carmen was American.

I regarded our newest family member. He had managed to tie the suitcases to the car. But in the process, he had also tied himself to it. His cheek was pressed against the metal. "Dammit," he said.

"Oh, Carmen, you moron," Aldo said in Italian, turning around. He released the boy from his self-made prison, smacked him upside the head, and secured the bags himself.

"Seriously," Stefano said to Sal as we took off down the highway, "what are we doing here?"

I had never seen a place like Albany, so bleak, closed off, colorless. It is a city held hostage by its weather—gray and slushy, its skies blanketed with flat clouds. Every structure is water-stained, the walls and roofs spattered with rusty marks.

After we passed by the flat strip malls and parking lots that line the main road, we hit the center of Albany, a curious combination of impressive government buildings and dilapidated housing projects, of grand, striking architectural triumphs and moldy dive bars. The redbrick governor's mansion looms above the multicolored row houses, an embarrassing reminder that this city is the capital of the state that includes Manhattan.

The people of Albany have a unique aesthetic, one dictated, at least in part, by apathy. I used to wonder if, one day, some rebellious hausfrau down on Elm Street had decided to strike. She was sick of sweeping the porch and fixing the house, and she wasn't going to do it anymore. She spread the word. *Everybody, from near and far: Don't bother.* And a revolution of lethargy swept the city, so that if you did, say, plant a few rosebushes in your front yard, you seemed like a snob. Who knew? To me, coming from a country where even the most destitute scrub their bathrooms with floral soap, the lack of care was mysterious. Yards were patchy, deck furniture was cracking. The main decorative touches appeared to be year-round Christmas lights and an assortment of flags featuring the Stars and Stripes, or Easter tulips, or cartoon kittens. Few houses used proper window treatments—people preferred to protect their privacy with sheets, towels, and T-shirts. When the cheap screen doors broke, nobody fixed them, so they hung wanly from their hinges, flapping back and forth in the wind.

Upon arrival, my parents were distracted by another complete surprise. They had seen America only in Cary Grant movies, which is why they were confused when we pulled up to a town house in the heart of an all-black neighborhood. I'd seen only one nonwhite person in my entire life—a visiting American soldier whom my father had taken me to gawk at back in Naples.

"That is what an African person looks like," he'd told me, his hand on my shoulder, motioning toward the man as if toward a rare piece of art. The soldier, surrounded by wide-eyed Italians, did not look amused.

But now, suddenly, there wasn't a white face for at least a mile. Two young men with well-puffed Afros leaned against the wall of the corner store. A brown-skinned woman clutching grocery bags and flanked by her children wandered by. A few dark faces peered from the windows around us. All the shopkeepers, every person on the street, was black.

"Where *are* we?" my mother hissed to my father as we unloaded our bags. "This isn't America."

"Yes, it is," Zio Aldo said. "This is our America." My siblings and I were huddled close, sweating profusely.

We stared at our new home in this dreary, gray town populated by people who appeared foreign and unreachable. It was a simple two-story white town house with red trim and a blue door. Thirty steps across the street was Zio Aldo's house, a two-story redbrick place with a brown door. Decades earlier, the neighborhood had been composed largely of Italian immigrants, but the government had built housing projects in the area and the Italians had moved away. The one reminder of that time was an old, abandoned rectory that the church maintained. When

Aldo arrived from Italy in 1953 with no place to stay, the church offered him the building for next to nothing; he bought it.

Suddenly, a stream of people flew out of that house—a ragtag bunch of light-haired children with huge grins on their faces. These were, it seemed, our American cousins. I'd first heard of them when, several years earlier, a box arrived stuffed with seventies-era clothing: lime bell-bottoms, floppy-sleeved button-downs, flower-power polyester jackets. We'd all chosen something from the box and walked around the streets of Barra in our groovy new outfits. So here they were, the original owners of those mustard platform loafers, smiling at us, and speaking in an indecipherable tongue.

"Welcome, Espositos," they exclaimed. We just gaped.

They weren't offended by our silence. Instead, each of them grabbed one of us and led him or her into their house. A girl of about nine appointed herself my guardian. She had an elfin face and long brown hair, parted in the middle.

"Hi," she said. I couldn't speak a word. "Sit here," she said, patting a chair.

I climbed onto the chair and stared. "Cinzia, me," she said, pointing at her chest. "Sergio, you." For the next hour, she circled my chair in silence, stopping every few minutes to tenderly pat my head. By dinnertime, I was nestled firmly in her lap, smiling like the satisfied pet I would forevermore be to her. Things were going pretty well, I reasoned. A new cousin to pat my head—this would be just fine. Then, my *zia* called us for dinner.

Zia Rosetta was an orphan from Italy whose relative had moved to Albany. He helped to bring her and Aldo over when they were in their late teens, and there they remained. Zia Rosetta was obviously unconventional, and she was unquestionably committed to—and terrified of—her husband for her entire life. Though the woman was no older than fifty, she lacked all but one tooth; and though she frequently came into contact with people, she rarely wore her dentures. She kept her white hair slicked back, and her personal style of dress consisted of an unorthodox housedress-and-rainbow-knee-socks combination. I came to love her dearly, as I suspected I would, for she was kind-hearted and generous. But from that first sniff of her kitchen, I knew that we had a major problem.

Due to her parentless childhood, Zia Rosetta had not been trained in the culinary arts. Further, she was stranded in the middle of New York State with little money and almost no way of acquiring fresh ingredients. She was not living the Italian life, in a small village surrounded by a community of clever, capable female relatives who could help her at any time, day or night. Instead, she alone was required to cook, daily, for between fifteen and twenty people—and this was in addition to her duties as wife and mother, bed maker, diaper changer, tear wiper, clothes sewer, shoe polisher, shelf duster, sweeper, mopper, scrubber, laundry doer, ironer, dog feeder, and practitioner of all the other small and large time-consuming tasks to which she devoted herself tirelessly and without complaint. While inexplicably good-humored despite her lonely and exhausting chores, she was not interested in concocting tasty meals for her brood. Her goal was to stave off everyone's hunger and make sure nobody suffered from scurvy. Her culinary style might be defined as military.

"*Buon appetito,*" said Rosetta as she plopped a steaming bowl of spaghetti and beans on the table. Next to it she placed a thick gray roast and then a salad made with wilted iceberg lettuce and pale tomatoes. Onto each of our plates she spooned at least two pounds of food.

I looked at my mother, befuddled. She shrugged her shoulders imperceptibly. Why had we been given seven times the amount of food we usually ate? Perhaps this was a strange ritual for guests. I pushed my fork into the pasta—it was mushy, as far from *al dente* as possible. My father twirled the dull strands around his fork. He chewed for some time and then swallowed with barely disguised effort. I followed his lead, but the pasta was like glue in my throat. It grabbed onto the sides of my mouth and coated my tongue. We were used to eating pasta from the town of Gragnano, where they laid the fresh pasta in the middle of the street so that the unique combination of Mediterranean and mountain winds would dry it in just the right way to produce the perfect texture when it was boiled. But this American pasta was made in a factory and could be overcooked within a second.

I looked at my family's sad faces. Anna's lips were pressed stoically together; Sal wore an expression of surrender as he chewed; Stefano's brow was contorted with alarm. My mother, who appeared to be holding back tears, kicked me under the table. I tried to swallow again, and coughed. Zio Aldo's family didn't notice, though. They were too busy chowing down.

❧

HERE ARE THE NEW food products I discovered in Albany: cottage cheese, barbecue sauce, marshmallows, dry cereal, peanut butter, ketchup. We didn't understand ketchup. Sweet tomato paste that you put on everything from eggs to meat? We especially didn't understand marshmallows. A white spongy hunk of gelatin that is difficult to digest and, on Easter, is dyed bright yellow and shaped like a chick? But *why*?

Here is what I learned in Albany: If you walk through an alley, you're going to get mugged, even if you're seven. If you walk into a middle-school bathroom, you're going to get mugged, even if you're twelve, and female. If you want to survive, you had better learn to fight. If you want to survive, you had better travel in a pack. If Zio Aldo is mad, run as fast as you can. If Zio Aldo is drunk, run as fast as you can. If you give Zia Rosetta a filet mignon, she will boil it. If you order a sandwich, you'll have enough flavorless meat to feed a non-American family of fourteen. If you take an Italian out of Italy and put him in upstate New York, he will spend all his time mythologizing Italy.

During those strange days, everything was new and different and violent. We stood out terribly with our brown leather shoes and our pale faces, and, none of us having learned English in school, we couldn't communicate at all. My mother had to work as a seamstress and my father got two jobs, one in the laundry room of a hospital and one as a dishwasher. Unless you counted Rosetta as a guardian, we kids were on our own. We were enrolled in public school and were slapped into regular classrooms; school officials might as well have drawn large red targets on each of our foreheads. Every day, we devised new routes home. We ran from the brick buildings as soon as the final bell sounded, clutching our backpacks and repeating the Lord's Prayer. We arranged to meet—me, Salvatore, Stefano, Anna, and our cousins—and provide a group shield for one another. But still we were often set upon by other groups, and we all had to learn how to brawl—me and Anna included. Our cousins were already experts. Cinzia could knock out a boy's teeth with one punch.

Then again, home wasn't exactly a safe haven either. Zio Aldo was unerringly charitable, physically incapable of not giving away whatever he had. He would go to the local farmers' market seven blocks away for a week's worth of groceries, and by the time he got home, he'd have only a head of lettuce; he'd seen people who needed the food more than we did, so he'd given it to them. He was incomparably generous like that, but he wasn't gentle.

Zio Aldo, with those baseball-mitt hands, ruled the roost, and he had spent his formative years as a young adult in Albany, a town in which fists were the preferred form of interaction. The man would punch anyone he thought had disrespected him—man, woman, or child—in the face. He'd been pushed out of Italy by his father, the fascist police marshal, after getting in trouble one too many times, and he was terribly bitter. Once, when he was furious over some mundane detail, he fired a shotgun straight through the dining room wall. We had a hole in the Sheetrock for years. He left it there, I think, as a reminder of his capabilities.

Zio Aldo was also the sort of man whose idea of family fun is shooting, dismembering, and devouring an animal. One day, about a month after our arrival, he came home from a hunting trip in the woods outside the city, a gutted deer slung over his shoulder. He threw it onto the kitchen table where we all ate dinner. Blood seeped out from the cut in its abdomen. We kids peeked at it from behind the wall. The deer did not show similar curiosity.

"Okay, everyone, get in here," Zio Aldo ordered.

We scrambled into the kitchen and stood in wait, a tiny army silenced in the presence of its beloved and potentially psychotic leader.

"Get busy cutting," he said, handing us each a sharp knife and motioning toward the corpse. All twelve of us stood around the table, and we butchered the deer. Zio Aldo strolled slowly about, offering guidance. As I sliced through the shank, I looked at the prowling figure in camouflage gear, the man who was my new, American *zio*. I knew it then: I loved this guy.

The feeling, it turned out, was mutual. He may have sensed my overwhelming need for his approval, or he may just have sensed my irrational, unconditional love for him. My father's two jobs meant that Aldo became the man in my life. His family's rituals became my rituals—and as with the deer butchering, I didn't think them strange. Like his children, I regarded him with a mixture of love, awe, and fear. And we all did as he said.

❧

EVERY EVENING, at suppertime, Zio Aldo arrived home, usually with a bum or two slumped against him. Albany was full of down-and-out people—drunks, addicts, all sorts of generally desperate, hard-living riffraff whom you could often see lying in alleyways, passed out in freezing weather, or weaving back and forth down Central Avenue, trying to make their way to the closest bar. Aldo related to these people, to their sorrow, to their circumstances, and felt compelled to feed them. So on his way home from the construction site, he scooped a couple of the less-fortunates up, swung them over his shoulders, and, upon kicking the door open, dropped them on the floor and pointed at whatever child or group of children was closest.

"Clean 'em up," he ordered, and then lay down on the couch to rest his back.

After we'd soaped up the dinner guests of the evening, we all sat down—Zio Aldo, his wife, his nine children, my family, and a couple of just-scrubbed bums—and dug in.

"Sergio, here," Zio Aldo said, pushing his wine glass toward me. We had fifteen glasses. If there were more than fifteen people at the table, it meant we had to share. If Zio Aldo drank wine—and he always drank wine—then I would drink wine, too. I held the glass in both my hands, careful not to spill, and took a sip.

That was when I fell in love with wine. It wasn't at a resort in the Alps or at a dinner party in Manhattan or during a bicycle tour of northern France; it was in Albany when I was seven. There was nothing informed or intellectual about my love, nothing so-phisticated or rational. I loved wine because Zio Aldo let me sip from his glass. He demanded that I sit next to him at the head of the table, where he ate his dinner in relative silence. Throughout, he drank wine, which was poured from a jug of California red. Because the wine, which was already pretty bad, was stored under the sink and next to the refrigerator, it was always cooked through. But I didn't know it then—and if I had, I wouldn't have cared. I knew only that I got to sit next to my *zio,* and that almost every night, I would share from his big goblet.

That's why I loved it: because he gave it to me, and because even though it was ruined, it tasted interesting. Still today, I remember those wines like I remember the smell of cigar—like musty cooked apples—on Zio Aldo's fingers.

As time went on, wine came to symbolize more than my relationship with my *zio*. It was a connection to Italy, a place I sorely missed. After a while, my cousins and siblings and I stopped getting beaten up all the time, and we made some friends; people called us "guinea" less frequently; my family moved away from the ghetto to a dismal suburban neighborhood; my brothers and my sister and I began to attend a Catholic school; I came to understand the previously mysterious allure of peanut butter, an all-American snack that, even I had to admit, was scrumptious. All of it made the fact that we didn't have the funds to return to Barra anytime soon easier—but not much.

We missed our Tschantrets and our fresh, still-warm mozzarella. We missed walking down the streets and knowing everybody, and we missed the Italian way of spending hours at the table. In Albany, there were few first-generation Italian families or Italian food shops or restaurants. Most people were decent, blue-collar workers or government employees, and the majority were of Irish or German descent. They valued humble simplicity and loyalty above all, and were largely struggling and insecure. You were supposed to be proud to be from Albany, and you were to take part in acceptable activities: drinking beer and bowling. The only tolerable form of hierarchy was a membership in the local Knights of Columbus.

We just couldn't get into it, and we didn't really want to. So we tried to re-create our Neapolitan life in some small way, however possible. As Italians have done forever, we remembered who we were through food. Of course, my mother couldn't find radicchio or huge lemons in Albany—she couldn't even find basil—but she was determined to make us our Sunday meal even if her hands were sore from days of sewing other people's dresses and slacks. She immediately located a family of Calabrians who had moved to Albany years earlier. In their desperation, they had managed to seek out every Italian specialty within a hundred-mile radius, and they were happy to share their information with my mother; in fact, they were also happy to share some of the *schiacciata*—a hard, brick-flattened, oil-soaked, spicy salami—they made themselves.

So on Sundays, my mother prepared dinner at our house, and we sat down to a four-hour meal. It was at once a meditation on our faraway home and a celebration of the fact that we were, at the very least, still together. Nobody ever missed it.

We ate olives and *sopressata;* prosciutto and sharp provolone; broken chunks of crumbling *parmigiano.* We ate heaps of spaghetti with a sauce of crushed fresh tomatoes; *pesce in bianco*—poached white fish dressed in lemon, olive oil, and parsley; fried miniature artichokes; fluffy, anchovy-battered zucchini and cauliflower; roast lamb shoulder cooked with onions, small slabs of bacon, juicy little potatoes, and big green peas; simple mixed salads; salted fennel dipped in oil; tangerines, pears, and apples; and tiny, round, glazed hazelnut and anise cookies. As we ate, we sipped simple red wines. They were one-dimensional, tasting only of alcohol and grapes, but I had no reference point: I associated those jugs of purple liquid with Zio Aldo, and with Naples, and with my family on Sundays. With the happiest, most full-bellied times.

THOSE TIMES DIDN'T LAST TOO LONG. When I was nine, Zio Aldo died of a heart attack at age forty-eight, and with him went one of my strongest links to Italy. Sitting at that long dinner table without Aldo at its head became too grueling for the entire family. Our Sunday lunches for twenty petered out, and soon it was just my siblings, my mother, and, if he had a rare day off, my father—no bums, no fresh-carved deer, no Zia Rosetta in her rainbow-colored knee socks. From my place at our table, I tried to recall the sensation of sitting next to Zio Aldo and sipping from his glass. At first I could almost pretend he was still there, but as time went on it became increasingly difficult to remember. In an attempt to regain what was lost, I began tasting wine on my own, requesting a few sips with every meal. As I drank, I tried to recall those three years by his side in the basement dining room. I could remember my *zio*, his squinty smile, his muscular arms, his silence. Moreover, through my intense concentration, I began to discover interesting tastes, smells, and dimensions in the wine. The drink, it seemed, was multifaceted—something I'd never before noticed. And the concept of consuming and experiencing something so relatively complicated mesmerized me. It was almost accidental, this new consciousness, but once I'd stumbled upon it, I wanted more.

What pushed me even further into the world of wine and food was, oddly, the movie *One Flew Over the Cuckoo's Nest*, which was played repeatedly on HBO. I liked all of it, but was most fascinated by the ending. Ultimately, the main character, Randle Patrick McMurphy, played by Jack Nicholson, a man displaying symptoms of antisocial personality disorder, is given a lobotomy, and he turns from the wild, violent person he once was into, essentially, a vegetable. I became obsessed with the concept of a lobotomy. *It can't be true*, I thought. *There is* no way *an operation can remove your personality*. At that point, I began to eschew my science homework and to instead research lobotomies at the Albany library. To her credit, the librarian never expressed any surprise that a local preteen was obsessively checking out books on an infamous psychiatric medical procedure.

What I learned about lobotomies was that they turned previously alive people into lazy, nearly catatonic beings, uninspired and without initiative. Such people, I read, didn't want to deal with anything new. They were incapable of learning fresh skills. They wanted every day to resemble the last. They desired to wear the same clothes, eat the same food, and watch the same TV program, and if you inserted novelty into their routine, they fell apart emotionally. On my way home from the library, it occurred to me that I passed those same people every day. They were all walking or driving the same route from work to home in the same uniform as the day before, to eat, I presumed from my experience at my friends' houses, the same steak and potatoes.

I'm living in a mental institution, I thought despairingly. *I've got to break free.*

Since I was clearly too young to leave home, I instituted a program that I figured would ensure that I wouldn't end up meting out my days as though I were lobotomized. The program involved, simply, exercising my senses constantly. If I could help it, I thought, I wouldn't end up chained to a life in which I ate a meal made with Hamburger Helper every Wednesday while wearing one of my eight pairs of brown slacks. Every day, I turned on music, tried to take note of the colors around me, smell the food I was eating. I liked to touch people—to give and receive neck massages, to hug my cousins and my mother, to pet our Chihuahua, Fifi. Once I began to search for stimulation, I found it everywhere. But mostly, I found it in food and wine.

While I enjoyed music, I didn't have an ear for it. I liked reading, but I didn't want to analyze the passages or characters. I appreciated art, but I didn't feel drawn to it emotionally. Music, literature, art: they were cultural necessities and lovely pastimes, but that's where it ended for me. Food and wine, however, had the ability to change me every day. When I came home from school and was met by the perfume of my mother's lasagna, my entire mood shifted. My brothers took a sniff and walked on by, but I was momentarily stopped. And I then moved on toward the kitchen to explore. Food altered my thought process, and if I was feeling a little down, a good meal could pick me up. Wine and food—the scents, the ingredients, my mother's mastery—pulled me in.

I found that apart from my tremendous interest, I also possessed the ability to learn how to cook easily, and to memorize aspects of wine immediately. From the age of nine, I worked as a dishwasher at the French restaurant at which Sal was a chef; by the time I was fourteen, I'd been promoted to waiter, and I then noticed that the wine was largely neglected. Naturally, I gravitated toward it, and began to study the variety they had.

❧

MY BRAIN, IT TURNED OUT, liked wine information. It held on to everything I entered into it. Once I'd had Cabernet Sauvignon, I was forever on able to identify it by color. Once I'd tasted a maderized wine—one exposed to too much heat—I could forevermore tell when a wine had gone bad in that way. I could determine pretty accurately at what altitude a grape had been grown—the grapes of an elegant wine were grown on a high hill, those of a less elegant wine were grown down in the valley. While all wines smelled basically the same to my siblings, all wines smelled dramatically different to me. To stick my nose in a glass and sniff for an hour seemed totally natural.

Every new bit of information elated me. I was sort of an amateur detective, dedicated to solving this new mystery, and with every step closer, I felt more fulfilled. I started to read all about food and wine, returning to the library to check out *The Galloping Gourmet, The ABC of Wine Cookery,* and *Mastering the Art of French Cooking.* With my math textbook as a footrest, I read about the history of Pecorino Romano, the preferred method of making a lemon soufflé, the origin of fava beans, the golden slopes of Burgundy.

As I was doing my reading, I also discovered a new movie, which was to replace *One Flew Over the Cuckoo's Nest* as my favorite. It was an Italian film shown on TV—*Mogliamante,* or *Wifemistress.* It starred the suave Marcello Mastroianni as Luigi de Angelis and Laura Antonelli as his beautiful, black-haired wife, Antonella. Luigi de Angelis is a wine merchant who spends his time traveling around Italy, buying wine, and having affairs with a long line of gorgeous women. When he is erroneously accused of murder, he goes into hiding in an apartment across the street from his home. Unable to tell even his wife where he is, he watches her through the window. As Antonella descends into poverty, she must take over Luigi's business, and in doing so, she discovers his affairs. As she becomes a success, she evolves from a meek housewife into a confident businesswoman, and she awakens sexually, inviting a succession of men into her life and—even better to my thirteen-year-old mind—baring her breasts on-screen. Here, wine was forever linked in my mind to liberation, equality, and sexuality.

When I saw a CNN clip on a New York City wine buyer who traveled to Europe to taste wines, I thought: *It's real! It's actually a job.* Then I wondered, *How do I make it my job?* To my knowledge, there were no colleges with wine-buying programs. I figured my best bet was to do as the CNN guy did, and go to Europe.

❧

I WAS DESPERATE TO TRAVEL on my own but didn't have the funds to do so, so when I was sixteen, I took my father up on his offer to take me and my brother Sal back to Italy. But after spending several days trailing my father through Milan's street markets, inspecting crafts and buying pecans from nut vendors, I was overcome by adolescent claustrophobia.

As we stood on the train platform, waiting for our train to Naples to visit family, I looked at the departure board. I then turned to my father.

"Babbo," I said, "I'm going to Pisa."

Having sensed that I'd made up my mind, having little time to argue, and secure in the knowledge that my overprotective mother was an ocean away, he nodded and told me that I was required to call and tell him as soon as I'd found a room.

A half hour later, I was Pisa-bound and giddy with excitement.

It was midafternoon when I got off the train. I watched with mild envy as a group of Italian teens greeted one another with kisses and hugs. But I was soon distracted by my own delicious freedom, and took off in search of a *pensione*. I wandered the streets until I found a suitably old woman sitting on a milk crate outside a delicatessen. In the window behind her was a stuffed boar's head. The smells of pungent cheese, dried blood, and cured fat emanated from the store. In Italy, guidebooks are unnecessary if you are able to identify true locals. True locals sit near a shop their family owns or at the nearby bar, and have done so for their entire lives; they inevitably know everything about their neighborhood.

"*Buon giorno, Signora,*" I said, and she pointed me in the right direction.

Once I'd settled into my rented room—a small space with a tiled floor and a single bed, and a bathroom in the hall—I returned to the *signora,* who slowly rose from her makeshift seat and cut me a piece of hard, fatty salami seasoned with garlic and fennel pollen. I ate near the Torre, the Leaning Tower, spreading the meat out on mellow, saltless Tuscan bread and washing it all down with a Fanta.

I then spent the hours until dinnertime wandering the city, stopping to sit blissfully on the great lawn of the Piazza del Duomo, weaving through the ancient Camposanto cemetery. As night fell, my stomach rumbling, I stumbled upon a small, sparsely populated restaurant on a side street. I'd never sat alone in a restaurant, but the waiter standing at the door looked warm and familiar, and I was hungry. I went in.

I told the man I'd like bruschetta and *lardo* to start. And then garganelli—small, hand-rolled tubular pasta—with *granchio,* crabmeat. Out of habit—in America, I wasn't legally able to order alcohol—I asked for another Fanta.

There was a short, slightly uncomfortable pause.

"You're not from here," the waiter said.

"I'm from Naples originally," I said. "I moved to New York when I was a kid."

"I see," he said. "Now, listen: Orange soda won't do here. If I let you have it, you'll complain that our food is no good."

"I would never—"

"We'll start you with a half glass of Sangiovese. Then, when the pasta comes, we'll see."

I nodded obediently and waited.

The bruschetta arrived without much fanfare—a thick slab of bread rubbed with garlic, grilled, and dressed in a thin blanket of finely sliced sweet white pork fat. I took the first crunchy bite and the melted fat coated my mouth. I reached for my Sangiovese.

The wine was so stern compared to the generous lard. They were made to be together—perfectly complementary and harmonious. Without each other, I recall thinking, neither of these honest things would have been nearly as excellent.

When I was finished, I waited excitedly for my second course. It came steaming in its bowl—a rich yellow pasta speckled with *peperoncino;* the crab and sauce were nearly invisible. As I picked up my fork, the waiter returned with a different bottle.

"This Merlot is sweeter and softer than Sangiovese, so it's better with red pepper flakes," he said.

Again, the drink and the food were a flawless pair. The pasta was fragrant, rich with crab-infused olive oil, basil, and parsley, and hot from the last-minute addition of the pepper. The wine was sweet and supple; its gentleness corralled the heat. I sat in that little room, taking each bite and sip slowly. I may have been there for several hours—I wasn't really aware of the time.

Eventually the door opened and the group of teenagers I had seen at the station came in. The waiter was friendly with them, and he introduced us.

"You must sit with them," he said. Italians never eat alone; seeing a single diner at a table makes them anxious. "Have a little more to eat."

I declined. I had to get going, I said. I didn't want to impose, and I was shy. But they were Italian—I should have known that I didn't have a chance.

"Absolutely not," said one pretty girl. "You're from New York, he says. Come and tell us about it."

Three hours, four courses, and six bottles of wine later, we all left the restaurant with full bellies and plans to meet the next day for a trip through Tuscany.

I didn't see my brother or my father for a week. I spent the whole week with the Italians and saw all of the region's jewels: Empoli, Siena, Florence, Greve in Chianti, Poggibonsi, San Gimignano. But my favorite trip was to a cement basement room in Montalcino.

I mentioned my interest in wine one day and one of the girls told me that her cousin worked at an estate.

"We'll go do a tasting," she said casually. The rest of the group concurred, as though sampling wines was a completely normal activity for six teenagers.

We drove through lush Montalcino and turned off onto a dirt road flanked by wild bushes. At its end sat a midsized stone house. The girl greeted her cousin, a rotund blond man in his late twenties, and he led us to the *cantina*, a chilly basement area lined with large wooden barrels. There, he handed us all wine glasses, and we headed to one of the barrels. He opened a spigot and poured a little wine into his glass. The wine was a darker, richer color than I'd ever seen before. He then circled around to all of us, emptying the wine into glass after glass, swirling it around so that it coated the inside, and then moving on. He was, I realized, getting rid of any lingering tastes—of soap, of leftover wine—that might be in the glasses. Then he went back to the barrel and took our glasses one by one, letting about a mouthful into each one. When we all had our glasses, I took a drink.

I felt I'd been hit in the mouth with a baseball bat. The wine from the barrel tasted like a heap of wood soaked in rubbing alcohol. It emanated sulfur and smelled like the barrel of a just-fired 12-gauge shotgun. As my new friends began to discuss the wine's body, its potential, its longevity, I stood silent. I could distinguish absolutely nothing. *This is a serious business,* I thought. *I have no part in it. I need to come up with a new career plan.* When we left I was dejected. I also wanted to brush my teeth.

But over the next few days, we visited more wineries—everyone seemed to have a friend or a sister or a friend of a sister who worked at one. And every time I tasted from a new barrel, I understood something extra. I could determine, bit by bit, within that murky alcohol, slight differences between the wines. They were still foreign and overwhelming, but each was distinct, distinguishable. I grew courageous; I had the ability to figure this stuff out, I thought. All I had to do was a whole lot more of this same thing.

When I met up with my father and brother in Naples, I was irrevocably changed.

☙

FOR THREE YEARS, I worked at restaurants in Albany during the school year, saved my money, and spent the entire summer backpacking through Europe, stopping off at as many wineries, trattorias, and osterias as I could. I was convinced that I wanted to dedicate my life, in some way, to wine and food. So, shortly after I graduated from high school, when my father was laid off from his job at the hospital laundry due to downsizing, I had an idea for his—*our*—new work. After more than a decade of working through the night, loading machines with hundreds of sheets and pillowcases and scrubs, he wanted to sleep by eleven and work decent hours during the day. Sal and I, amateur foodies that we were, proposed what we thought would be the ideal alternative: a wine store. We pooled our money with our father's and rented a carpeted space in a one-level strip mall, next to a manicure parlor. We called our wine store Ciro's, after my father, and got started buying and stocking wine.

As should have been obvious, I could not live out my *Mogliamante* dreams there. This was, as it had always been, Albany. And because of where we were, I was unable even to order many wines; the distributors decided what we would be selling. Back then, as in most of America, there were few distributors, and each carried a key product (Absolut vodka or Captain Morgan rum). If you, as a liquor store owner, wanted to stock a basic, necessary drink, you were told that you could purchase it—as long as you also purchased three no-name products and two dozen cases of cheap Merlot. But ultimately it didn't matter anyway, because the inhabitants of our town did not want to spend their hard-earned money on wine, and, as I had noted earlier, they were a people of habit. We really sold only two brands of wine: Franzia, which was a bag of wine in a box with a spout, and Bully Hill, a local producer that came out with about fifty types of whimsically named wines (Lighthouse White, Meat Market Red, Love My Goat). Anything that differed was regarded with suspicion, and our clientele was unwilling to spend more than $3.99 a bottle.

"If I pay six dollars," they would say, staring at me as though I was quite possibly a swindler, "it had better be really damn good."

My brother, father, and I drank any beautiful wines we'd managed to get, since they just collected dust otherwise.

And so it became clear over the next year, as I sold box after box of Franzia, that I couldn't stay in Albany. I wanted to find a way to repeat the experience I'd had in Tuscany with my Italian friends. I wanted to sell wine to people like that waiter in Pisa—people who understood what they were talking about, who could teach me something. I wanted to talk to people who loved wine as much as I did. The solution was New York City. If there were wine lovers anywhere in the States, I thought, they were probably there. I left my father with the shop (he closed it five years later) and headed south.

Chapter 4

NEW YORK CITY

———— ❦ ————

I WAS TWENTY-TWO, with a longtime girlfriend named Diva and
a VW Fox, which we drove down Route 87, Steely Dan in the
tape player. I had researched enough to understand that the
Upper East Side was the place to be for a successful person, so
when we landed our first apartment on Seventy-fifth Street between Second and Third, I felt I had at least halfway made it.
Never mind that the apartment was two hundred square feet,
and dark even at midday. Never mind that black bars covered
the windows, or that the paint was cracking. Never mind that
my fantasy didn't include an eighty-year-old landlady, Mrs. Lau,
who spoke little English except to repeatedly exclaim, pointing
one finger to the sky in triumph, "I am former Chinese Ladies'
Tennis Champion!"

"That's tremendous news, Mrs. Lau," I said.

"Champion," she said.

So it wasn't quite white-glove luxury living—but it also
wasn't Albany. I was content.

A few weeks after I got to New York, I was browsing through
the yellow pages, and I came upon a listing for a wine distributor called The House of Burgundy. I had read enough to know
that Burgundy was the world capital of fine wine, and I called
to ask if they were looking for salesmen. They said no. I hung
up and picked up the classifieds. A day later, my phone rang.

"Yes, this is The House of Burgundy," the woman on the other end of the line said. "You called about a job?"

"I did," I said.

"Well, we've had one suddenly open up," she said.

"That's great news!" I said.

"Not exactly," she said. "One of our salesmen just died."

The next day, I arrived at an old warehouse on West Fifty-eighth Street, wearing my best suit.

From then on, I spent my days dragging suitcases stuffed with the distributor's number one brand, Prosper Maufoux, from restaurant to restaurant. We also sold wines from Bordeaux, Provence, and California. I popped open bottles of Château Saint-Georges, Domaine Ott, Mondavi Special Reserve, or Opus One four times a day, ate elaborate meals with top restaurateurs, and was definitely no longer a skinny kid.

Sometimes I went out to lunch with the main producer, Vincent Maufoux, a stocky man with a considerable nose and mottled red skin. We sat at Le Cirque—he, commanding the wait staff to bring us plate after plate of frog's legs and coq au vin, and I, eating. Then, with an air of grandeur, Maufoux would pop open a $600 bottle of his best Burgundy. As I took a sip, I would smile at him and think, *I guess it's* okay.

At night I often lay in bed in my studio and read about wine. I read Burton Anderson's *Vino,* Hugh Johnson's *World Atlas of Wine.* Whenever I learned something completely new, I felt a great rush of excitement, as though I'd been presented with the perfect gift.

From my endless self-designed course of study, I learned that throughout the wide world of wine, most people agreed that French wines were the Oscar winners, so to speak, and Italian wines the less prestigious TV soap stars. Enthusiasts pursued the high holy grail of Burgundy, the supreme thrill. When journalists or lecturers deigned to mention Italian wines, they made them sound, frankly, kind of unappealing. "They are too wild," wrote one critic. "Inelegant," wrote another. "Catastrophic, full of animal aromas"; "defective"; "lacking finesse and harmony"; "acid monsters"; "bitter, tannic nonentities"; "a free-for-all." So who wanted to wade into that murky territory? I hadn't experienced that supreme thrill of the great French wines consistently, but still, I thought, *One day, I'll open a shop and sell the finest Burgundy in the world.*

Yet the dream was getting tarnished. No matter how much I resisted, I had to admit it: Burgundy disappointed me. After all I'd been fed about the majesty of the great French *crus,* after all the meals with aficionados, all the evenings spent poring over books and magazines, after all the effort I'd put into comprehending the magnificence of these wines, I still didn't get it. There were some brilliant Burgundies, for sure, but on the whole, they didn't awaken within me what I hoped they might have; they didn't enlighten me, though I couldn't say why. After a year at the company, I resigned.

∂৵

A FEW WEEKS LATER, I found myself in Midtown, near Columbus Circle. I had just finished consulting on the wine list at a large, popular, modern-American bistro where magazine editors and publishing executives enjoyed three-martini lunches. It was a drizzly fall day in 1992, and the whole city seemed to blend into a haze of taupe overcoats and black umbrellas. I pushed my collar up and dug my hands in my pockets as I cut around the crowds. I hit Central Park South, where the damp carriage horses were lined up; there weren't too many tourists out for a stinky ride around the soggy Great Lawn. As I crossed the street, I took a deep breath. I was heading for San Domenico, the finest Italian restaurant in America, where I'd heard there was a job opening. I walked through the marble entranceway, introduced myself to the maître d', presented my credentials, and was told to return in **two days** for a trial period as a captain. I would be working in the front of the house, something I had learned how to do, if on a different level, in Albany. I didn't know exactly what this would lead to, but I knew I wanted to learn the ins and outs of sophisticated Italian cuisine, and I'd had enough of pushing lavish French wines I didn't much believe in.

San Domenico was the brainchild of a ruthless and savvy Italian businessman named Tony May. Established in 1988, it was, in the 1990s, the most esteemed Italian restaurant in the United States. Mr. May was not an innovator, nor did he want to be. He wanted only to show Americans what Italian food really meant. To do so, Mr. May formed a partnership with a famous restaurant called San Domenico in Imola, Italy. He brought over its top chef, Valentino Marcatelli, who, for two years, helped develop the restaurant. They duplicated the menu and the wine list, and, upon Marcatelli's departure, Mr. May hired chef Theo Schoenegger to lord over the kitchen like the Kyocera-wielding dictator of a hot, garlicky country.

Theo and Mr. May didn't concoct lychee-partridge foams or infuse a single edamame bean with essence of Burmese lake trout. They perfected the art of roasting a branzino. The restaurant's signature dish was simple: a single huge raviolo stuffed with ricotta, spinach, and a soft-boiled egg yolk, topped with brown butter and *parmigiano-reggiano*. They wanted to make spaghetti, tomato, and basil—but only if it was the most harmonious spaghetti, tomato, and basil in the entire world, so that people would realize that though they'd eaten it thousands of times, they had never before understood the essence of that candid dish. They didn't use spaghetti, exactly, but the pasta called *spaghetti alla chitarra*—so called because you made it by slowly pressing semolina-flour dough through the top of an instrument with strings like a *chitarra*, or guitar. Theo made a rich tomato sauce, a mix of olive oil, garlic scent, fresh tomato, and *peperoncino*, and when it was all done, he whipped in grated *parmigiano-reggiano* and fresh whole squares of butter, flipped in the pasta, topped it with basil, and watched as people begged for more. It seemed so basic, but Theo was a scientist: you couldn't duplicate what he did, no matter how hard you tried. One day, the staff stood by as an elderly man got up from his table and announced to the dining room, with a mixture of joy and sorrow: "I am almost eighty years old, and I have only just now eaten the best meal of my life."

❧

THOUGH TONY MAY HAD GROWN UP in hard-knocks Torre del Greco, on the outskirts of Naples, and had made his way to America working on cruise ships, he fit effortlessly into the glamorous world of San Domenico, dining daily with ambassadors, movie stars, singers, journalists, fashion designers. Luciano Pavarotti was his buddy. Tony May was wealthy, having made his money as a part owner of New York's legendary Rainbow Room. He was handsome, sharp-featured, tall and broad, with tightly curled salt-and-pepper hair and a pair of authoritative silver-rimmed glasses. He always dressed in one of his many intricately tailored gray suits. And he was a brilliant conversationalist. This part I can only guess is true, considering the company he kept and held rapt at his dinner table every night. But he never had much of a conversation with me, or any of his wait staff, unless to say, in his wiseguy accent, "Don't fuckin' talk about it, just fuckin' do it."

He was also very difficult to approach about vacations.

"What do you need that for?" he responded when I asked for a week off.

"Well, I haven't taken a day off in four months and my girl is really bugging me to spend some time away from the city," I said.

"Okay," Mr. May said begrudgingly. "But you really don't get anything accomplished on vacation."

He was equally stony about raises.

"Why do you need more cash?" he asked. "You're here all the time. What do you do that requires money?"

But what hurt the staff the most was when he was nice, really nice, to other people. We would all stand, steaming, in our respective stations, watching as Tony May greeted a young stranger from California, a wannabe cook who had come to pay homage. Suddenly our Grinch morphed into Babbo Natale, a generous paternal figure with all the time and connections in the world, helping the kid land an internship in Italy or an all-expenses-paid tour of restaurants.

"What a fantastic guy," the student would say, grinning. "Tony May really set up my life."

We seethed—we were slaving away all day in the hot kitchen, serving guests so that our boss could make his fortune, and then some nobody who'd done nothing came by and profited from all of Tony May's connections. We were the bitter, neglected step-kids; we simultaneously despised him and craved his approval, even though we knew he was never, ever going to bestow it on us in any satisfying manner.

He was a hard boss, and I can't say I liked him, but later in life Tony May's existence came to symbolize for me a fundamental question about means, ends, and art. If, say, Matisse was a jerk, does that mean anything about his paintings? Are they still valuable? Was it all worth it? For all Tony May taught me not to do, maybe the mark he ultimately left—on the world of Italian food, on my brain—was the truly relevant thing. And maybe the reason the staff all complained about him was also the reason he was so important.

Tony May was a traditionalist in the strictest sense. He was relentless because Italian culture, in its truest form, is also relentless. Italians are a people bound—nearly to the point of strangulation—to their past. They are terrified of change, and in an increasingly globalized world, they cling to all that is Italian. In most places around the world, you can find a few ethnic restaurants. England and the United States, lacking their own strong food customs, are packed with everything. Not Italy. Sure,

Rome and Milan house a few places, but even midsized cities keep serving the same stuff, again and again. In an Umbrian city, for example, you will find twenty restaurants that all serve variations on the same exact regional menu—some more expensive, some less expensive, some with a *fritto misto* that includes fried spinach balls and some with a nut bread starter, but otherwise it's roast pork, grilled pork, pork sausage, chicken breast, lamb, bruschetta, and thirty types of pizza. There is the possibility that you could locate an unpleasant Chinese restaurant, but it survives only as a sort of proof that other ethnic cuisines are inferior. Each and every Italian in the city must try it once or twice, if only so that they can say that they have indeed sampled and hated foreign cuisine, and now, given their new perspective, they can declare definitively that Umbrian food is the world's best.

This is the true strength of Italian food. Italians don't get bored by their recipes—when something's good, why change it? The goal is not to improve on Great-Grandma's recipe; it doesn't need improvement. The goal is to replicate exactly Great-Grandma's recipe. It's almost Darwinian: the best recipes survive forever, handed down again and again and creating a historical dish that balks trends. Tony May knew this better than anyone.

We all thought, *We work so hard all day and he just sits in his office.* But in fact we were slaving away in exactly the way he dictated. He was a cultural watchdog, terrifyingly alert, and he never let us fall into trends. A little flamboyance was immediately struck down. We all had our own ideas, and we all wanted to make a name for ourselves. But anytime we tried, we were punished.

If the maître d' went off the color scheme, he was reprimanded. If the pastry chef tried a new topping on the *cassata,* he was called into the office. Once, Theo tried to change every item on the menu, convinced that with some new, inventive dishes, he could transform the place into a four-star affair. Tony May sat down with a new creation every night and systematically said,

"This tastes like crap." The rest of us ate Theo's new dishes, and they were fantastic. We figured that Tony May, that shadowy, daunting figure, was an imbecile for being unable to see that. But now I know that he understood precisely how good Theo's stuff was, and he didn't give a damn. His objective was to protect a ritual. Because of this, he was on the board of the Culinary Institute of America's Italian program, on the board of a famous cooking school in Alba, and the founder of the Gruppo Ristoratori Italiani, a society dedicated to improving Italian food in restaurants. For his ardor, he was awarded the Italian government's highest honor for expatriates who do great work for Italian culture. Tony May knew that management was a game; he recognized what he wanted, and every day we tried to make him forget it. But he was iron-willed and coldhearted, and he would always win.

Furthermore, he taught me about a whole new food culture: the intellectual aspect of epicureanism. I was working at a restaurant that valued—truly valued—rice; we even held risotto tastings, which involved eating the same risotto dish made with five different types of rice. I once witnessed Mr. May and a food historian discuss—for three full hours—the best way to slice a tomato: how you cut one, when you wedge one, why you dice one, each point elaborated on in painstaking detail.

Our goal as captains was to control what the customers consumed. We hoped to gently dissuade them from ordering for themselves, and to concoct for them a symphonic experience—a meal that layered dish after dish and rose to a perfect pitch. Meals at the restaurant were put together with mathematical precision. The average patron would be prone to order something he was comfortable with, but that didn't go with something else he was having; he was unaware that ordering lobster salad followed by rabbit made about as much aesthetic sense as pulling on a pair of red slacks and a pink-checkered polo shirt. We wanted to make his experience beautiful, and so we would suggest that he trust us. We would then serve him beef carpaccio and foie gras slices, drizzled with raspberry vinaigrette; then roasted Alaskan spot prawns and rosemary-stewed cannellini beans; followed by garganelli with poached salmon and caviar; a beef glaze risotto; and duck breast wrapped in spinach and puff pastry and topped with a black olive sauce. No one dish was massive; we never wanted to make anyone ill. At the end of each dinner, we served our guests *pinzimonio,* small raw market vegetables on crushed ice, with new olive oil for dipping, and sea salt. The vegetables cleared out your system, cooled your stomach, and cleaned your mouth.

San Domenico was about such attention to detail, and such respect for the Italian way. It was not, I realized, similarly dedicated to wine. In fact, Tony May didn't even know which varietal many standard wines were made from, and he still probably knew a lot more about the genre than almost any other Manhattan restaurateur. San Domenico may have been unique when it came to food, but even though it had the biggest Italian wine cellar in the United States, it was like everywhere in America at the time: nobody gave a damn about Italian wine. I would learn just how much they were missing when I became, to my own surprise, a sommelier.

❧

AFTER I'D BEEN WORKING on San Domenico's floor for two weeks, a sommelier arrived from Italy. He was young and skinny, with a permanent hangdog expression and four pin-striped suits. I followed him around eagerly for a few days, hoping to learn from him—he was, after all, rumored to be one of the finest up-and-coming sommeliers in Europe and I had awaited his arrival with an almost groupie-like enthusiasm. But it quickly became clear to both him and me that he actually knew very little about wine; I was more informed. He was embarrassed and I was determined to get his job. So I led him to Tony May and together we told him that I should be handling the cellar and he should be working as a captain.

"Let's give it a try," Mr. May said as he finished his meal with his daily plate of sliced papaya. With wine, he wasn't picky. He regarded us, adjusted his glasses, and waved us away.

That night, I passed Mrs. Lau on the stairwell.

"How was your day?" she asked.

"Actually, Mrs. Lau, I got promoted," I said. "I'm the sommelier at the restaurant now."

"Congratulations!" she said. "I'm former Chinese Ladies' Tennis Champion."

"I suppose we both have something to be proud of," I said.

I went to my apartment, kicked off my shoes, and lay down on my bed with the San Domenico wine list. It was heavy, bound in thick brown leather, and seventy-five pages long. It was an exclusively Italian list, which was unheard of in those days. Italy has over two thousand varieties of grapes growing in its soil, and I was unfamiliar with many of the wines on the list. I fell asleep with the list open on my chest, and when I woke up, I knew how I could make it even better.

"Mr. May," I said the next day, "I have a proposal."

"Let's hear this," he said, taking a puff of his cigar. He blew the smoke out in a line of perfect wispy gray circles.

"I think we should expand the wine list to include French wines, too," I said. "It would raise our prestige."

"Sounds good." He nodded. "How about this? You get to know the wines on the list, and as soon as you run out of good Italians, you tell me, and we'll order some French."

❧

DURING MY EARLY DAYS as a sommelier, I tasted every wine that I served to my tables, which meant that I was trying about forty bottles a night. Again and again, I felt my heart lifting. I wanted to know how to impress people, how to read a diner for the wine she would most enjoy, how to understand the codes people give you when they ask about wine. I needed to know which wine of San Domenico's eight hundred would make a certain table the happiest. I was dedicated to raising my customers' understanding of both wine and food. Before, food and wine had been purely an exercise of passion for me; no matter how much I read, I ate with feeling, not thought. Now, I had begun to integrate the emotional and the philosophical. Many Americans, raised on a mix of puritanical restraint and hamburgers, may think food only nourishment, and wine only intoxication, but Europeans consider food and wine the stuff of life, worthy of attention and study. I was working with that approach.

Because Italian wine had been largely ignored in the United States, I had to scramble to find any older vintages. There had been, really, only one dealer, a Queens-based importer named Lou Iacucci, but he'd died in 1989. He had been obsessed with improving wine lists throughout New York—at Lidia Bastianich's first restaurant, Buonavia; at the Brooklyn institution Tommaso's; at Long Island City's famous Manducatis. Manducatis was my watering hole.

On a slow night, my friends in the wine industry and I would take a cab through the Midtown Tunnel and hop out on Jackson Avenue in front of Manducatis—a gray-brick corner restaurant, its windows lit by blinking red beer signs. Three of us would typically open ten bottles—Barolos, Barbarescos, Brunellos—all chosen by Iacucci and purchased by owners Vincenzo and Ida Cerbone. The Cerbones refused to charge astronomical prices. Bottles I was selling for $450 as a sommelier in Manhattan were $60 at Manducatis. Better yet, Iacucci had convinced the Cerbones to cellar their wines properly, and had taught them how to hold them for a long time until they were perfectly ready to drink; back then, they were the only Italian wines with good provenance. My friends and I learned Iacucci's invaluable lessons alongside the restaurateurs.

Next, I started a wine-tasting group with ten other people in the industry. My importer friend Dino Tantawi and I headed up the group. Once a month, we were to meet at a restaurant and each bring a bottle that corresponded to a theme: Left Bank Bordeaux, perhaps, or the best wine we owned from 1985. The bottles were to be secured in paper bags, so that each tasting would be blind.

We all sat down—Dino, an Egyptian bistro manager named Kareem, a Greek-American restaurateur named Chris, a California wine representative named Jordan, and a ragtag bunch of sommeliers and me—opened our bottles, tasted, and scored. In blind tastings, I was always drawn to Italian wines—the simple Barberas, the complex, regal Barolos. I was not alone. Many times, one of our Francocentric friends would point to a glass filled with Italian wine, his expression a study in the sublime, and declare it his favorite.

I had also begun a side business helping people—mostly diners at the restaurant—organize their cellars. Instead of asking for, say, $600, I would ask for $300 and the opportunity to try some of their best vintages as payment. Often, I'd slip a glass of Brunello or Barbaresco into the largely French mix. The unsuspecting collector in his cellar, surrounded by his sparkling treasures from the hills of the Rhône and the valleys of Napa, would ask me, "Which one of my babies was that? That one was incredible." When he found out that his favorite drink came not from a famous château but from a small estate in the heart of Tuscany, his face would crumple into a mess of consternation and disbelief. "Italy?" he'd say. "From *Italy*?"

Those years were my personal university, and the most valuable course I took was taught by San Domenico's second-biggest personality: Theo Schoenegger, the best cook I've ever worked with.

Theo came from Alto Adige, the snowy northern region bordering Austria. He had worked as a child at his mother's restaurant, a highly regarded trattoria, and was one of the chefs whom Tony May brought to New York under the guidance of Andrea Hellrigl, the chef at his other restaurant, Palio. These guys were technically Italians, but on the inside they were German: serious and frighteningly precise. Theo was skeletal; he jogged ten miles daily, mid-shift. He was always dressed in slacks, a skinny tie, and a white coat, and he looked more like a lab worker than a chef. He liked to circle the restaurant, hands behind his back, and pop up behind various employees to ask nonsensically, "Now do you see my point?" To which most people would answer, "Um, yeah, I guess." He was a perfectionist and he was merciless.

"My cat's having kittens," a runner once said.

Theo laughed.

"Why are you laughing, Theo?" I asked.

"I'm just remembering that back in Alto Adige, when a cat had kittens, we put them in a bag and then we hit the bag against a wall until they stopped crying. That's when you knew they were dead."

The kitchen was eerily silent. Theo laughed again and went back to work.

I developed a rapport with Theo. It had its upsides and its downsides. Its downsides included spending a good deal of time with a kitten killer and being his go-to for hiring Spanish-speaking dishwashers.

"Ask this boy if he has a problem with authority," he commanded me. We stood in the basement—me, Theo, and a quivering twenty-year-old immigrant who had spent the last week strapped to the underside of a bus, speeding farther and farther away from his home and family.

"*¿Tienes problema con autoridad?*" I asked in my best restaurant Spanish.

The man looked at me and said, "*Non tengo problema.*"

I turned to Theo and said, "He doesn't have a problem."

"Ask this boy if he has a problem with people of authority," he said.

"*¿Tienes problema con personas que tienen autoridad?*" I asked.

"*No tengo problema con personas que tienen autoridad,*" the man said.

Theo looked at me questioningly.

"He doesn't have a problem with people of authority," I said.

Theo nodded. "If I ask him to pick up a box, will he pick up the box?"

"*¿Se el te pregunta di prender una caja, tu la prendes?*" I asked.

"*Si, yo la prendo,*" the man said.

"Yes, he will pick up the box," I said.

"And ask the boy if he will come to work every day."

"*¿Tu vienes a trabajo todo los dias?*"

"*Yo vengo.*"

"He'll come."

Theo looked at the man skeptically for a moment. The man imagined his wife and barefoot child back in his home country. He broke into a light sweat.

"Fine," Theo said. "Tell him that he should be here tomorrow at seven a.m."

One of the upsides of having a relationship with Theo was that he allowed me to taste his food. And his food was spectacular. It was perfect, literally perfect. My friend Scott Conant worked at the restaurant; he's a celebrity chef in his own right now, and back then he had enough talent to get into that kitchen, but it took him three months to learn to make a veal stock the way Theo wanted it. Theo prepared treasures. He made little fish ravioli in calamari broth, these tiny pockets bursting with intensity, with freshness and seafood and the depths of the clearest ocean. He made duck ravioli with whipped foie gras and port sauce fused together topped with *parmigiano-reggiano*. He made rabbit and goat and roebuck. And he may have thrown those cats against that wall, but when you ate his *spaghetti secchi* with cuttlefish ink and mussels, it seemed that maybe, just maybe, all of his sadism could be overlooked. He was, after all, committing noble acts of kindness for mankind just by feeding me.

He also taught me. He gave me food, I gave him wine, and we ate and drank together at the banquette tables after hours.

"What is the mistake?" he would ask, presenting me with a spoonful of sauce. "What do you think?"

"I think it sucks," I would say. Or, "I think it's remarkable." Or, "I have no idea, Theo. Tell me."

Then I would do my thing. "What about this wine?" I'd ask. "And this one? And this one?"

❧

WINE TOGETHER WITH FOOD is the Italian way. I was comprehending exactly how the two could work as a team, how they could be synchronized, how I could help create an astounding experience for a diner through the correct combination of flavors.

But as time passed and my knowledge grew, I began to sense that the wines I had fallen for were changing. When I had begun reading about wine in the late 1970s, everything I read concentrated on the importance of how wine made you feel. When I had toured Italy, I'd witnessed traditional winemakers—pretty much the only type of winemaker there was at that time—making wine in the traditional way.

Historically, the first known quality winemakers were priests and alchemists, men who believed that nature was central to all understanding. For priests and alchemists, wine was relevant because it was the most alive consumable substance. Everything else—save for cheese and yogurt, with their enzymes—is dead. Meat is dead, vegetables are dead, baked bread is dead, cream sauce is dead. But wine is alive, full of yeasts, and ever changing, evolving like a plant or a person, a divine creation.

Priests and alchemists made and analyzed wine according to

what they considered its three properties: spirit, soul, and salt. The wine's spirit was its alcohol; its soul was its individuality, its fragrance and *territorio,* how it demonstrated the land from which it came; and its salt was its body. To the contemporary mind, the philosophy of alchemists is difficult to grasp. It sounds flighty and nebulous. But at the base of it all was a belief that the best wine came from the best *materia prima*—the best raw natural material. What the discourse about salt and soul meant practically was that these winemakers considered their wine a being, and treated it with respect as such, and that they concentrated first and foremost on growing the best grapes possible, because wine's power came from nature.

Long after the alchemists were gone, traditional winemakers made wine in this way. The drinks they crafted were unaltered expressions of their earth. When you drank them, you reacted to the intangible qualities they possessed. Were they masculine, feminine? Complex, unpredictable? Mysterious? These winemakers maintained the faith that their predecessors based everything on, the faith that nature would give them what they needed to make the best wine, that nature would help them create something that was alive.

But during my time at San Domenico, I saw many of these wines changing. What had once been reserved and gracious was suddenly a richer, newer, extroverted version of itself. Almost all the Chiantis had changed. The Barolos—Ceretto, Prunotto, Sandrone, Clerico, Scavino—were no longer rusty pink, but deep purple instead. They were thick, robust. They were . . . modern.

Modern wines were made by those who followed a philosophy quite opposite to the traditional one. Rather than maintaining faith in nature, modernists put their faith in technique. They thought traditional winemakers were ridiculous, mystics in a world of atheists; the best way to make wine was with technology. They didn't think wine was "sunlight, held together by water," as Galileo had said. They thought wine was grapes and chemical reactions, controllable by the newest and best machines and additives. Some producers, especially those in California, even took the position that *territorio*—a wine's sense of place, or the particular qualities a wine picks up from its land, its specific environment—did not exist at all. Wine, in their eyes, was a product of how you made it and nothing else.

The new wines were produced by technologies that allowed modernists to exaggerate everything in the wines while de-emphasizing vineyard care. Any flaws in the fruit could be corrected by tools. These wines were analyzed by their fans in concrete ways: High or low in tannins? Silky? With the taste of pear? When someone looked at his glassful of inky liquid, he thought, *Well, maybe it is better than the old drinks.* In the mid-1990s, even the skeptics were into the modern stuff.

Then, most people thought that vibrant was better because they were human beings, and humans, visual creatures that we are, like bright things. Things that we consume should be, our instincts tell us, as fresh and young as possible. Nature offered visible cues to our ancestors as they wandered the woods and plains. If given a choice between a large, soft peach and a small, hard peach, you could safely bet that the large peach was going to taste better. It would be riper, juicier, healthier, and just plain yummier. Now, people were stalking food every day on the new hunting ground: the supermarket. And they wanted apples as red as a Crayola crayon and the size of a newborn's head, a bunch of jade broccoli that could serve twenty, a chicken that could have put up a fight against a Doberman. Everything was to be unblemished, shining, like a cartoon. And wine, too, was supposed to engage in the competition.

But it was a trick—and, if just for a second, everyone fell for it. Whereas once these observable traits were usually indicative of quality, laboratories changed that. The bulk and brilliance of an orange no longer indicates its superiority, and may, in fact, imply its inferiority. A wild orange can be gorgeous, but it will never be as huge and symmetrical as the kind made by a scientist. And if a scientist designs a seed with the purpose of growing an aesthetically pleasing piece of citrus fruit to appeal to the masses in the produce aisles, he necessarily sacrifices the true orange flavor of the thing. Nature leaves clues, sure, but she's more subtle than that. The truth is that these days, with the amount of corporate manipulation that goes into food, it's better to go for the smaller, weirder apple, the scrawnier chicken. These are signs that the stuff is real, not factory-made. And since flavor likes to condense itself, the littler, organic things taste better. Compare a tiny strawberry plucked from a vine to a huge strawberry plucked from a crate: it's the difference between a strawberry and a mass of watery red pulp.

The same goes for wine. Everyone thought, just looking at our newly crimsoned glasses back then, that it had been improved. But they were blinded. In fact, wine, too, was easy to screw around with. Some people had altered their products in natural ways, but most had begun experimenting with enzymes, laboratory yeasts, and concentrators. The grapes weren't purpler—chemical additives made the product that way. The juice wasn't sweeter—that was the sugar pumped in. And if the winemaker didn't rely entirely on artificial methods, but had used the new French barriques incorrectly, often the wine didn't taste like its territory anymore. These wines were sweeping the nation—everyone was nuts for appealing, soft, easy concentrates.

After the initial thrill and confusion, I stepped back. These wines were effortless, but what did that really matter? The beauty of wine had never been that it was uncomplicated. I could drink orange juice if I wanted a fruity, simple drink. The new wines were like the hot, popular kids in high school—they appealed to an enthusiastic but unsophisticated appetite and then aged badly. Plus, my job was to protect tradition just as Tony May did. You couldn't very well serve the most classic dishes from Italy with these new wines. As the journalists were slapping high scores on the new wines, I retreated to my older collection. Every time I drank an old Barolo, I was overwhelmed with remorse. There was the Italian in me: Why change such a perfect thing? What could I do to make sure these guys who followed the old way, these holdouts, didn't disappear altogether?

Chapter 5

SCAVINO

———— ❧❧ ————

I QUIT SAN DOMENICO, and while I supported myself with consulting work and a job at an importing company, I began to think about having a store. By the summer of 1998, I had developed a business plan that centered on the concept that this store would present Italian wines as they'd never been presented before. There would be no warm, dusty bottles pushed together, no "2-for-1" specials, no $4.99 Chianti. I would build hundreds of small individual shelves, where I would display one of each bottle (the rest would be kept in a temperature-controlled cellar); I wanted to send a message that the wines displayed were important enough to be considered works of art.

All of my employees would have intricate knowledge of the many regions, of the range of artisanal methods, of the thousands of grape varieties. We would sell modern Italian wines, but mainly as a sort of gateway drink, just a step on the path toward a love of traditional wines. Your average California Cabernet drinker, presented with a deeply traditional Barolo, would be too shocked by how different it was to recognize its beauty, and he'd probably conclude that he didn't like Italian wines. Instead, if the California Cabernet drinker came to the store, we'd give him a Merlot-Sangiovese blend from Tuscany, rich and contemporary, that would at once show him something new and offer him the comfort of the familiar. Then we'd progress with him, in whatever time necessary, to the wilder, older, more distinctly Italian drinks. My employees and I would be patient, and keep in mind hospitality: an Italian vendor wouldn't dream of charging an extra $2.50 for a gift box, wouldn't rush you through a decision, would sit you down in his office, offer you a glass of his favorite wine, and talk to you. The shop wouldn't offer French wine or Californian wine or any wine that wasn't made on Italian soil. And I would go after connoisseurs and opinion makers, people who could help change the image of Italian wine, and the concept of great wine in general.

A year earlier, I had met, through work, my partner Perry Porricelli, a guy I immediately realized would be perfect to balance me out. Perry was calm, steady, and experienced, and he had the ability to pick the right wines for different people. But most important, Perry was a great salesman—a quality I lacked. I was too emotional; if a client didn't like a wine I knew was great, I turned red in the face. I felt as though he'd spoken badly about a member of my family and I never wanted to talk to that person again.

That approach, I recognized, didn't work well in day-to-day dealings, and it wouldn't help me reach my goals. So Perry was a necessity, my personal wine diplomat. If someone didn't like a wine Perry knew was great, he would shrug, smile, and find a wine the client liked better. If somebody didn't immediately understand a wine, Perry had the patience to pull him through. He was the kind of person, I foresaw, who could spend years helping a client make his way to the complicated stuff. It helped that he was unerringly honest, and that he believed in my idea enough to quit his job and come along for the ride.

We found investors on Wall Street and a space on West Twenty-second Street in Manhattan. The investors were into the idea, but they had never quite comprehended how the shop would be different from other wineshops, or why I wanted to offer only Italian wine. Nonetheless, by the winter of 1998, they were officially ready to put down some money.

The day the lease was being drawn up, I went to a wine auction. I often found myself bidding against Joseph Bastianich, then co-owner of two Manhattan restaurants: a wine bar and restaurant called Becco, and a new high-end Italian place called Babbo. At this particular December auction, I was buying for a very rich private client who had made it clear to me that price was no object—he just wanted the right wines in his collection. With this on my side, I won each lot, even if I paid more than the wine's value. Afterward, Joe—a portly young guy with a shaved head—came up to me. We'd met more than once at the Blue Ribbon, a late-night joint in SoHo that served, after 2 a.m., almost exclusively chefs, waiters, and managers getting off shift at their own establishments.

"Sergio, what are you doing paying so much for this stuff?" he asked.

"I have a buyer with no limit," I said.

"Private consulting?" he asked. "Working on anything else?"

I told him about my upcoming shop. I had perfected a two-minute pitch, concept and explanation included.

"So only Italian wine?" he asked.

"Italian wine and nothing else," I said.

"Raising the profile of Italian wine," he said.

"Changing the idea," I said.

"I want in," he said.

"I have a group of investors already," I said.

"How about you come to Babbo tonight," Joe said. "It won't hurt to talk."

That night I went to Babbo, Joe's restaurant with chef Mario Batali, off Washington Square Park. Mario, now possibly the most famous Italian chef in America, was relatively unknown back then, but he was still a larger-than-life character, with his signature red ponytail and orange kitchen clogs. I thought he'd send me out a platter of antipasti, I'd talk to Joe for a half hour, and then I'd be off. But the experience was quite different.

Joe and I sat down at a round corner table in the low-lit place. He poured me a glass of a simple red wine, and Mario sent out his most advanced dishes—lamb's tongue salad topped with a poached egg and surrounded by chanterelle mushrooms; handmade beef cheek ravioli; stewed tripe; and his own *testa,* a terrine made from a calf's head, drizzled with vinaigrette and accented with pearl onions. I'm an adventurous eater, and I relished the chance to consume such rare dishes. But, I wondered, how come the dining room was full? There was no way that a bunch of New Yorkers were ordering up anything composed of the inside of a sheep's stomach. I scanned the room and saw that, indeed, very few of them had. Instead, most of them had chosen the safer, more familiar options: the braised beef with asparagus, the striped bass with leeks and pancetta. Mario was giving his public exactly what they craved in the hopes of getting them to eventually recognize the value of what he really loved—brains and intestines, the stomach lining, the most deeply flavored, underused parts of the animal. His food was almost like modern wines—it offered at once novelty and comfort, and it could bring Americans over to new experiences.

These guys get it, I thought. *They get how to push the limits without scaring anyone. They understand how to make an American like Italian food, and how to make an American branch out.*

"How will you find your wines for this place?" Joe asked.

"The same way I find them now," I said. I told him how I hit up ten wineries a day on my trips to Italy. I told him I had a one-step system for what wines would always be good: Get to know the winemaker. Is he taking shortcuts? Does he want to make a quick buck? Is he just following the market? Or is he steadfast, true to his principles, devoted first to wine and next to profit? This was how I found the great wines that you could depend on year in and year out—by finding the great producers.

As the meal neared its finish, Joe leaned in to me. Mario had sent out biscotti and a sweet dessert wine. "Listen, Sergio," Joe said, "you sure it wouldn't make more sense to have me and Mario invest?"

Joe was right. I thought about my financial backers. They were money guys, big money guys, with a money guy mentality. They didn't care about food or wine much; they cared about making a profit. On the other hand, Joe and Mario, though they may have been born, respectively, in Queens and Seattle, had a lot of Italian in them. And they clearly understood the relationship between food and wine.

I didn't sign the lease for the place on Twenty-second Street. Instead, I took Joe and Mario up on their offer. I found a first-floor storefront on East Sixteenth Street, right off Union Square. I set it up—demolition, drywall, paint, and all—with the help of Perry and my first-ever employee, a workhorse of a man named Gildardo, who today runs the cellar. In October 1999, we opened our doors. It was not a fairy tale.

From then on, I slept three hours a night, gained thirty pounds from the stress, and at one point owed my purveyors $160,000. When I dated, I constructed elaborate tales as to why we couldn't go out to a pricey restaurant dinner. The only things that I ever treated myself to were boxing lessons and, counterintuitively, a daily Krispy Kreme glazed doughnut.

One of the main reasons for the Krispy Kreme and the unhappy purveyors was that all my spare cash was going into travel. Some years, I flew back and forth to Italy fifteen times; I traveled around the country for weeks on end, meeting producers, discovering new estates, new varietals, new characters. It was there that I finally caught a glimpse of a change, of a circling back to the ways of old. I'd been searching for the traditional wines all this time, and now, I sensed, the traditional wines were getting easier to find. I learned the reason why on one such trip in 2002, sitting at a restaurant table with a man named Enrico Scavino, whom I had come to visit earlier that day.

～

THE PAOLO SCAVINO ESTATE—named for Enrico Scavino's late father—sat just off a main stretch of industrial road in Barolo, nestled at the end of its own small street. The house and winery consisted of a Spanish-style hacienda from which two wings stretched out and hugged an open stone driveway filled with luxury cars. I stepped through a dark wood door to an interior courtyard, where three white cats played and a fat old dog on a chain nervously paced up to a tree planted in the center and then back to his water bowl. A teenager in a purple rock 'n' roll T-shirt and backwards baseball cap was wheeling a stack of boxes through.

"Are you here for an appointment?" he asked.

"With Signor Scavino," I said. "Sergio Esposito from New York."

"He'll be right with you," he said.

I strolled around; an old dachshund running free licked my shoe. Two minutes later, Scavino himself emerged. *"Buon giorno. Come sta?"* he said, greeting me and asking how I was in the formal style. The way he moved was almost Japanese, arms at his sides, back tense and straight. He reached out and we shook hands.

Enrico Scavino was a square, sturdy man, not quite six feet tall, balding, with gray hair and delicate, unremarkable features. He was dressed in a maroon sweater, yellow collared shirt, and dark pants with creases, and he wore heavy brown leather shoes. He was incessantly, almost helplessly polite. It could take up to five minutes to pass through a door with him, as he steadfastly refused to go first and I, as his junior, felt I had to follow suit. We had initially gotten stuck at all entrances and exits, which was time-consuming, considering that his winery was a labyrinth of new rooms.

"You first," Scavino would say, standing to the side.

"No, please, you first," I would counter, standing to the other side.

"No, you, of course."

Then, smiles pasted on our faces, we would both hold out. Since he always won through sheer willpower, I gave up altogether and automatically went first, hating myself a little.

We walked up a flight of stairs to a room full of metal tanks. To one side was a small glassed-in laboratory and in it a woman, perched on a chair, examining a test tube. From behind, you could see only a mass of brown hair.

Scavino tapped on the glass and the woman swirled around and smiled broadly. Enrica Scavino was famously *bona*, or hot. She had a snub nose, sultry cat eyes, and an excellent figure. Even better, she was charming, polished, and naturally seductive. In a world frequented by dweebs, she was a true celebrity. At any event she attended, she found herself surrounded by a gaggle of the bespectacled, the crooked-toothed, the socially inept—the dorks who made up our glamorous industry—all reveling in the fact that someone like her was talking to them, and therefore was maybe, just *maybe,* interested.

Enrica waved at us and opened the door.

"She's so talented. When she returns from selling trips, we just see orders flying in," her father said.

"*Benvenuto,* Sergio," Enrica greeted me. In addition to speaking three languages and acting as Enrico's translator and head of global marketing, she had studied accounting and economics. She kissed me on both cheeks.

"Well, shall we start a little tour, then?" she asked.

Enrico was in the midst of a major operational overhaul. He had recently invested in a new vineyard and was constructing new rooms and purchasing new equipment to handle the grapes.

Enrica's lab was a windowed room within the greater fermentation facility, a warehouse-sized space lined with gleaming silver ceiling-height vertical tanks and gleaming silver ceiling-height horizontal tanks, the rotary fermentors.

"Sergio, do you remember how we used to have to mix the grapes by hand, four people, all day?" Enrica said. The machines did everything for them now.

"*È una cosa perfetta,*" said Enrico. It's a perfect thing.

To the side there was a smaller room that contained another spotless silver apparatus. A series of open containers connected to what looked like a tiny, sloped, factory production belt.

"A top-of-the-line grape-drying machine in our grape-drying room," Enrica said. Before, they couldn't even pick fruit when it had rained because no matter what you did, the wine would be too watery. "Now, using this, five hours and there's not a spot of external moisture to be found," she said.

"*È una cosa fantastica,*" said Enrico. It's a fantastic thing.

Nearby was another area with a spiderlike contraption, a metal object with many buttons and short, open hoses. It was a bottle-drying machine.

"It's Italian but the air compressor is American," Enrica said. "When it purifies the air, it uses enough electricity to heat a small house in winter. But it's worth the price because this ensures that not one drop of water enters our wine."

"*È una cosa bellissima,*" said Enrico. It's a very beautiful thing.

We headed down the stairs, through an enormous modern brick area punctuated only by a lonely shelf holding several dusty old bottles of ancient Barolo, and past a bright concrete garage that could house five big rigs.

"This is where the trucks deposit the grapes," Enrica said.

Enrico opened a heavy wooden door and we descended farther underground to the *cantina,* an area the size of an airplane hangar, lined with barrels and barriques. Unlike most *cantine,* it was relatively warm. The floor was heated to start fermentation.

"We keep the wine in barrique for one year to get more air and clean the smells off," she said, speaking of the small oak barrels that had become popular in Italy after they were imported from France in the 1980s. "Then we move it to *botti* for a year." *Botti* are the older wooden barrels that most Italian winemakers had used for centuries.

"Bravo," I said. "I've seen a lot of people massacre the wine, keeping it in barrique too long."

"We're always experimenting," Enrica said. "We buy ninety percent of our barriques from two of the best vendors and ten percent from new vendors, and then we do a trial. You can see how different wines emerge, according to the wood that was used—some more vibrant, more elegant, more excited."

Enrico Scavino was something of an innovator in the use of barriques, which he first tried out in 1982, when the rest of Barolo was still dedicated to the *botti.* He spent years testing out the different types of barriques, Nevers and Alliers—some that produced wines that stank of vanilla and toast, some that overwhelmed the Nebbiolo grape, some bigger so as to have a smaller wood-to-wine ratio, some with more expensive material. He saw that barriques made wines he considered more open, more accessible, and as his *botti* got too old and porous to use, he purchased more barriques. By 1994, he had thrown out his old *botti* and was using only barriques.

The Italian government demanded that producers of Barolo age their wines for a minimum of two years. Scavino began to see that when aged in barrique, the wine became oxidized, the typicity masked—the fruit's signature characteristics were lost. Nebbiolo is a delicate grape, its greatest trait elegance; unlike the heartier Merlot or Cabernet, it can't handle the strength of the barriques for two years. By 1998, Scavino reverted. He had seen that Barolo needed, at least in part, to be made by its traditional methods in order to retain its essence. He decided to bring back his *botti*. He was reverting to the old method; he'd seen that he obtained better results from his grapes that way.

֍

"WELL, YOU MUST BE HUNGRY," Enrica said, looking at the silver watch wrapped around her delicate wrist. "We have a lunch to make." She ushered us out to the driveway and into a silver Audi, which Enrico then casually drove at one hundred miles per hour to the typical Piedmontese restaurant where he always ate. Like most of the great winemakers I have known, he was a creature of habit when it came to restaurants.

Antica Corona Reale da Renzo was a one-floor stucco building off a flat industrial farming road in Cervere, next door to Bra, a town that houses, most notably, the offices of the Slow Food movement, an organization dedicated to encouraging natural, small-scale farming practices. The proprietor, a woman with spiky black hair and thick navy eye shadow, kissed Enrico. The waiter, a tall, gangly young man with dimples, grasped his hand.

"Signor Scavino, thank you so much for coming," the waiter said.

We were shown to our table in the second room, a small space with a brick ceiling and creamy yellow walls decorated with enormous, realistic paintings of food: one of a fruit tart, its grapes and blueberries glistening with glaze, the other of plump strawberries. There were a pair of men, surrounded by wine bottles, holding unlit cigars in their mouths, and a couple, the proper woman sitting decorously in her chair, and the man simultaneously eating a small slice of leek frittata and talking on his wireless headset. "I'm eating," he was saying. "It's just delicious."

After it had been decided that we would have the tasting menu, Enrico reached into the bag he was carrying and took out a Barbera, two single-vineyard Barolos, and his reserve Barolo.

He would be supplying us with his wines for lunch, but he wanted to start with a sparkling wine.

"My old friend, Migliorini," he said as the owner poured him a taste of Brut Zero.

Valentino Migliorini was more than an old friend. He, along with Enrico Scavino and about ten others, was responsible for a movement that changed the character and direction of Barolo forever. They were dubbed the Barolo Boys—the winemakers often credited for making Barolo internationally popular. They were modernists, marketers, and technology lovers, and they were, as much as any winemaker can be, icons of pop culture. From their ranks, Scavino himself, the boxy gentleman with the soft smile, had risen to become a global rock star. His Barolo reserves sold for $150 a bottle, and he headed a virtual empire, which included $100 regular Barolos, $30 Barberas, and $25 Dolcettos. He sold to America, England, France, Germany, Belgium, Norway, Sweden, Denmark, Russia, Japan, Hong Kong, Malaysia, and Singapore. He was a media darling, a renowned winemaker, and a very rich man. But this international success was perhaps more surprising to him than to anyone else. When he was thirteen years old, Enrico Scavino had left school to work on his father's farm, where he shoveled manure, fed the chickens, and picked grapes. At the time, he imagined he'd be doing pretty much the same thing some fifty years later.

"My parents asked me what I would prefer: to continue with school or to work in the cellar and fields with my father," Scavino said as he began to eat his *anguilla marinata alle verdure,* silver eel wrapped in a long spiral and served cold with sweet and sour onions. "I still remember the smile on his face when I said I wanted to work with him. And he took me aside and he said we would be able to keep all our cows now. Because, you see, every year we had been forced to sell a cow to pay one of our workers. But now with me working for no pay, we'd have a cow worth one hundred twenty thousand lire." That was a saving of $600, a

Barolo farmhand's annual wage in 1952, and a small fortune to the Scavino family.

Enrico's grandfather Lorenzo came from a village near the town of Barolo. He and his brothers had shared a farm in their hometown, but Lorenzo wanted his own place. In 1921, he bought a one-hectare, or roughly two-and-a-half-acre, plot in Barolo for about $100. There, he and his son Paolo grew wheat and Nebbiolo grapes and tended to fowl, sheep, and cows. They made a little wine, poured it into demijohns, and shipped it to local restaurants. Lorenzo died in 1949, when Enrico was eight, and Paolo took over. Five years later, Enrico and his father began to produce five hundred bottles of wine a year. They still had twenty thousand bottles' worth of liquid in bulk, but they were curious as to whether they could sell individually bottled wines to private customers. And they did so easily. The next year they decided to come out with seven hundred bottles, and the year after that, nine hundred. They closed down the animal farm—it stank like the barnyard that it was and the odor entered the wine—and decided to concentrate on the vineyards. Enrico's mother, Giuseppina, ran the house, receiving customers in the kitchen and acting as the head vendor. His sister Angela picked fruit in the mornings and cooked the family meals in the afternoons. Enrico and Paolo covered everything else.

"My father taught me details—how to clean the buds off the plant so you get grapes growing on the shadowy part; how to keep the grapes out of direct sunlight so they don't lose their color; how to clip, cut, dig, mix, ferment," Enrico said. "And he taught me about cleanliness in the winery, obsessive cleanliness, and he gave me a work ethic. At midnight, after working all day, I would want to pass out, but he would still go down and get grass to feed the rabbits. And last, he taught me generosity; he was the kind of man who wouldn't eat his own piece of meat so that we could have more."

Little by little, Enrico and Paolo expanded. They bought a

small vineyard in 1960, a plot less than a hectare in size. In 1967, they picked up another. There wasn't too much competition back then; they were buying for about $300 per hectare, and continued to do so into the 1980s, when they accumulated six hectares in total. The area was true agro-country, the hills covered in broken-down barns and bored, skinny horses. The people drove around in three-wheeled trucks or got to where they were going on foot; they slaughtered their own animals for meat. Certainly there were several big, old estates—Marchesi di Barolo and Borgogno—but for the most part it was a poor, highly rural community. Enrico and Paolo figured they would make their locally bought and sold Barolos, Barberas, Nebbiolos, and Dolcettos forever.

Then, one day in 1982, a journalist knocked on the door. He was a slim, mellow, middle-aged man with light brown hair, a big nose, and puppy-dog eyes. His name was Luigi Veronelli and he was curious about Scavino wines. He'd tasted them in some Barolo restaurants. Veronelli, unbeknownst to Paolo and Enrico, was a Milanese enologist, an anarchist who had studied philosophy at university, the former editor of several magazines on socialism and gastronomy, and the world's foremost expert on Italian wine. After encouraging a group of Piedmontese winemakers to revolt against corporations in the 1970s, he devoted his life to wine journalism and to promoting small-scale vintners, to finding the hidden, the bizarre, the beautiful wines in the crannies of his country. When he knocked on the Scavinos' door in 1982, he had already written several books and was considered the most influential wine writer in Italy; in fact, he was considered the originator of Italian wine writing. "If he had been born in France, where they really care about these things, he would have an official holiday named after him," one of his disciples once told me. "That's what he did for wine."

"We didn't really know who he was," said Enrico. "But then again, we didn't care. We'd never had anyone but a client buying a couple of bottles. And then here was a journalist, coming to see us, for the first time. It was better than if the president of the United States paid us a visit." He blushed at the memory.

Paolo and Enrico took Veronelli down to the *cantina,* where he tasted young wine from the barrel. Then they all went up to the kitchen, where Giuseppina gave Veronelli a platter of cheese and salami. There, he drank from some older bottles the family had managed to save. Veronelli asked hundreds of questions, scribbling down the answers in his notebook.

A year later, Paolo and Enrico bought Veronelli's guide at a local bookstore. They brought it home, sat at the kitchen table, and turned to their page. Veronelli had written glowingly of their wine. He thought their product was exceptional.

"No amount of money could have ever made us that happy," said Enrico, shaking his head. "Not thousands, not millions."

Enrico and Paolo kept in touch with Veronelli after that. "He is a great man," Enrico said. "He loves producers. He has foresight because he always pays attention to the agriculturalists, not the big guys. He's a humble person, not like many of them, that are interested in you for just two years. He has relationships forever."

A week after Veronelli's review came out, a man from the Florentine importer Enoteca de Rham called the Scavinos. He told them he'd read about their work and asked if they'd like to sell wine in the United States. He invited Enrico to take a trip with a group of other producers; they would be hitting New York City and San Francisco. Enrico agreed. It would be his first time on a plane.

"When we got near the airport in New York, we had to circle around in the air for about twenty minutes because there was no space to land, and I kept looking down at the water. I thought: If we fall, I'm dead. I can't swim."

When he got to Manhattan, he was treated to a city tour in a helicopter.

"There were four of us in there but I was the closest to the door," he told me. "I was pretty sure that if one of us was going, it would be me."

Then he was escorted to a hotel on Central Park South.

"I still remember that the room they put me up in cost three hundred fifty dollars a night in the early eighties," he said. "I was scandalized." He sat on the colossal bed, regarding a complimentary, chilled bottle of Champagne and wondering if you drink Champagne when you're alone.

The producers went to fancy dinners, met with collectors, conducted tastings. Enrico had imagined New York as a luxurious, prosperous place full of diverse and intriguing people; he hadn't imagined that, without English, he'd never be able to communicate with them.

"I felt completely handicapped," he said. "Everyone else was a doctor, a lawyer, just investors in these estates, never set foot in the field. They could all speak English and I couldn't even order a bottle of water. I was so furious that the day I came home I hired Enrica an English tutor. I told her, in a rage, 'You will speak perfect English in one year!'"

A year later, Paolo had passed away and Enrica was fluent in English. By the time she was twelve, she was working on an as-needed, unpaid basis as Enrico's translator. She could soon speak French and German, too.

"She met all these important, wealthy people, and she got so into this world," Enrico said.

"I just liked people who had a passion for the best things, like wine, food, education, and travel, the highest lifestyle," Enrica said, daintily eating *lumache di Borgo San Dalmazza ai porri di Cervere,* small snails served with leeks. "It really had nothing to do with money." She handled all of her father's public relations.

But Paolo's perspective and Enrica's linguistic skills weren't the only things that changed with that trip. Enrico saw that the United States held a lot of possibilities for growth. He saw a market opening up. He wanted in. He may have been a farmer, but he was one with an entrepreneur's heart.

He began to expand his production. "With so few bottles, most importers would just say, 'What do you want me to do with an amount this small?' So we upped it." They didn't have the money to do anything major, so they added new space bit by bit.

At around this time, new winemaking technology was becoming available. Every week, Enrico attended lectures by other winemakers, scientists, engineers. In 1982, people suggested using blocks of dry ice to bring down a wine's temperature and prevent it from fermenting too aggressively. Enrico found an ice vendor several towns over and every day when the wine was fermenting, he drove a truck to the store, loaded up on eight blocks of ice, went home, put them in a special sack, and dunked them into his vats.

"I was so tired," he said. "Just moving those things into the truck was hard labor." Soon thereafter, he bought a new machine that allowed you to cool your wine with cold water kept in an outside compartment.

"It required literally tons of water," he said. "The water itself was costing me a fortune."

Finally he learned about temperature-controlled tanks. They were much like refrigerated tanks for wine, with a sophisticated system of buttons and knobs. Understanding when and how to raise and lower the degrees was in itself a feat, but it was nothing compared to the physical toil required to handle ice blocks, or the ludicrous cost of cold water. Scavino loved the freedom his new equipment allowed him, and he was officially on a constant search for new, better machines to buy.

His dream was to discover something that would relieve him of his most arduous task: punching over. Punching over involved standing on a ladder over your vat of wine, holding a stick. You plunged the stick in, and then, using all your strength, churned the wine. In essence, you were required to mix the enormous weight in liquid constantly for up to twelve hours a day, inevitably dyeing your arms purple and straining your back in the process. If you missed an hour, your wine was taken over by aggressive odors, and thereafter smelled like vinegar.

"I spent hours sketching my ideal invention," he said. It was a metal machine that automatically and constantly turned wine. "Then, in 1993, we had this Greek intern, an enology student, who was married to a German woman and lived in Stuttgart. I said to him, 'Can you figure out how we can produce something like this?'" The intern slapped Scavino on the arm.

"Enrico," the intern said, "this machine exists, and they build it in Germany."

The next day, the intern brought a catalog in and showed Scavino a device known as a rotary fermentor, a big, horizontal tank with what looked like a gigantic corkscrew running the length of it. Electricity-powered, the corkscrew turned the wine.

"That was one of the greatest joys of my life, to know that I wouldn't have to do that by hand anymore," said Scavino. He and Stefano Conterno, the son of the famous winemaker Aldo Conterno, drove to Stuttgart. Enrico needed two fermentors but he purchased only one. "I was ninety-nine percent sure it would work, but it cost twenty-five thousand dollars." He brought it home and conducted an experiment: he put half of his wine into a manual fermentor and half into his new rotary fermentor. After three months of various fermentations, he invited his friends over—the winemakers Armando Parusso, Domenico Clerico, Luciano Sandrone, Roberto Voerzio, Elio Altare—and served each of them two glasses.

"Tell me which wine is better," he said.

They looked at their glasses. "This one," they all said, each pointing to the glass of wine made in the rotary fermentor.

"But you didn't taste it," said Scavino. "How do you know?"

"Because it has a richer color," they said.

There it was, the same thing that happened to me and everyone else: they were blindsided by that natural preference for the darker, richer-looking wine. It was the human instinct, the one that leads you to the big, shiny apple. The winemakers fell into it, too.

"Batsoà fritto su rape violette di Cervere," said the restaurant owner, interrupting Scavino's reminiscences. She and the waiter placed the plates in front of us. *Batsoà* is the skin of a pig's hoof, pounded flat. Here it was served breaded and fried with leafy purple broccoli rabe.

"Buonissimo," I said with the first bite. It may have sounded weird, but when you thought about it, you were basically eating pigskin, and it's an indisputable fact that few things are more delicious than fried pigskin. We drank Scavino's 2002 Barbera d'Alba, bright, sharp, unusually dense and tannic—awkward in the glass.

Scavino smiled, but he was distracted. Maybe it was the talk of that first taste test, of the winemakers' preferences. That discovery, made in the process of modernizing his winery, was in part responsible for his current situation and all it involved. He leaned closer to me. *"Come va il mercato?"* he asked quietly. How is the market?

"In the States or here?"

"Here," he said. His eyes betrayed a tension I hadn't picked up before.

"You've had five great vintages in a row," I said. "But it's still not easy. Tuscans, for example, are having real problems; sales are down with the Super Tuscans. And the south has its economic issues."

"You think the Tuscany thing has to do with tourism?" Scavino asked.

Loads of Italians had received state loans and funding to create *agriturismi*—farms and wineries that also serve as guesthouses. The Italian government had made the money available initially in order to bring an increasingly citified population back to the land; *agriturismi* tended to be beautiful, reasonably priced, and accessible. Soon, the Americans, British, Germans, Dutch, and Swiss were coming in droves and the Italians were expanding operations accordingly, upping their production of wine and improving their properties. But when September 11 occurred, tourism fell drastically. Cellars were filling up with wine, and vendors, in a panic, had begun to sell at next to nothing just to free up space.

"I don't know if it's tourism for sure but I can tell you that in Barolo, at least, guys that used to sell for twenty-three are selling at twelve euros a bottle to wholesalers," I said.

Scavino tapped his fingers on the table. "What about the Americans?" he asked. "What do they think? Are they interested?"

"They're moving stuff," I said. "They're doubling sales."

"This new building is a stretch," Scavino whispered—he didn't want any industry people at nearby tables to hear him. "I pushed it bigger than I needed for my daughters. I want them to be able to work there for the rest of their lives without having to worry about adding on, but the place is costing me. And now I'm wondering if there even will be a market for our stuff," he said. "And the American press? Am I going to have difficulty with them?"

"They tend to love you," I said.

"What do the Americans *want*? What can I do to make them buy?" Scavino asked.

"They want to trust you, they want to know what they're getting, they want your guidance," I said. "You do so well with them."

"It's just that I'm selling what I expected to sell, but I have some new vintages out and I wonder how people are going to react."

"I tasted the new vintages, and I'm sure you'll be fine," I said.

He moved closer to me, his voice almost a whisper again. "Did you know I bought another property recently?"

"You did? How much?"

"Four acres."

"That's not too small."

"Do you think I'll have trouble? I can tell that this land is great, really has potential. But can people handle more now?"

"Enrico, you have to keep making the greatest wines you can," I said. "If you do that, you'll never have anything to worry about."

He sighed. "You can't imagine the enormous amount of wine I need to make and sell just to keep up, the land I have to acquire, the tons of new equipment I have to purchase, the methodological changes . . ." He ran his hand over his head. "It's endless."

Risotto Carnaroli ai pistilli di zafferano e carciofi croccanti was set on the table—a bright saffron carnaroli with lightly fried artichokes. We drank two different Barolos, his single vineyards, both from 1999. The first was his Barolo "Cannubi," from the area's most prized vineyard; well structured, it would be a perfect wine to introduce Italy to a California Cabernet drinker. The second, his Barolo "Bric dël Fiasc," was confident and honest.

"I thank God that I was born in such a wonderful place," Scavino said, as the wine revived the happy side of his brain. "But it's not easy."

"Our expansion really represents the future," Enrica said, moving us into more positive territory, maybe out of habit. "Tell us about the store."

We talked about other things from then on: the business, my goals, Enrica's travels, her sister's backbreaking work in the vineyards, the Piedmont gossip. We ate *Chateaubriand di fassone piemontese*, a special cut of the fillet—carved from the inner top of the cow, where it rests close to the organs and is softer, less worked—along with lightly roasted carrots and fennel. We had *finanziera*—a simple stew of innards and vegetables—and Scavino's 1990 "Rocche dell'Annunziata," a potent giant of a wine. Whenever I drank it, I felt as if a pair of hands had reached out from the glass, grabbed my ears, and pulled me closer.

Eventually, the dessert tray emerged: an array of miniature meringue and whipped-cream pastries, dark chocolate truffles, and almond cookies. We finished our wines and stood to leave.

Scavino drove me back to his sprawling hacienda and invited me in once again, but I declined. I had other appointments, other producers to see, and I'd already spent hours with him; I was sure he, too, had lots to do. As I left the drive, I waved at the Scavinos and they waved back, smiling widely.

I could see them in the rearview mirror, the gentleman and his worldly daughter in front of their shiny car and their gleaming estate. I imagined the scene twenty-five years earlier, a jalopy with a windburnt old farmer and his son making their way on a dirt road to their stables. It had been like that for generations for these people, until one day a journalist knocked on the door, wrote an article, and the world came calling, always wanting more.

Chapter 6

LAGO DI GARDA

꘎꘎꘎

BY 2002, MY PARENTS' FORTUNES had changed considerably
and they had left Albany, only to settle in the one place on
earth that is Naples's opposite: Tucson, Arizona. Years earlier,
Sal and Stefano, lured by the area's booming business, had
moved there with their families. And my parents, lured by the
promise of constant access to four of their grandchildren, had
promptly packed up and resettled.

There, they lived in a gated community of identical condo-
miniums painted a muddy "Desert Sand" and arranged around
a communal swimming pool, Jacuzzi, and tennis court. Of
course, my parents mostly stayed in, watching Italian satellite
television. They stayed in because, despite the fact that they
lived in a suburban-American oasis, past their patch of lawn,
behind their heavy brown door, lay a blinding chunk of dear
old Napoli.

The house was my mother's domain, an homage to her
particular aesthetic. The place was a labyrinth of marble, mirrors, glass, and crystal. Though the two floors couldn't have
covered more than twelve hundred square feet, the dining room
table, made of a slab of charcoal gray stone with elaborate
swirls of cream and surrounded by gray fabric–covered, high-
back chairs, could seat at least sixteen. In the middle of the
table sat a heavy glass vase, filled with translucent beads and

two dozen fake long-stemmed red roses, each accentuated with droplets of glue dew. The floor itself was faux black-and-white marble, from the door to the kitchen, and reflected upon it was the sparkling light of twenty-two tiny bulbs ensconced in the chandelier presiding over it all. You could see your reflection in almost any surface, as well as in the four mirrors that hung on the walls, some of them reflecting one another.

My parents spent most of their time perched on the brown couch, nestled between twelve perfectly arranged red throw pillows. From their spot, they gazed at the dozens of ornately framed family photographs arranged on glass tables. Or they watched the endless loop of their Italian channel on their oversized television. Or sometimes they listened to a cassette tape of Neapolitan music on their boom box.

There were several activities they engaged in when they weren't on the couch. My mother, spilling out of one of her flowered sundresses, her red lipstick perfectly applied, aggressively shined the reflective surfaces, or cooked. My father, shirtless, in a pair of shorts, sat on a chair for up to eight hours reading an Italian newspaper, either *America Oggi* or *Gazzetta dello Sport.* But they were multitaskers: while they went about their routines, they managed to bicker absently and without end. Their favorite subject was what my father was wearing. Outside of the house he was always dressed in pressed slacks, an ironed shirt, and shiny leather shoes. But his secret was that despite the fact that he was a small, skinny guy, he was always overwhelmingly hot. After fifty years of marriage, my mother still refused to accept it.

"Put on a shirt, you'll catch a cold," she said in Neapolitan.

"I'm already hot, don't need a shirt," he said.

"Well, before you go out, you need to put on that thermal underwear I bought you."

"I would faint and die in thermal underwear."

"You'll die *without* the thermal underwear."

"*Stupida!*" he said.

"*Stupido!*" she said.

They alternated that fight with the fight about what my dad was eating.

"Have some lasagna," my mother said, serving my father an eight-pound mass of pasta.

"*Maronna mia,* that's too much," my father protested.

"*Dio mio,* it's not even close to sufficient," my mother responded, heaping more onto his plate.

"*Basta!*" he screamed. "I can't possibly eat all of this!"

"You have to or you'll get so thin you'll disappear," my mother said. "Wine?"

"Yes, thanks," my father said.

For another chunk of their time together, my mother pretended she didn't know how to do things, and my father went around heroically accomplishing such feats for her as turning off lights and making telephone calls. My mother had been capable of everything all her life, but as soon as my father retired, she became an invalid—my siblings and I were positive she just wanted to give him a sense of purpose.

"Oh no, Ciruzzo! I need to check the mailbox but I'm afraid it's too modern and complicated for me to open," she'd say sweetly. "Do you think you might help me?"

She also liked to send him out to pick up an ingredient for a recipe, though he had never in his life succeeded in this. If you asked him for basil, he brought back salt. If you sent him out for milk, he returned bearing a loaf of bread and some cottage cheese.

On certain days, they went to work, sort of. My mother moisturized and perfumed herself and pulled on her sheer stockings and her heels; my father showered for an hour and then knotted his pressed silk tie. She stalked any motes of dust that might have descended upon her marble in the middle of the night, and she made the bed with hospital corners. He organized his wallet, which wasn't really a wallet at all. The size of a binder, the leather object contained thirty-two untouched credit cards, a checkbook, his passport, a copy of his passport, his driver's license, a copy of his driver's license, a small pen, a notebook, his Social Security card, a copy of his Social Security card, and a calculator. He carried it under his arm at all times.

When they finished, they got into their beige Lincoln Town Car, with its spotless beige leather seats and its glistening beige dashboard, and drove fifteen miles east to Roma, a one-level Italian-American trattoria owned by their friend Gino. Several times during this drive, my father would panic, certain that he had lost his wallet, and would feel about desperately for it until he located it.

When they arrived, my mother entered the restaurant, kissed Gino on both cheeks, walked purposefully through the swinging metal kitchen doors, tied on the white apron hanging from a hook, and began to concoct one of her many specialties: meatballs, stuffed shells, veal parmigiana. The food would be preserved until evening, and then served to the customers.

While my mother rolled out sheets of pale yellow pasta dough, my father, peeking over the steering wheel of his boat of a car, scoured the city for his Italian-language newspaper. For mystifying reasons, he was never able, in his thirty years in America, to locate the newspaper at the first or second newsstand he visited. After his extended search, he returned to the restaurant and my mother served him an espresso, which he drank as he read the paper. Then my mother put the finishing touches on her dishes, they ate lunch together, and they drove home. My father inspected his car from all angles and rubbed off any blemishes with a cloth. At about six, a small group of Italians from around town showed up and played the card games *scopa* and *buraga*. Bedtime was midnight.

My parents were content and comfortable, and their house was so clean that you could have licked up soup from any randomly chosen place on the floor; in fact, you probably could have eaten a meal off the roof of my father's car. They appeared to have slowly and relentlessly tamped down their longings for Italy until they could no longer sense them at all. In the space that those longings once inhabited, they constructed their own small approximation of Naples in the American desert.

ॐ

IT WAS 2004. I was planning my buying tour of Italy—a two-and-a-half-month exploration of wineries, with a stop at Vinitaly, the annual national wine festival—and this year, I was trying something new. For a decade, I had always thrown some socks and underwear into a duffel bag twenty minutes before I left for the airport, and traveled around the country in a rickety rental car, deriving sustenance from packages of chewy fruit candy and shots of sugary coffee, and crashing at roadside *agriturismi* with my mouth stained purple from a night of tastings. But now, having been married for three years, I was more settled. And my wife, Stephany, had only months earlier given birth to our second child, Liliana. I weighed the options: hot, rushed, solitary travel as my baby, far across the ocean, forgot she even had a father, or a slower tour of the country with my family in tow. Furthermore, I figured, I could bring my parents along. I could show them the Italy I had discovered on my own: ancient wineries, seaside villages carved from mountains, hidden castles. They had been back only four times, and then only to Barra. I would show them what their son had accomplished, the connections he had forged with his homeland. They would be proud, they would be impressed; at night they would whisper to each other about how I amazed them. I would whisk them away from arid Tucson and the monotony of their days. This was the sort of surprise they'd been waiting for.

I picked up the phone and presented my idea to my mother:

a grand journey through my Italy. The sunny Mediterranean sea, the sparkling Alpine lakes, the pale green Tuscan olive groves.

"Sergio, that's the nicest invitation I've ever received," she said.

"I knew you would—" I began.

"But no thanks," she continued.

My father got on the upstairs telephone. They liked to talk to me together. "If you have so much free time, come on over here," he yelled. He always yelled on the phone. "We'd love to see you!"

"We'll visit Capri," I said. "We'll see the Friulian fields. I'll take you to villas in Umbria. We'll try all sorts of regional cuisine."

"I don't understand why you don't just buy tickets to Tucson," my mother said. "The weather is excellent here now. Very dry, mild."

"Yes, it is," my father said. "We can't wait for you to come!"

The next day, I called them again. "I don't think you understand," I said. "You'll be my guests. We'll cover the country. It will be stupendous."

"I'm sure, *amore*," my mother said. "But I can make some of that lasagna you love right here at home."

"The kids can swim in the pool," my father added with a holler.

"You're giving up Italy for your condo pool?" I asked.

"I don't see why we have to do something so complicated," my mother said. "We'll set up the guest rooms."

"The guest rooms are very sunny," my father yelled.

"That's the truth," my mother said. "I'll even buy some fun new sheets for Salvatore. What's his favorite color? Does he still like trucks?"

I thought back to my childhood. When all the kids at school were going to the amusement park for a field trip, my mother tossed the permission slip aside.

"So can I go?" I asked.

"Nah, stay here with me," she said. She didn't understand why I would want to go through all the hassle of rides and lines when I could just as well hang out with her all day.

Then I thought back on my early days in Manhattan.

"I've gotten us reservations at the most amazing new four-star restaurant," I'd said to my visiting parents. "Most people wait two months to get in and we can go tonight. The chef is my friend."

"No, no, I'll just whip up pasta with chickpeas," my mother answered. "You've always loved it."

"I'm sure your fancy friend can't make *pasta e ceci* like Mama can," my father added.

I should have known that the idea of a whirlwind tour of the finest spots in Italy wouldn't appeal to this duo. They absolutely did not care. For them, glitzy things—and glitzy could even include an amusement park—didn't hold any worth when you compared them to sitting at home with your family eating spaghetti. So, tailoring my approach to their values, I called again.

"Mom, Dad, I'm desperate," I moaned. "I have no choice but to make this trip. Stephany and I just can't handle both Sal and Lili all summer. We need your help."

Within several hours, the flight arrangements had been confirmed. A month later, my parents arrived at our door in Manhattan: two small, expectant faces; four immaculate suitcases.

❧

LAGO DI GARDA IS A LARGE REGION comprised of fifty villages that surround Lake Garda, a basin that stretches, thin and cerulean, along the feet of the rough black Italian Alps. In the town of Garda, pale, delicate cottages ascend the mountains. This was our first destination.

I drove our rented minivan from Milan. Everyone, exhausted from the journey and the time change, had entered a dreamy state, and the car was quiet. In the backseat, Stephany had fallen asleep, her head resting on her arm, which was resting on Lili's car seat, in which the baby was also asleep, her pacifier having dropped from her mouth. Next to her, Sal was curled up in his own car seat, falling in and out of consciousness, his heavy-lidded eyes opening and closing, controlled by opposing forces: curiosity and the desire for dreamy oblivion. To our left and our right, the small hills that flank the autostrada rose and fell; burnt farmland appeared and disappeared. We passed by herds of sheep and lazy cows; the grass turned green, then gold, then brown, then green again. I navigated around the wild Italian drivers as well as I could. Once in a while, a couple on a motorbike would swerve by us, their bodies clasped together, leaning forward with the machine, and weaving, as if in a video game in which no one can really get hurt, in and out of traffic. My mother looked absently from her backseat and said nothing much. My father sat, straight and dapper, next to me, gripping his massive wallet and wishing, I am certain, that he was in the driver's seat.

After three hours, we turned off the highway and all the colors seemed to brighten—the dry greens turned to jade and emerald, the sky lost its touches of gray. The smog and the dirty humidity of Milan rolled away, and the air, alpine, was at once warm and crisp. As we drove closer, the land became more mountainous.

We drove up to Hotel Regina Adelaide, a grand, terra-cotta-colored establishment that overlooks the seemingly infinite lake. This would be my home base for the week, and my parents, Stephany, and the kids would get established here. We all looked at the building, and then again at the water, and there was nothing to say. Any comment would only illuminate how useless our words were.

"Dinner's at nine, but let's have a light lunch at two" was all

I could come up with. The valet took our bags and we headed upstairs for a day of naps.

For dinner I had planned an evening at the hotel restaurant. Like most lower- or middle-income Italians, my parents have eaten *la cucina povera,* or peasant cuisine, every night of their lives. The goal of this cuisine is to perfect the preparation of simple ingredients—a feat that a Michelin-rated chef, with his demiglazes, often cannot master. But the food is simple, and my parents are not culinary explorers. For them, this would be a new taste experience.

That evening, we convened in the hallway and headed downstairs to the softly lit dining room. The room contained several tables covered with white tablecloths and set with a dozen pieces of silver. Our waiter, a pudgy young man with prematurely graying hair, was wearing a cream suit jacket, black pants, and black bow tie. He presented us each with a heavy, bound menu and brought us water. My parents regarded the menu seriously. In the background, the chords of "Con te partirò" echoed softly. After some meditation, my father reached a decision.

"I'll take the tagliolini with shrimp and zucchini, I believe," he announced in Italian.

"No, have the veal, Ciruzz'," my mother said.

"Alma, I don't want the veal," he said.

"The veal is full of protein and it's prepared simply, so it won't bother your stomach."

"Okay, Alma, I'll take the veal, then."

"But have the tagliolini first."

"But I'm not that hungry."

"But you need it."

"Alma, *fermati!* Just the veal."

"The tagliolini and the veal."

"Fine, fine, fine. Both."

The waiter stopped by the table. *"Signora?"* he asked my mother.

Though my mother has lived in America for over thirty years, she has never learned fluent English. Now we were in her home-land and she could finally speak freely in her own language.

"My hoosabund will have the scrimps," she said in English.

"Mamma, speak Italian," I hissed.

"Oh!" She giggled. *"Pasta con gamberi e zucchine! Scusi!"*

"Better," I said.

"Dopo il vitello, e con una insalata," she said.

"But I don't want a salad," my father said.

"You may not *want* a salad," my mother began, "but—"

"Excuse me," I said to the waiter. "Can you please give us a minute?"

"Of course," he said, and disappeared.

I slammed my hand on the table. "Mamma, Babbo," I said, "could you please both do me a favor?"

My parents gazed at me, wide-eyed.

"For forty years, you have known that Babbo doesn't have a huge appetite," I told my mother. She gasped. "You can't force him to eat!" She didn't move. "And Babbo—" I pointed at my father. He, too, sat very still. "You cannot order only one thing because you know that your wife"—I pointed at my mother, whose eyebrows were raised—"cannot live with herself if you do."

Stephany was watching us all with great delight. Neapolitans are steadfastly respectful of their elders, and she had never heard me so much as raise my voice to my parents. But this was a drastic moment: we needed to nip this problem in the bud or we were in for seventy-five days of hell.

"Avete capito?" I asked. My parents nodded. "Tonight, I'll be doing all the ordering. And don't worry, Mamma," I said, "I won't let Babbo starve to death."

The first way my father averted malnutrition was through Prosecco, admittedly not nutritious but certainly good at stimulating the palate. The waiter poured us each a glass of the bubbly wine—bright, nondescript, perfectly acidic. Then we started in on *vellutata al basilico,* a deep green creamy soup that contained small shrimps and was accented with crispy bits of bread. By then we'd finished the Prosecco and were drinking a 2002 Quintarelli Bianco Secco; in fact, we'd be drinking wines made by master winemaker Giuseppe Quintarelli all night.

I remembered the first bottle of Quintarelli I'd ever drank, a 1980 Amarone della Valpolicella. The year was 1992 and I had gotten my job as sommelier two weeks earlier. Tony May called me over to his table.

"Taste this," he said nonchalantly, handing me a long-stemmed glass full of murky red liquid. Obligingly, I took a sip. Then I didn't move, I'm sure, for quite some time.

If a normal wine is a paper airplane, Quintarelli's wine is a spaceship. Every quality is overblown—its sweetness, its sourness, its acidity, its tannins, texture, flavors, smells—and at the same time, all the qualities work in tandem. The drink was an exercise in contradiction, and the question it brought up for me was: How, in the blast of confusion created by such exaggeration, could there exist perfect poise and harmony? It was a mellow symphony. I looked at Tony May in total disbelief.

Quintarelli is known for making wines of *appassimento,* a purely Italian method. *Appassimento* refers to the process of drying grapes before you make wine from them. It's a risky business because you're working, essentially, with rotten grapes that exude sugar and thus alcohol. Done badly, an *appassimento* wine is completely disjointed. Done well, it's concentrated and balanced. Done by Quintarelli, it's a magical elixir.

Why his wines are so remarkable has never been determined. In the lab, scientists have re-created the environment of his small working farm. They have reproduced his chemical conditions, his materials, the climate. They have used the same grapes, grown in the same way. And they've never made anything close to a Quintarelli.

"I personally envision him as a wizard in a long cape who waves his wand over the barrels," a friend told me.

It was puzzling, but it could also have been as simple as accepting the fact that the essence of a winemaker does indeed enter his wine.

"He could have been the pope," said Quintarelli's U.S. importer Robert Chadderdon once. "He has more than a normal person's love of life and people."

I wasn't the only one who responded to Quintarelli's wines. They were the hardest Italian wines to find in the world, and his cultlike following was constantly scrambling for more—for his Amarone, his Valpolicella, his Cabernet Franc, his sweet reds, everything.

We drank the Primofiore 2001 with our starter, a terrine made of thinly sliced pork belly doused with spices, placed in the middle of a white porcelain plate. Then came our *frittate*, small slices of grilled crustless tart, made with eggs and finely chopped leeks, and topped with shredded radicchio, sharp and magenta. We ordered Quintarelli's 1995 "Ca' de Merlo," so named for a vineyard in which a blackbird (*merlo*) lives.

We drank Quintarelli's Valpolicella with mezze maniche pasta, long, thin strands mixed with a spicy sauce of anchovies, red onion, dilled bread crumbs, and olive oil. Then came the small portions of potato gnocchi, miniature dumplings in a sharp taleggio cheese sauce. We worked our way through oil-poached salmon, deep orange and cooked rare, topped with crème fraîche and caviar, and resting on an emerald bed of flattened zucchini slices. And finally, we had seared sweet veal medallions, plump and glazed brown, and cooked quickly with butter, lemon rind, and parsley. We paired the meat with a 1980 Amarone Riserva, which gave me the sense, when I drank it, of talking to an old rock 'n' roll legend.

"So what do you think, Mamma?" I asked when the last plate, swiped clean, had been carted away. "Will Babbo survive?"

"*Maronna mia,* Sergio," my mother said, her eyes closed.

"*Ottimo, ottimo,*" my father said—the ultimate. He slumped, rested his head in his palm. I looked in his eyes and I could see it, something new, something I'd never quite seen before. Was it enlightenment? Maybe, but more clearly the man seemed to be . . . drunk. His posture was practically relaxed. I hadn't seen him drunk more than once before. I kicked Stephany under the table.

After dinner, full-bellied and weary from our long journey, we took a stroll to the edge of the lake and sat together on a bench. Then I hooked my arm in my father's, Stephany hooked her arm in my mother's, and we all waddled, weaving, back to our rooms. My parents hugged and kissed us and went next door to their suite. Stephany and I checked on Sal and Lili, both knocked out in their cribs, and slipped into bed. I opened the French doors to the balcony to let the breeze in, and crawled into bed with my wife. As I put my hand up to touch her hair, an agonized shriek pierced the night air. We froze, our hearts in our stomachs.

"ALMA! ALMA!" It was my father's desperate call.

My adrenaline propelled me to the balcony in under a second. There, I clasped the railings and yelled out. Had they been attacked by vacationing lakeside robbers? Had my mother hurt herself? I saw a curled shadow there, my father on his knees on the grand terrace.

"Babbo! What is it?" I yelled.

His words were jumbled, his speech slurred. I couldn't understand. Stephany stood behind me, barefoot in only her negligee, her eyes wide with fear.

"What is it, Babbo? Answer me," I pleaded.

Again, he mumbled in fast Neapolitan. I leaned in. "'*O burze* . . . *'O burzellino mio.*" He was almost heaving. My mother stood near him stoically, her hand on his shoulder.

"His what?" Stephany asked. "Sergio, tell me."

"'*O burzellino mio,*" he moaned.

"His *wallet?*" Stephany asked.

"He's missing his wallet, yes," I said.

"My life, my whole life," my father moaned.

"His big, brown man-purse," I said.

"*Sì,*" he said.

"You screamed that way for the wallet?" Stephany asked.

"*Sì,*" my father said.

Stephany searched my face for an answer, but found nothing. I understood my father well enough to know that if we didn't find that wallet, we would cart a ruined man around this beautiful country. Without his wallet, my father was broken; every day would be a battle against panic, with him consumed by the worry that someone, somewhere, would demand at least two copies of his Social Security card, and that he would be unable to provide them.

Then, without thinking, I looked down below, to the bench upon which we had been sitting. There, illuminated by a street lamp, sat my father's shiny leather escapee, all alone, looking out at the water and feeling, if wallets can feel, a sense of freedom for the first time.

"I see it, Babbo," I said, pointing at the bench. "Let's go."

He rose from his fetal position, and, to his credit, controlled his urge to run. He walked swiftly with me, both of us dressed smartly in pajamas and dress shoes, through the hotel lobby and down to that bench, where my father grabbed his wallet and held it to his chest.

"Let's just sit down for a moment," I said. "Let's take some deep breaths."

He looked wan, relieved, shaken, like a man who had just escaped death. I tried to remember Stephany's Lamaze techniques—two swift snorts through the nose, a big release of air through the mouth.

For twenty minutes, my father regained his composure. We smoked a few cigarettes, slowly and carefully, and we sat together in our PJs. I patted his back as he cradled the wallet. Behind us were the clear windows of the hotel, lit up, but we looked forward. The lake was black, illuminated by the moon. We were silent, leaning against each other. After some time, my father turned to me.

"*Overo 'na bella serata,*" he said. Truly a beautiful night.

❧

THE NEXT MORNING, I rose at the crack of dawn. Vinitaly began that day at the edge of Verona, and I was certain to be exhausted by evening, after all the meeting and greeting and tasting, after moving through the throngs of professionals and enthusiasts from around the world. I slipped out of the bedroom and rushed down the hotel's marble steps.

"*Buon giorno,*" I said to the front-desk clerk.

"*Buon giorno, Signor Esposito,*" he answered with a smile.

The cobblestone streets were empty, the shutters were closed to the cold morning light, and the only sound was that of my shoes clacking along. I'd parked the car across town, which meant a three-minute walk along the lake, which was lit up fire-orange from the sun's reflection and rippling in the barely perceptible wind. It was brisk, as early mornings in lake towns are, even in the dead of summer, and I hurried along dutifully, rehearsing my plans for the day. Everything was perfectly organized: my arrival, the stalls of vendors I would hit, my lunch and dinner dates, and my return to the hotel just in time to see my children before they fell asleep.

As I approached the empty lot in which my car had been parked the evening before, I became perplexed. I didn't see a trace of my minivan. In its place was a burgeoning fruit and vegetable market. Men and women were unloading eggplants and nectarines and heads of lettuce from their tiny white trucks, setting up rickety plastic tables, assembling pyramids of produce. I looked down the street and behind me. No minivan. I took a deep breath.

"Sergio, try to carry this rubber ball for unexpectedly nerve-wracking situations," my stress therapist back in New York had told me. She had handed me a squishy red toy, which I was to squeeze when I felt anxiety approach. Why hadn't I listened to my stress specialist? Where had I left that stupid red ball? I walked back, slowly, counting down from two hundred to the hotel.

"*Scusi,*" I said to the desk clerk. He wore a pressed blue shirt, and a pair of wire-rimmed glasses teetered on his bulbous nose.

"*Si, Signor Esposito?*" He adjusted his glasses.

"My car is gone," I said. "There's a market in its place."

"Ah, yes." The clerk nodded. "Thursday is market day."

"So you were aware that there would be a market there today?"

"*Certo, Signore.* There is a market every Thursday," he said.

"Then why did you tell me, last night, to park there?" I asked.

"*Signore,*" he said solemnly. "You asked me last night, Wednesday. As I said before, Thursday is market day."

"How could I possibly know that?" I asked.

The clerk shook his head gently. "I'm sorry about your car, but there is always a market on Thursdays, and it always takes place in that lot. It then follows that if you park there, the mechanics will have to tow your car to make room for the fruit stands." He looked at me with a mixture of disdain and compassion, as though I were an especially slow but respectably determined person. This was going nowhere.

"Well, can you at least help me get the car back?" I asked.

"Yes, I'll call Gianfranco," he said. "And then I'll call you a cab to get you to Gianfranco."

As I stood impotently on the corner, I felt that his reference not to a towing company but to a person named Gianfranco did not bode well for me. I stood there for a long time, gazing drearily at the water and watching the town slowly rise for the day, windows flung open, women stepping onto the *terrazze* to sweep, or to water the languid purple flowers that hung, dripping, from the railings. People took off for work, in minuscule cars or on motorcycles, and tourists began to drift onto the various hotel patios, where they were served dark coffee and bowls of melon. A cab, it became clear, was almost impossible to come by because all available ones in the region had been reserved days earlier by visitors on their way to Vinitaly. By noon, a rusty Fiat van pulled up and we rattled down the highway to Gianfranco's, a three-car garage next to a sheep farm.

Gianfranco, I presumed upon arrival, was indeed present at his business, but had taken an early lunch and was therefore not to be bothered. He was sitting at a small plastic table to the side of the building in unbuttoned coveralls, his hands stained with black grease. His wife and two children were there, too, all hunched over their plates, shoveling pasta into their mouths and drinking red wine from plastic cups. I peeked around at them and Gianfranco threw me an uninterested wave before he resumed eating his tagliatelle. I settled onto a small bench out front, where I would wait, head in hands, for another hour.

❧

I ARRIVED AT VINITALY at 2 p.m., not 8 a.m. Back in 1993, when I first visited Vinitaly, I saw approximately two Americans wandering through the sparsely populated area. The first event, meant to be an industry affair, had taken place in 1967. By 1969, the organizers had attracted 130 producers of Italian wine, who introduced their products to the buyers and sellers attending lectures and meetings. Now, there were nearly four thousand producers—and, it seemed, at least one-third of the global population.

I found an overflowing building, crowds pulsating in and out, English words tossed around. There were thousands of people, from New Jersey, New York, Hawaii, Missouri; from Germany, Norway, Singapore, South Africa. The buildings—makeshift green metallic structures erected for just this purpose—sat upon a fairground, a sort of Las Vegas convention-hall affair. Wildly attractive women staffed the entrance, all of them in a standard-issue uniform: a pine green cloak, tight black skirt, pressed white shirt, and red cap. Throngs of people were registering at the different doors, their notebooks and digital cameras in their hands, their faces plastered with that avid look most often spotted on rock music fans pushing to get into a venue for a Stones concert. Above it all rose a billboard, one hundred feet wide and thirty feet high, across which was sprawled in burgundy: VINITALY.

The fairground was divided according to regions of Italy—Calabria, Sicily, Campania, and so on—each cordoned off in an area the size of an airplane hangar and connected to the others by outdoor spaces in which vendors were selling an assortment of pork products, including sandwiches made from one of the many eight-foot-long mortadellas to be seen throughout. After being bandied about in a line to the door—I was behind a group of Ohioan enthusiasts who, judging from smell and appearance, had begun to sample wine much earlier in the day—I started to wend my way toward Campania. And that's when I heard it, loud and heaving, rising above the bustle of the crowd: the laugh.

I turned swiftly, following the stream of guffaws until I located him.

Our eyes met. "Daniel Thomases," I said.

We were supposed to meet for lunch but I was already so late that I had decided to avoid him. He wasn't particularly forgiving when it came to punctuality. Years earlier, I had arrived to pick him up in front of his hotel four minutes late. I found him standing in the middle of the street, his hands behind his back.

"Daniel, what's wrong?" I asked.

"*Sempre un napolitano,*" he said angrily.

"What do you mean?" I asked.

"Constantly late," he said. Then he got in the car and refused to talk for thirty minutes.

"Sergio," Daniel said, walking in my direction.

He looked the same as always. He was balding, corpulent, and dressed like a New England prep-school teacher in his cotton-turtleneck-and-blazer combination. He wore his characteristically discordant expression: a crooked, toothy smile and dark, apprehensive eyes. We shook hands and hugged.

Daniel was an American transplant in Italy, a sort of chance Italian, a foreigner who had come here to study and, owing to a confluence of unforeseen circumstances, simply never left. He had a Harvard degree, an apartment in Florence, and a French wife. He taught classes, worked at a leather company, and then, after writing for *Wine Spectator* and *International Wine Cellar*, and composing the Italian entries for the *Oxford Unabridged Encyclopedia of Wine*, he met Luigi Veronelli, who recognized his abnormal capacity for learning and memorizing. Daniel then spent years working as a cowriter with Veronelli, writing about and appraising wines. When Veronelli became too old and weak to circle Italy, Daniel reviewed five hundred wines a year for him. He became a walking wine dictionary.

But Daniel was no longer anybody's co-anything. Instead, he had been appointed by Robert Parker to cover Italian wines for the *Wine Advocate*, the most popular wine publication in America.

Robert M. Parker Jr. is often referred to as "the Master" or "the Emperor of Wine," and not without irony. Born in Baltimore, Parker was an average mid-Atlantic boy when, while at college, he followed his then girlfriend (now his wife) to an exchange program in Paris. There he began to learn about wine, and developed a passion for it that he brought back to the States with him. In 1978, when he was a lawyer in Maryland, Parker launched his newsletter, initially an amateur undertaking read by his friends.

Before 1978, the American wine market was weak. There were very few wineries represented in supermarkets and liquor stores. People tended to buy cheap wines: jug wines; farm wines; wines that tasted like sweet sherry, went for $1.12, and got you wasted.

But for many reasons—including the wild popularity of French cuisine, which was brought into the public consciousness by Julia Child and Jacques Pépin—Americans became more and more curious about wine. But they were scared; wine was the dominion of the American aristocracy, of people with cash and maybe class and the ability to travel. It was for Europeans and sophisticates, for socialites throwing dinner parties on Park Avenue and for jet-setters who frequented European restaurants. (Or, to some, it was for alcoholics.) It was not a drink for everyone, as it has always been in the Old World, but one for the chosen few. The chosen few "got" wine; they spoke a secret language and appreciated qualities that were undetectable to the untrained American palate. The average person was okay with this separation; he didn't want to try that hard to understand a drink. He didn't want to be confused when he ate a steak after a long day at the office.

But Parker had an idea for him. Wine drinking didn't need to be an obstacle, and it didn't need to be a sophisticated enterprise. Wine drinking could be better: it could be a competition and a hobby. Around the country, ears pricked up.

Parker used accessible language, words pulled from a common vocabulary, to describe wines. He is the reason that people from Florida to Maine, when drinking a glass of Australian Merlot on their porches, say things like, "This stuff has notes of chewy apple, leather, and tobacco, for sure, and it finishes with a smooth explosion of blackberry for at least fifteen seconds." But then again, he's also the reason that people from Florida to Maine were inspired to try wine in the first place; he's the reason they have a good bottle of wine at all.

Parker's unique approach of offering simple descriptions ("woody," "fruity") and scores (50 to 100 points, 100 being perfect) appealed to average Americans who had previously considered wine an intimidating subject. Parker gave Americans a way to communicate their thoughts on a wine; even if they were guessing, at least they had words with which to guess. It was democratic and fun, a competitive game that appealed to the American desire to succeed, and to the American distaste for shades of gray. Wine was no longer a liquid mystery; it had definite tastes that were either right or wrong, and everybody could at least try to identify them. If you could detect the taste of grapefruit, you could eventually (or, better yet, immediately) understand a wine. If you thought a wine was fantastic and Parker gave it 96 points, you were officially correct. The wine was indeed fantastic and so were you, a little, just for knowing that. Wine had quantifiable, definable properties, and could be accurately judged to be good or bad. In this way, Parker became famous. And Americans began to buy more wine.

For the wine industry, this initially seemed like a boon. Now, it's a monopoly. Today, due to his popularity, Parker can launch a producer into the limelight, so when he's having a "raspberry moment," vintners around the globe scramble to inject their drink with synthetic fruit-flavored chemicals, hoping to catch him and therefore his followers. Producers have begun to model their wines after what he prefers: highly concentrated, with soft tannins and low acid—as smooth as milk.

California wines, which bloomed out of the lush Napa hills and flatlands, are appealing to Parker because they're often creamy. They've been manufactured to match their culture. When you travel to the Napa Valley, you recline on a pale-wood lounge chair, gaze upon the landscape, and take a sip; food is an afterthought. French wines, like Bordeaux, are obviously in luck—they are the stick against which Parker measures everything. They are the reason he began his newsletter, and for this attention to the nation, Jacques Chirac personally presented Parker with the coveted Legion of Honor.

Problematically, Italian wines are often the opposite of most French and California wines—of "Parkerized" wines. They're meant exclusively to be drunk with food. (One exception to this custom is in Friuli, where truck drivers take shots of white before their morning routes.) The wines, therefore, are acidic, sharp with tannins, low in alcohol—precisely the qualities that Americans have been trained to flinch from, and the qualities that make Italian wines complement meals so perfectly.

But even more problematically, Parker's approach has corrupted an old idea of wine as artistic, strange, and indefinable. Before, there were bad wines and great wines, but there were not right wines and wrong wines. What you liked was, in large part, a question of taste, a complex concept generally agreed upon to be a reflection of individual preference. And part of tasting and understanding wine involved being open to the idea that some wine requires patience and work, and is not instantly gratifying.

Finally, there is the real question that Parker's work raises. Perhaps a wine is reminiscent of a lemon, tanned leather, and the seaside. Say that a researcher can demonstrate that these three scents exist most obviously in a specific drink, and say that you have the ability to identify them. If you have identified the wine as being a tart, cowhidey, salty-aired drink, then what? What is the next step? Even if it is possible to be unarguably correct in figuring out aromas, what do they *mean*? Does the simple fact that a wine tastes a little like red fruit signify anything bigger than the fact itself? What line of logic brings us from red fruit to excellence? Parker's success is built, in part, on the assumption that because a person is able to recognize elements, he is also able to recognize beauty. As Lawrence Osborne notes in his wine-world adventure *The Accidental Connoisseur*: "It's clear that the cheery jargon of aromas and tastes, the blackberries, tannins, phenol contents, flowers, tars, and so on, is little more than an airport-novel language that tells you nothing about wine."

But the fact remains that Americans have now been trained to crave such descriptions. And they want to compete with one another, because what good is pleasure if you can't win at it?

My friend Carlo Maggi, a merchant of rare wines, once told me that many Americans liked to visit his Umbrian shop and taste a hundred of his wines. They would take ten pages of notes, go home, wait for Parker to release his scores, and ultimately buy the three wines awarded 98 points. Carlo suspected they wanted to convince themselves that they were actually choosing the wine.

"Why drink so many fucking wines?" he asked. "Why do so much work if you just wait for someone else to tell you to buy a certain three?"

"Yes, why?" I asked.

"I don't *know* why!" he yelled. "You need a psychiatrist for that!

"In America they say, 'I use my talent to understand wine,'" Carlo continued. "In Italy we treat it like an art. Wine is easy, not difficult. I knew that I would marry my wife ten minutes after I met her. And I need to study wine for five years to pick the correct bottle? Why?"

"Well, why do you think?" I asked.

"Wine isn't obvious, is the problem," Carlo said. "A three-thousand-dollar bottle and an eighty-dollar bottle are both made from glass, both sealed with corks. If you see a Ferrari and a Fiat, you can immediately spot the better car. But when you actually drink wine, it's simple. It's not difficult. You use your nose, your mouth, and your eyes, and you know if you like it or not. You don't need someone to tell you everything."

"Some people feel that they do," I said. "They're intimidated."

"The people who profess to help them are leading them astray," Carlo replied. "Because if a person is really passionate about wine, he wants to help other people enjoy it, too. And that person will make the experience really simple for you. He who says wine is complicated needs through wine to have power. *Vaffanculo!*"

⁓

DANIEL THOMASES LOVED WORKING with Parker. Since the only substantial market for quality Italian wines is the United States—before, Germany and Switzerland had topped the list, while France took the lion's share of the cheap stuff—Parker and his disciples dominated. Since Daniel was solely responsible for scoring new wines, the words he was now writing essentially controlled a large part of the Italian market. For some, this would be a disturbing responsibility. Not for Daniel.

Now that he was working with Parker, he had newfound power. I had met Daniel four years earlier. I knew he was on the beat for Veronelli at the time, and later for Parker, and I knew he visited almost four hundred wineries a year. It was enough to make me want to get to know him better. I started to call him in Florence. He was a great source of information and updates.

"Do you want me to do an event at your store?" he asked, a year into our phone sessions. A month later, he strode through the door, let out a chortle, and started talking wine.

Now, he and I began to walk together through Vinitaly. I recalled my first time there. I had wanted to see as many new and emerging producers as possible, to taste wines I couldn't get in the States, to try out the high-end stuff that most people find too cost-prohibitive to sample. It used to be full of Italian winemakers, sellers, restaurateurs, barrel producers, corkscrew makers, bottling company reps, enoteca owners. Now, in addition to that crew, there were tons of American waiters, Italian teens, everybody in town. I used to slip in, drink quickly, and stay only if I was interested. Now, I usually couldn't even reach the table.

But things looked different from my new perspective, beside Daniel. At first the movements of the winemakers we were approaching blended into the commotion, but then a pattern began to emerge. When the people at each table saw Daniel, they quickly went to work. Usually one person was dispatched to the back and returned with a bottle or two, which he surreptitiously opened and arranged. Then, everyone stood at attention and waited for Signor Thomases, whom they demanded be let through the crowd.

Unless you set up a factory and maniacally pour chemicals into your grape juice, you cannot make identical wine. Within a harvest, every producer has a best and a worst barrel. They know which is which, and they keep track of the bottles these wines are poured into. When someone like Daniel Thomases, someone they need to impress, comes around, they usually dig up the greatest wine they have. In other words, the quality of the samples Daniel and I were tasting as we stood at those rickety tables—the samples Daniel was noting and marking for his magazine—was not in any way indicative of the quality of wine that people would be buying in the store. "Daniel, these people see you coming," I said. "They have the best bottle hidden in the back."

Daniel ignored me and continued strolling, hands in pockets. I followed him in a daze, past hordes of people—Italian schoolkids playing hooky; British couples with Cockney accents; groups of American guys on a sort of middle-aged, moneyed pub crawl; and the hobbyists with their stuffed notebooks and furrowed brows. The space was hot, and I broke into a sweat. Daniel was ahead of me like a well-fed Moses, parting the crowd, and, as though it were a choreographed modern dance piece, producers on the left and the right jumped lithely from their seats, reached behind their curtains, and brought out the top bottles. They knew that each point he awarded would earn them hundreds of thousands, even millions, more in sales.

I desperately needed an escape, so I suggested to Daniel that we go for a meal in Verona. I recalled a little restaurant I had visited years ago, Antica Bottega del Vino. I wanted to revisit the experience, to get a breath of Italy again, away from the packed fairground.

But as Daniel and I edged into Verona center, which consists of two piazzas, I realized that mine was a pipe dream. The smooth stone streets and the delicate shops were obscured by the drunken masses. It was like Mardi Gras, without the beads and breasts. We pushed our way into the restaurant, which appeared to have been taken over by Americans. There was a line around the block, two hundred people in a courtyard, a room stuffed full of stools and minuscule tables, each bearing little plates.

Our seats had been reserved, which meant that, within minutes, Daniel had tucked a napkin into his collar. We talked about the trade, as we always do. I found myself distracted by the conversation around me, which seemed to be getting louder by the minute. I was enveloped in an off-key opera of American wine-speak: "I tasted three hundred wines today!" "I went way past three hundred—almost hit five hundred!" "I tasted six vintages of Sassicaia!" "I was in Angelo Gaja's booth half the day as his guest!" By the time we left, I had a splitting headache. We didn't finish our meal until 10 p.m. I did not make it back to Lago di Garda in time to put my kids to bed.

The next day, I woke up at 7 a.m., took a shower, and dressed. Vinitaly is a five-day-long affair, full of industry people. For many professional reasons—networking, marketing, exploring—I needed to make the drive back to the big green metal buildings outside Verona. I looked at my sleeping wife. Lili was beginning to stir in her crib. I picked up my suitcase, walked to the door, put my suitcase down, and went back to bed.

After a decade of Vinitaly, I'd had enough. There was nothing negative about the popularity of Italian wines, but Vinitaly had become a party—good for the partygoers, but bad for me. It was too wild and overrun for me to even taste wines, much less learn anything. I wouldn't go back, I decided, ever again.

When everyone woke up an hour later, I had a suggestion.

"I think that today, we should go to Gardaland," I said. While Daniel Thomases presumably was making his second round through the swaths of wine tourists huddled together, I watched my father turn pale green while riding in a spinning bunny at the area amusement park. Sal got a glob of cotton candy stuck in his hair. Holding Lili, I watched my parents restrain my sobbing son as my wife poured seltzer on his head, and I was certain that I'd made the right choice.

Chapter 7

FRIULI

———— ❧ ————

A WEEK AFTER the cotton-candy-meets-hair incident, we made our way north to Friuli, and there we met an unusual sight: the chilly Friulian hills, their slopes lined with vines dripping golden grapes, were swarming with Americans. Or, more accurately, a concentrated area was: a small, dark chalet, its courtyard full of roses and out-of-place palm trees, its name painted on a wooden sign: LA SUBIDA. The California winemaker Steve Clifton was getting married here, and his friends and family were milling around excitedly. We'd shown up for the festivities, among other things.

Before Steve opened his two Santa Barbara wineries, he was the singer in a mildly successful rock 'n' roll band called the Movement, which once allegedly opened for the Red Hot Chili Peppers. He no longer wears his hair long, but you can still see the rocker in his thick features, his expressions, his walk. He is also willing—nay, itching—to sing an eerily accurate rendition of Tom Jones's "It's Not Unusual" while standing on a table. Several minutes after we met in 1999, we were close friends. Soon after, I took him on his first trip to Friuli.

Abutting Slovenia on the northeastern tip of the Italian peninsula, Friuli is simultaneously a curious combination of two countries and a place unto itself. Its people are warm like Italians and severe like Russians. Through their blood runs the memory of all the wars that have been fought on their soil. The hard land is carpeted with the vines that make most of Italy's and Slovenia's robust white wines. Any remaining inch is used as pastureland for horses and pigs, or planted with tobacco or grain. This, combined with a faraway highway and industrial center, gives Friuli a distinctly picturesque quality—crisp air, a brightly colored landscape set against dark mountains, the cerulean sky. Steve promptly fell in love with the region on our first escapade, which was why he was, five years later, holding his wedding in its heart.

My only problem was that I couldn't make it, exactly, to the ceremony itself. I deposited Stephany, Lili, a very energetic Sal, and my parents at the chalet, in a pair of rooms outfitted with enormous fireplaces, and I took off. I had an appointment with a mad genius, and I didn't want to be late.

❧

JOSKO GRAVNER—NEARING SIXTY, tall and broad, with buzz-cut gray hair and hound-dog eyes—looks like a country-dwelling intellectual. He wears thick sweaters and hiking boots, and when he dons his checkered cap, he might be one of any number of men who take daily constitutionals down tree-lined streets in Denmark, Ireland, northeastern Connecticut, or your average Midwestern university town.

From 1975 to 1997, Gravner was widely recognized as the best maker of whites in Italy. Famously eccentric, he has always been considered a mysterious and hermetic character who shuns the press and holes up at his Friulian estate. If you did a little re-search, you might think he was a humorless militant: in the few photographs that exist of him in the public sphere, Gravner, with his army-issue haircut, is standing in his cellar, unsmiling, brow furrowed. But now here he was, this so-called enigma, cur-rently ostracized by his colleagues for his radical methods, stand-ing outside his house and waving to me. Flanking him were a little black mutt and a puffy, grinning Akita. In the decade that I'd known Gravner, he had always been gentle, sweet, and smiling—he had, I noted, large, perfect white teeth.

He welcomed me into his office, a spacious room on the first floor of his house, next to the kitchen, where his slim, bespectacled wife was making lunch. The office was unremarkable—a long desk with a computer, a table with several chairs for tasting wine. The little black mutt shyly put her front paws on my lap and gazed at me.

"She just had puppies," Gravner said. "They were the cutest things." He offered me a plate with some bread spread with homemade quince jam and a glass of his Ribolla Gialla.

The house itself was also unremarkable—clean and simple, with terra-cotta tile floors and white walls. It was a two-story stucco structure near the street, one side covered with red ivy, thick fir trees all around. Next to the door sat a pair of Birkenstock clogs.

Of course, what was remarkable was the unassuming man I'd come to visit. Beneath this fellow's calm exterior, I knew, rumbled the heart of an obsessive mastermind.

※

JOSKO GRAVNER WAS BORN in this house. For generations, through war after war, his family had been making wine here. In 1901, Gravner's grandfather had begun to ferment grapes in the basement, but when World War I broke out, he abandoned his vineyards to join the Austrian army. The rest of the family fled to Piedmont, and the Collio, as this hilly area is called, was razed to the ground. The Gravner house was the only structure left standing, mainly because the Red Cross had taken up residence there. Everything else—trees, vines, stables—had been destroyed. "This is the problem with the Collio," Gravner explained. "All of the wars were fought right here."

After they'd replanted the vineyards, the family continued

producing decent whites. Then Josko came along. He was like other Friulian winemakers in his approach. But in his execution, he was not. Josko Gravner was the best of a different species of winemaker: the ahead-of-the-curve northerners. They were usually at the forefront of technology. And this was both a blessing and a curse.

Friuli was initially a collection of *cantine sociali,* the cooperatives with communal tanks that catered to the community. The area grew an abundance of white varietals and shipped its wine throughout Italy. It was known within the country to be a hotbed of white wine–making, but nobody outside the borders knew much about Friuli. The wines were too rustic, too obscure for foreign tastes. Then, in the 1970s, Friulian winemakers discovered a new method of making whites. They were the first in Italy to adopt the Austrian-perfected technique of cold fermentation.

As noted earlier in these pages, with cold fermentation a vintner can, using temperature control, stop the fermentation of a wine. For white wines, this is especially important because before this practice was adopted, the wine would often evolve past its peak, becoming oxidized and nutty. Suddenly, by halting oxidization, winemakers were able to preserve the taste of young fruit in their wines, to seal it in. In doing so, Friulians made sweet, fresh wines that appealed to sensibilities outside of Italy. They began to bottle their cold-fermented wines and opened the international markets. Friulian whites were immediately popular; money started pouring into a land once decimated by war. Now Friulians were excited: What else could they get their hands on? What other new practices could they cook up? What was the next big thing?

Enthusiasm swept through the region. They brought in everything: barriques; steel tanks; temperature regulators; pumps; woods from France, America, Slovenia; different sizes of corks; acids; tannins; extra water; sugars; man-made yeasts; flavoring agents. Anything that popped up, the Friulians pounced on it. They were operating in a feverish state, Gravner among them. Gravner bought it all, and he bought it first. He perfected each new system before anyone else had even assembled the pieces. Because of this ability, he was known to many as the master, and he trained a new generation of Friulian winemakers, eager young men who tracked his every move. Many of the students of what became known as the School of Gravner turned out to be important winemakers in their own right: Damijan Podversic, Edi Kante, the Bensa brothers of La Castellada, Stanislao Radikon.

His protégés followed him religiously. Gravner alone could comprehend the intricacies of just about every approach. He could make the finest wine possible every time—whites that were fresh, well-balanced, superb. While most Italians did not understand how to utilize a barrique and thus made wine that tasted heavily of wood, Gravner quickly became as accomplished as a Frenchman, integrating the wood so flawlessly that you couldn't sense it. He grasped the scientific precision necessary for properly adding yeasts to a wine—when, how much, the desirable combinations with each year's grapes. He knew how to bring temperatures high to start fermentation, exactly how to bring them low again, how to manipulate the wine through heat and cold. Simply put, he had the golden touch. And through it all, he never showed an interest in money. He was trying everything because he hoped eventually to find the great new secret, the ultimate technology. The world's wine industry applauded him: they called him "the King of Italian Whites."

The problem for most Friulians was that with all this constant change, they were messing up a lot. Their wines were full of errors. They had become unstable, some hitting peaks, others dropping down. The winemakers—less talented than Gravner, desperate, confused—didn't have time to understand one approach before a new one exploded onto the scene, compelling them to move on. The wines, now a mishmash of techniques, had lost their regional identity and become anxious drinks, reflective of their makers' unrest.

Even for Gravner, the business had grown frustrating. Just as soon as he had understood a new approach, he scrapped it and took up another. By the time he had purchased something, he was already too late. This is the nature of technology: as soon as you discover something, a better version of it is already well on its way. In the mid-1990s, Gravner realized that he had lost sight of his goal of making the best wine in the world. Wasn't wine about the natural product? If he found himself endlessly disappointed going forward, perhaps, he thought, he should look back. He began to research ancient methods.

Gravner started experimenting, cultivating natural yeasts, extending maceration periods, prolonging grape-skin contact with the juice. In 1997, the German winemaker Udo Fiersch sold him a 230-liter red clay amphora, one of the enormous jugs in which the first wines were made, five thousand years ago. Gravner began to test out the peculiar process. Hardly anyone in the world was making wines this way anymore, so Gravner learned about amphorae through old texts—how to bury the amphora in the deep earth, what sorts of grapes to use, when to remove the juice. He was intrigued; the amphora method seemed simple but required expertise, the finest grapes, the most intricate handling. One day in the year 2000, he and his son Mika were escorted by bodyguards through the freezing-cold Caucasus mountains of the perpetually warring Russian state of Georgia. The mountains housed some of the few winemakers in the world who specialized in the use of amphorae, and Gravner wanted to taste what they were up to.

"The Georgian wine was bad," he told me matter-of-factly.

"Bad grapes, bad wine. But I saw potential. I knew then that this was the path."

This was why I was at his house, eating jam on bread, because I wanted to know what his epiphany had led to in practical terms. This man had once been the most technically advanced winemaker in the country, and now, it seemed, he had flown as far back in time as a winemaker can go. Gravner was making wines in the ancient Roman style. He was convinced that it was the only true way to make wine.

In this, he was on his own. His once-devoted followers, with the exception of Podversic, had abandoned him. Further, some understandably resented him. He had guided them to the heights of modernism; they had invested in what he recommended, had hung on his every word. And now, Gravner had unapologetically scrapped it all. He was saying at wine tastings—with the press in the room—that he would no longer allow his family to drink wine full of the laboratory-made products he had once used.

"My old wine is garbage," he would tell a roomful of buyers, winemakers, and journalists. "Wine and food have to be natural products. In flying a plane, one needs technology, but it's absurd to think that man can ever improve what is natural. Wine and food we put in our stomachs. How could I continue doing my work if I have knowledge that what I make was slowly poisoning my children?"

Gravner felt he had to withdraw from his apprentices. He couldn't be bound by relationships and personal loyalty if he was to make known his views.

"You can make wine because you're researching what the market wants or you can make wine you believe in, and I believe in my wine," he told me, shrugging. "To make wine this way, you must be able to break free from your so-called friends and go it alone."

What I really wanted was to see the amphorae, and so we started for the cellar. The cellar, which was connected to the house, could be reached by walking across the driveway, which housed an old white Lexus with the insignia ripped off the front but a Lexus logo baseball cap in the window, down a small slope, past a lone worker in coveralls, and into a permanently under-construction back building. Compared to many other cellars—sparkling, spotless showrooms—the place was downright ramshackle. It was a minuscule venture: several dank old stone rooms, centuries of moisture packed into their walls; some barrels. The few windows were draped gothically with spiderwebs so thick and dusty that they looked like worn black scarves. We walked until we came to another room, a little lower down. This was the amphora room.

Josko Gravner's amphora room was a strange, medieval, windowless underground space, the floors made of large planks of rough wood laid over dirt. Every few feet, there was a substantial opening in the wood surrounded by a circle of dry red clay. A quarter of the room was merely a gaping cavity, a deep opening of damp soil and rock, with a shovel balanced in the corner.

"Here you go," Gravner said.

The circles of dry red clay were deceiving: each was, in fact, the lip of one of Gravner's twenty amphorae. The actual structure—which resembled a primitive vase so big that a human could fit inside (and often did, to clean it)—was buried in the earth. Some of the tops of the amphorae were covered with slabs of cardboard, cut from moving boxes. Other amphorae were open and filled to the brim with juice; the amber grape skins had risen to the top and formed a cover so thick it was impossible to glimpse the liquid below.

"The ground has all the life you need to give birth to grapes," Gravner said. "A vine needs the earth to make a grape. Once you have that grape, you need the earth again to make wine." The ground maintained constant cold temperatures if the amphora was made properly, and of the correct clay.

To make the wines, Gravner had taken to harvesting tiny yields of extraordinarily high-quality grapes from his vineyards each fall. Growing small amounts of such precise fruit was a complex undertaking, and it required constant surveillance and a great command of the land. But it was necessary.

"This wine is all about *la materia prima*," Gravner explained. "An amphora is dangerous. Unlike a barrique, which at least imbues the drink with some wood, an amphora gives nothing to the wine. If you put in one bad grape, you can taste it."

The juice, along with all of its elements—pulp, skins, stems, and seeds—underwent a maceration period, sitting for between six and nine months. During this time, thousands of things could go wrong; wine is a volatile animal, which accounts for why the industry is dedicated to eliminating such risks, and why most winemakers macerate for two weeks. Gravner was not interested in eliminating hazards. Throughout the maceration process, the grape skins first floated to the top and then, as they became heavy with must, sank. At the end, Gravner manually pumped out the juice; then someone fairly limber lowered himself into the amphora and scooped out all the skins.

Pinot Grigio is a red grape. If the skins are kept on, the drink emerges as a rosy-colored wine. Since rosés tend not to sell, the skins are generally discarded immediately, and the grayish-yellow wine widely recognized as Pinot Grigio materializes. Because Gravner didn't remove the skins from his grapes, his Pinot Grigio was rusty pink, which was guaranteed to freak out many potential customers. Gravner, however, didn't care if certain people refused to see that a Pinot Grigio didn't have to be yellow. He apparently didn't care about anything but his wine. In his mind, it was his ethical obligation on this earth to make wines in this way. Anything else, as he had mentioned at the conference, was toxic: How could he knowingly produce a product that hurt people? If wine was pleasure and beauty and art, it had to be safe and right.

"If you look at the life of most wines now—from the vine to the bottle—it's like they travel in a polluted river," Gravner said. "You begin with a pure stream, the grape, and on its way to the ocean, technology pollutes it. For me, finding this way to make wine was like searching around the world for the clearest water. Finally, I saw you don't seek the purest water in a waterfall. No, you go to the source. Clarity is down there, in the ground."

We tasted the wine, taken from the earthenware containers. It wasn't like his old wine. In fact, it wasn't like anything I'd ever drunk before. How would he describe the difference between this and his old wine?

"I don't have the words for that," he said—*Non ho parole.* "How can you describe a soul? I can tell you only that these wines have real spirit."

And what about other people? I wondered. *What about the people who will be baffled by this stuff? The people who are expecting their California white when they pop the cork?*

"I think of it this way: I make wines for me," he said. "I sell what's left over."

Gravner was laconic—now, more than ever. He wasn't bothered. What did he have to defend? What did he need to explain? He and I both knew it: these wines were his greatest achievement yet, his legacy, his private laurels. This was why he could never go back. He had found satisfaction, he had finally begun to achieve what he'd been chasing after his entire life. He wasn't interested in money or public opinion. His freedom to make this wine was his freedom from mass influence, from the common desire for cash or glory. What more could he say?

We trudged back up to his porch and sat down, looking out at the stone driveway. His Akita put her head on his knee. We talked a little about our families and then I left for the wedding reception. I waved at Gravner as I turned right from his driveway.

And there he was, tall, smiling, waving back, in front of his humble house, his hand on the dog's head, not a thing out of the ordinary—a brilliant disguise.

❧

THE AIRY ROOM at La Subida was full of well-dressed Americans and a few fair-haired Slavic Friulians, gorging themselves on the regional specialty: delicate prosciutto di San Daniele made by the artisan Gigi D'Osvaldo, who lived down the road. To the side was a swarthy Italian playing a guitar and singing in a thick Puglian accent—almost Arabic, unmistakable. I sidled up to him.

"What are you doing up north here?" I asked him in Neapolitan dialect.

"Moved years ago," he said cheerily. "Like the place."

I nodded, unsure as to how a southerner, a person used to the heat and noise of his birthplace, could comfortably move to this cold and silent land. Then I got distracted by a plate of fried regional montasio cheese, and one of zucchini blossoms filled with white dollops of ricotta and salami. The displaced Puglian continued to sing.

I said hello to my friend Valter Scarbolo, a proud, blue-eyed Friulian winemaker from Butrio who owns the trattoria La Frasca in Lauzacco and creates remarkable salami, sweet, thick, and fatty. His son Mattia, a gangly fourteen-year-old, sat loyally by his side. Mattia had been spending his summers in California with Steve Clifton, apprenticing and learning English.

Someone tapped a fork against a glass; it was time for speeches. I had located Stephany by the prosciutto spread, and together we found our way to our table—we were seated with all the northern Italians—and got ready for the requisite speeches.

Greg Brewer—Steve's partner at Brewer-Clifton winery—was best man, and he stood in the front of the room first, looking, in his tailored suit, exactly like a grown-up Richie Rich. He took the microphone.

"A lot of people don't understand Steve," he said. "A lot of people don't understand why Steve is always late." I was ready for a roast—American wine guys, a wedding party full of bubbly—but Greg grew more serious. People got frustrated with Steve when Steve gave them their stuff late, Greg said. But Steve, Greg went on, wasn't late because he was some irresponsible, careless jerk. No, Steve was late because Steve couldn't say no. Steve simply couldn't say no to anyone—his heart was just too big. You asked him for the littlest thing, you asked him for the biggest favor, and he'd drop what he was doing and help you. Steve was just this sort of person. When someone asked for help, he could only say yes.

Suddenly, Greg choked up a little and then, without warning, began to cry. Steve was the best friend he'd ever had, he said through tears. Steve was an amazing person; Greg was so happy that Steve had finally found love, real love. I looked around the room. The faces of Steve's family and friends were contorted with emotion. Steve was a beautiful man, Greg said. Steve was a great man. Steve's family sniffled. Greg stumbled off the stage.

Next, Steve's new sister-in-law stood up. She began to talk about Chrystal, her little sister and Steve's new wife. Chrystal was deeply kind, she said. Not just sweet—though, God knows, she was sweet, too—but the sort of person who'd help you when you were at your worst. She recounted how Chrystal had nursed her back to health after a near-paralyzing injury. Chrystal's sister let out a hoarse sob. Chrystal deserved this happiness because she gave this happiness to so many others. Chrystal and Steve were so perfect together. I looked around again. Chrystal's family had erupted into tears, which appeared to have spurred on Steve's family. The room was full of bawling people in formal wear.

Steve stood up. His face was red and damp. "I love everyone here so much," he said. He couldn't believe the love he felt for and from his friends, his family, his new friends, his new family. The room experienced a new rush of hysteria. People grasped one another's hands.

At my table, the Friulians were confused. They looked at me for some explanation, as though I could bridge for them this unexpected cultural abyss.

"What is happening?" whispered one alarmed woman in her Slovenian accent. "Is this normal on such occasions?"

"I thought of your people as more restrained," said a man in a tuxedo. "I had no idea."

But I was just as baffled as they. Stephany and I had never seen Americans behave in this way, and in public. We shook our heads. Had Italy gotten to them?

"I have made a new wine," Steve continued. "I want to tell you all right now about this special wine. Because I want to name this wine after someone who is close to my heart. This person has become like a little brother to me and I am so grateful that he has come into my life and taught me new things about myself and about the world." Steve paused to collect himself. "This wine is dedicated to Valter's son, Mattia."

Mattia, all limbs and adolescence, bolted from his table and collapsed in a corner, howling. Valter, the formerly staunch restaurateur, went after him and soon found himself, too, weeping and cradling his son.

And as though operated by some switch, my table turned on: the Friulians lost it, I lost it, Stephany buried her head in her hands. Mattia had the mike, and was trying to explain, in his broken English and through his whimpering, how much Steve and Chrystal meant to him. I could hardly hear through the cacophony, but I did feel a tap on the shoulder.

I turned around and there stood the stocky Puglian musician, the only dry face for miles.

"*Si?*" I blubbered.

"This shit is worse than Puglia," he said, shaking his head. "You Americans and northerners are babies, man. I'm going home."

He had a point. We'd upstaged southern Italians in the communal-emotion game, something I'd previously considered impossible. Maybe they'd slipped something in our fizzy water. "Waiter," I said. "Let's get some bottles of tequila out here, stat."

We passed the bottles around. Soon, everyone had dried their salty cheeks, and we drank until dawn.

❧

SOMETIME BETWEEN THE MASS BREAKDOWN and the morning headaches, my friend the Slovenian winemaker Aleš Kristančič arrived at the party. He lived close to La Subida and knew Steve well enough, and he may or may not have been swilling Prosecco until sunrise—nobody there is a trustworthy witness. But the one thing I did remember when the haze of the festivities lifted from my head was Aleš's blurry, grinning face, requesting my presence at his estate, Movia, the next evening. The image was distorted and contained no specifics, as it took place approximately ten seconds before my memory abandoned me for the night.

"Babe," I said to the breathing lump beneath the covers, "do we have dinner plans tonight?"

"Eh," the lump responded. A small hand reached out and attempted to swat me away.

"Did Aleš give us a time?" I asked.

"Think eight," the lump groaned.

I left my wife with several bottles of water and a packet of Italian aspirin by her head and bumped around to a few wineries. When I returned seven hours later, she looked a little pale but otherwise prepared. For someone pressing five feet tall and one hundred pounds, she was having a respectable run.

"Hi, honey," she said weakly. "I'm ready for more."

We drove for exactly three minutes to the Slovenian border and hopped out of the car.

The Slovenian border crossing in Cormons—consisting of a gate and a tiny shack where a man in military garb sits at apparently random intervals—looks like a displaced, old-fashioned railroad crossing. Since the barrier is put down at night, you need to leave your car behind if you plan to return to Italy between midnight and 6 a.m. The entire setup appears a mere formality, because if you wanted to smuggle anything—diamonds, kilos of cocaine, kidnapped businessmen—from one country to the other, you could calmly do so on foot several yards from the guardhouse. But Aleš's estate, in any case, is only a five-minute walk into Slovenia, and even if it took two hours, it would be a worthwhile trip.

ℛ

ALEŠ KRISTANČIČ IS, AMONG OTHER THINGS, a champion ballroom dancer, a devoted husband, a hapless womanizer, the doting father of two, a painter, a dog lover, the unofficial Slovenian ambassador, a poet, an art collector, a deep talent, a rebel, a reflective thinker, a Luddite ("I am now beginning to learn e-mail but I find it oppressive"), an amateur physicist, a philosopher, and someone you want to hang out with all the time. But he is above all a maverick winemaker.

We found Aleš waiting for us at Movia, a sprawling collection of two-hundred-year-old pink stucco houses on the edge of his vineyards. He has the build of a middle-aged athlete and a Russian face with a boxer's nose, and what is left of his hair is shaved close to his head. He was wearing tattered beige Dolce & Gabbana corduroys with his Gucci belt, a black fleece sweatshirt, and black kitchen clogs. His hands are at once enormous and elegant.

"*Zak-zak!*" he yelled excitedly.

"What's *zak-zak*?" Stephany whispered.

"*Zak-zak* is his word," I said. "It means what he wants it to mean. In this case, I think it means, 'You made it!'"

Stephany nodded.

Aleš dashed over to us and kissed Stephany's hand while bowing.

"You are really beautiful," he said in his thick accent, grinning. "I am so happy that you have come." He spun her—gently and forcefully—into a one-step dance, and caught her in a dip. Stephany swooned and then swiftly recovered. Aleš hugged me and led us inside.

The inside of Aleš's entertainment house, where he serves food to presidents, actors, writers, winemakers, and friends, looks like a modern restaurant. The main room holds several tables, including one long, rectangular twenty-seater, and is attached to a terrace that overlooks the winery's property—a collection of bright fields that cross into Italy. In the main room, Aleš's wife, Vesna, displays a rotating assembly of art done by a Slovenian artist—sculptures, paintings, drawings. Every San Martino Day (Saint Martin is a priest who fought for farmers' rights), when there is a new batch of wine in the cellar, Vesna hangs new art on the walls. The bathrooms smell heavily of musk and lilac, and upon one table, surrounding a vase of flowers, are stacks of shiny photographs of parties that have taken place in the room.

"The good life is like a red carpet, running through everything you do," Aleš once said to me.

"You mean like a thread?" I asked.

"The good life is like a silk thread, running through everything you do."

Already, a couple of Sicilian winemakers were seated at the table—dark, squat fellows hoping to learn a little bit from Aleš. An American journalist from Colorado was talking to my friend Paolo Domeneghetti, a Gérard Depardieu look-alike originally from the Adriatic seaside town of Ancona. Paolo is a wine importer, though he previously owned a place in New York called Boom and a Miami sister establishment called Bang, both of which are known to be the first places European models realized that it was fun to dance on tables and engage in after-hours orgies. Paolo's art-history-trained, Ohio-born wife, Allison, who wears her hair in a black bob and favors miniskirts, was standing at a counter talking to Jeff Meisel, a guy who used to be a waiter with me at San Domenico and who now invited me to his house in Westchester for Passover every year; since Jeff looks exactly like Jesus, Passover with him was always a little disconcerting. Outside, a blue-gray Great Dane named Tango and a white West Highland terrier named Cash waited eagerly to get in on the action.

"Ever since Tango made a faux pas, they are banned from attending parties," Aleš whispered.

"What faux pas?" I whispered.

"Aggressively sniffed the vagina of a Danish diplomat wearing all white," he said. "Very bad for international relations." He brought out a magnum of his sparkling wine Puro.

"Watch this, now," he announced to the room. "I want to show you a special maneuver."

Vesna emerged with a large glass bowl filled with water. She was wearing a black belly-baring pants-and-T-shirt combination, her dark hair falling limply around her round, tanned face. She was serious, steady, calm—the opposite of Aleš's wild noise.

Aleš's drink was true to its name—*puro,* Italian for "pure"—and each bottle thus contained about a half inch of naturally occurring sediment. This kind of sediment, in almost all other bubbly drinks, is sucked out and replaced with a mix of sweet new alcohol—cognac or older wine—so that buyers don't drink solid bits of dead yeasts when they buy a bottle. But Aleš didn't like this artificiality and ease. He had other ideas.

"The sommelier used to be a person who linked the farmer and the customer, and whose role it was to protect both," Aleš explained as Vesna set the bowl in front of him. "The sommelier was someone who understood good cork, bad cork, good wine, bad wine. Now he understands numbers, not the reality of wine."

Aleš dunked the neck of his Puro beneath the surface of the water. "Puro is a game, you see. I'm giving this contemporary sommelier work. He must learn how to serve my wine. He must learn that a perfect product is not necessarily a good product. If you make something scientifically flawless, you miss the life. Just as if you have a perfect person, they are lifeless, plastic."

Aleš took a cloth napkin and wrapped it around the submerged cork. Everyone had gathered, rapt, around his table. "You can measure your ingredients and time your fermentations. You can make a practical wine that you take to a picnic, you put in your paper cups, *cin-cin, zak-zak,*" he said. "But wine is not practical or mathematic. I mean, I like practical engineering in cars. But wine and food is life, and a practical, engineered life is no life at all."

He jimmied the cork. "This is a Jesus Christ way of doing things," he announced.

Stephany looked at me.

"I don't know," I said.

In one fluid movement, Aleš released the cork within the bowl. A flush of fizzy sediment rushed out into the water, and Aleš pulled the bottle out. He held it up. It was now as clear as Champagne.

"And *zak,*" he said. He poured us each a glass of the transparent bubbly. Vesna brought out some little pieces of toast with dollops of caviar balancing upon slabs of butter. The Puro was as always: crisp, confusing, complicated, and so alive it woke me up.

❦

THIS COURAGE OF CONVICTION—the determination to make a drink that directly contradicts convention because you believe in its unerring and morally necessary authenticity—is in Aleš's DNA. Eight generations earlier, a Kristančič man married a Movia daughter, and their family has run the place ever since.

Aleš's grandfather Anton risked his life to make his wine. At the beginning of Josip Broz Tito's infamously repressive and brutal communist regime in the 1950s, Anton mounted a wine-based resistance. He had been making his own wine from his own grapes for decades, as had his father and grandfather, and he wasn't about to dump his juice into a *cantina sociale* because of this new political philosophy. When the postman arrived with the state-sanctioned newspaper, Anton would spend hours cutting out the parts he hated, and the next day would instruct the postman (under threat of violent death, of course—"My grandfather said to that postman, 'I'll slit your throat if you don't follow my orders, and I know where you live,'" Aleš recalled) to return the paper to the politicians. "To tell them what he thought of their news," said Aleš.

Eventually, Tito paid Anton a visit. Would he be personally hauling him off to jail? Was it torture-and-murder time?

"Actually, it turned out that Tito just wanted some wine," Aleš said. "Tito came and said to him, 'Look, you can make your wine. I won't touch your land. But you can't go around with your individual labels because we don't want it to be clear that you can do what other people can't.' And then Tito told my grandfather that the government would secretly buy it and drink it themselves because it was so good." Because of this, the Kristančič estate, unlike the others from the area, had a little time capsule in its cellars: wines from Anton's era, a time when most other expression had been squashed, an extra helping of history.

Then dinner was served: sliced avocadoes sprinkled with fresh cracked *peperoncino* and sweet basil; corn and asparagus risotto; Aleš and Vesna's farm-raised chicken stewed in white wine and served with polenta; their own roast suckling pig surrounded by roasted spring vegetables. We drank Aleš's savage, serious 1999 Sauvignon; his funny, unsophisticated 2001 Veliko Bianco; his 2001 Tokai Gredic, like a thousand-piece orchestra warming up; his stern, impatient 2001 Ribolla. And then the oldies: the 1988 Ribolla tasted like someone running for a train, frazzled and almost there; the 1959 Ribolla made me feel like I was in a beautiful, soundproof safehouse as the world crashed around me; the 1963 Merlot, at once vibrant and elegant, was the best Merlot I'd had outside of Pomerol, Bordeaux.

At the end of dinner, Stephany leaned over to me. "I get everyone else's connection, but what are those Sicilian guys doing here?" she asked.

"People come from around the world to learn about this stuff from Aleš," I said. "He could charge thousands if he wanted."

"Aleš, Sergio tells me people come here to learn about winemaking," Stephany said. "What exactly do you teach people about?"

"People like these gentlemen here?" Aleš asked. The Sicilians smiled in unison. "Whatever they want. Today, for example, we discussed the theory of the grape."

Stephany, normally shy, was emboldened by the wine. "Aleš, I've been married to Sergio for three years now and I know next to nothing about how wine is really made," she said. "Would you be willing to give me a lesson?"

"For such a beauty, how can I say no?" Aleš said. "Tomorrow morning?"

"I'm coming, too," I said. "I don't want you putting your paws on my wife."

"Sergio, don't worry," Aleš said. "Can't you smell that? It is the smell of my brakes. If I get too close to your wife, I am like a cable car, stopping fast. *Screeeeeech.*"

❦

ALEŠ, IN HIGH RUBBER BOOTS, was sitting on a stone wall at his house at eight the next morning. He looked inexplicably fresh, considering that after we had left, he had continued on to the Slovenian town of Ljubljana, where he told us he had spent the rest of the night eating foie gras and dancing to techno at some sort of "super-fashion party."

"But how did you manage to go on after all that we ate and drank?" Stephany asked. "I needed to crawl directly into bed."

"It's not too complicated," Aleš said cheerily. "Your body's saying, 'Hey, maybe I should go to sleep.' And you wait it out and stay awake and your body says, 'What are you doing? I said we needed to sleep!' And you say, 'I don't want to sleep. Let's go out dancing!' And your body thinks a little and then it's like, 'Okay, I'm in!'"

"Oh," Stephany said.

Her education began with the vineyards. We passed into the nippy winery and then down some concrete steps and out into the fields. Surrounding the rows upon rows of winding little vines were olive trees, fig trees, white rose bushes. There were two cheerful cherry trees with their red leaves ("A little disco," Aleš said, pointing at them) in the middle of the vineyard, and apple trees, apricot trees, and white flowers sprouting up from all over.

"Is there a reason for all this fruit?" Stephany asked.

"Of course," Aleš said. "The vineyard must have some friends." He paced down the curved land slowly. He lost his intense playfulness. This land was not a game to him, or some silly thing. He was suddenly the college professor everyone longed for—the teacher imbued with eternal youthfulness, fiery passion, an instructor who wanted more than anything for his students to learn, and who regarded their naïveté without judgment; someone who could turn a subject with such high boredom potential into a beautiful story. He began with the earth.

"Man arrived and wanted to plant the soil, but when he began to dig he found rock. This was limestone." He bent down to the cracked and parched earth and picked up a hard chunk. Beneath it lay gray dirt. "With sun and rain, this type of earth forms a solid layer on top, like this piece. When you till it you find this dirt below, but it's really poor. You can see." He let the dirt fall through his fingers. "It's bad for potatoes and corn and lettuce and tomatoes. It's bad for almost everything."

Stephany and I bent down to feel the earth; it was crumbly, dry.

"Potatoes and corn need easy soil, brown, supple, rich. And you'd think vines would like it, too. They do seem to. If you plant a vine in such soil, you get big, juicy grapes. Everyone's happy. But then you eat them and they have no taste—only sweet water."

"Sweet water," Stephany said. "Like supermarket grapes. Why?"

"Yes, correct," Aleš said. "They seemed so happy, they grew so fast! The berries were so large and gorgeous. But now they have no richness. They're not fantastic grapey grapes. Just sweet and juicy. Why? Why?" He held the dainty branch of a vine in his hand.

"Why?" Stephany asked. She was having a little trouble balancing in her black Prada ankle boots—made of some kind of "all-weather" microfiber that she had announced would hold up well on our tour through nature—but was otherwise completely engaged. She had been to many tastings by my side, but had never really traipsed through a vineyard, had never seen the details so close.

"Exactly my question," Aleš said. "You must understand this: If any plant in all the plant world were to rise up into the animal kingdom and become a human being, it would be the vine."

"How so?" Stephany asked.

"It is the plant closest in character to man," Aleš said. "If it has this comfortable life, and this undemanding land, it is never challenged. It's like a spoiled socialite: healthy, beautiful, and vapid. It's a machine, not a thing of natural beauty—just eating and producing fruits. And yes, absolutely, you can make something from this fruit. You can mix it up in a barrel and get drunk from it—but this thing you make is not wine. *Hai capito?*"

"*Ho capito.*" Stephany nodded. She dug a heel into the ground and acquired some traction. I watched in amazement as she didn't look twice at the mud stuck to her boot.

"On the other hand, if you plant a vine in poor soil, that's a different situation. In this tough limestone, it must reach with its roots deep into the earth for nutrients. The best things are there, down in the ground, far from man. The elements that give a wine complexity, beauty, intrigue, flavor—they're all hidden from our view. And vines like to search for them when given the opportunity. Potatoes, no. Potatoes don't want to go burrowing around, but vines do. And that's why we call this land 'absolute wine-growing position.' Because this land is meant for grapes. Nature intended them to be here and she tells us that by fating everything else. Melons, broccoli, cauliflower, spinach, grain—they all fail here. But grapes that grow here flourish, and they taste of more than water and sugar."

"What exactly is more than water and sugar?" Stephany asked. "What's grapiness?"

"The taste of earth is more," Aleš said. "The taste of the depths of this place, of the minerals that tell us what was here before, how this soil happened. This taste of earth is what every-one refers to as *territorio.*"

"*Territorio,*" Stephany murmured.

"The specific taste of this place," Aleš said. "The taste comes from down there, and we can't see it."

"So simple!" Stephany said.

"Exactly," Aleš said. "So now we have our land. We need to plant the vines. Ready?"

"Ready," Stephany said.

"Why do we plant vines in lines?" Aleš asked. Stephany stared at him. "We plant vines in lines because it's easiest to work them this way," he said.

"Clearly," Stephany said, gazing at Aleš. Had she ever looked at me this way?

"Aleš, I think she loves you," I said.

"*Screeeeeech,*" Aleš said.

"Sergio, shhh," Stephany said. "Aleš, go on. The vines."

"Every vine needs his place on this planet. He needs surface room, space to breathe. He can't be close to his neighbors like lettuce. He needs to stretch." Aleš lit a thin, girlish cigarette. "You know, smoking is the cellular telephone line to God," he added. "Anyway, you can't figure out how many vines you plant per hectare using mathematics and economy, using equations, determined to fit as many vines as possible. You can figure out how many vines to plant, and where, only by understanding your individual land and the personality of vines."

"How do you do that?" Stephany asked.

"You work your land for a long time," Aleš said. "I can't tell you more than that. How do you understand a person? You talk to him, stay close to him, spend time with him. Then you can begin to comprehend.

"So, only a happy life gives good, healthy products. If you plant tons of plants close together, each plant will be like an industrial chicken. The industrial chicken has never seen a rooster and she will produce in a tiny box by artificial means for her whole life and die without ever once feeling love. When you eat her meat, you don't get positive energy or passion; you get calories and no more. A plant is the same—he must be open, he must go deep, he must experience freedom. And then he will give to you beautiful fruit. So now we have planted our vines. Next, we must harvest. *Sei pronta?*"

"*Pronta!*" Stephany said. We wandered down the hill a little and Aleš finished his cigarette. He looked below him. His vines rose and fell in waves into the valley.

"We do this work for our children," he said. "You need one generation to plant and a second to receive the best fruits. Here's why: During the first years of its life, a plant can go deep fast if you work the soil right, move stones, cut stones, prepare the soil well with good technology—tilling machines. If you do this, the plant becomes secure enough to survive and to make her own way. But she is still young. She is moving through school to university, always learning, developing her own character, finding out who she is. Yes, she has us and nature, teachers and parents, outsiders, to help guide her for the first twenty or twenty-five years, but ultimately she must search for herself.

"In this time, she has lots of energy. She's growing lots of new leaves, each of which is like a small factory that produces more sugar and more vegetation. So she's growing sweet, sugary grapes in a frenzy. Excellent, right?"

"Wait, is this a trick question?" Stephany asked.

"Yes. It's not excellent. Sugar is just one element. You must consider what she's producing, your vine. You must consider her mental state. See, she has lots of vigor for love but sometimes she's not selective enough."

"Frisky," Stephany said.

"She's just young! Don't judge her," Aleš said.

"Sorry," Stephany said.

"If you are stupid and greedy, you pick her grapes, all of them. You keep picking them because she's producing and producing and you want to also produce your wine and make some cash. For twenty years you strip her bare every time she offers you something. And then what?

"Then one day you find that your vine is not young anymore. You didn't allow her time for a childhood. She grew up too fast and now she is prematurely aged and she can hardly produce at all." Aleš sucked his cheeks in, slumped, and mimicked a weak, old woman. "She gave too much and now she's almost barren.

"Flowering is something the plant must do. It must do this to create nature, new life. But when she is flowering, we must understand she is just maturing. She has the curves of a woman, but she is not a woman. She is still a child, and we must treat her delicately, as such.

"Because if we allow her to mature and we don't rip from her all her bountiful fruit, she will have a long life and she will, over time, become more discerning. She will make fewer grapes but each grape will be richer, more intricate, her individual creation, her wise choice. She learned that by making a smaller amount of grapes she could give us the best possible fruit. We didn't have to control her to make her do this. We only needed to be tolerant with her. We needed to have faith in her. And only then, when she is ready, can we take from her these fruits."

"Now we pick," Stephany said. "But ideally, we're picking from vines our father left for us?"

"Correct," Aleš said. "We plant the vines for our kids. We harvest from the vines our father planted for us. To do so, we use natural methods, not pesticides and chemicals. Because if you kill twenty things to get one thing, your approach is counterintuitive. You upset the fragile balance and, little by little, destroy your land.

"The most important thing for a wine producer to leave behind is not a beautiful cellar, or the latest machine or wads of money. It is a vineyard. A vineyard is not about wealth and profit and immediacy. A vineyard is your heritage. Your parents need to have planted, twenty-five years before you, vines that you can use. And you need to plant, twenty-five years before your children will take over, vines that will be ready for them.

"When you see 'Since 1820' on a wine label, that's not just marketing. Sure, if the company that makes your sweater is old, maybe it has more chances to be good; but just as easily, a new designer could make a better sweater."

"For example, Stella McCartney does better collections than, say, Escada, in my opinion," Stephany said.

"I was never a fan of Escada," Aleš said. "But in the wine world, 'Since 1820' means that with this estate you have the chance to drink something made from the fruit of mature vines. You have the chance to drink a serious wine. So now let's get to that part—the making of the serious wine. We should talk about this in the appropriate place."

We wandered up the slope to the winery, which stood at its peak, a towering structure in the classic Movia pink stucco. Inside, a series of rooms connected to one another. The first room was bleak and industrial, high and concrete-walled and empty but for two immense metal vats and several cardboard boxes. The only sign of life was a hunched woman, sweeping the floor.

But the room led into another, lower room, which was part museum, part cellar, full of towering Slovenian oak casks and accented by several lit candelabra and an ornate sculpture and collage—a wooden rod, decorated with a series of dice and holding up a slick dark wood rectangle, nailed to which was a canvas. This was Aleš's art. Upon the canvas, he had pasted enlarged newspaper type of Slovenian words and numbers, and atop that he had painted a bright caricature of Vesna, dressed in black, with a mass of dark hair, red lips, and enormous black eyes. Above her head was painted, in yellow, *Dedicated to V, the Queen of My Heart.*

As we proceeded deeper into the cellar, each room had its own adornment made by Aleš's friends. An intricate brass sculpture of a winged Greek god hung at the entrance to the older part of the cellar. On one wall was a mosaic made with a medley of blue and turquoise tiles—water and sky—flanked by reddish-brown tiles—earth. There was a wood-and-hammered-silver whale's tail. A copper box nailed to the wall contained the clay likeness of a man in a copper coffin, a glass bottle of wine pouring liquid into his mouth, his hair wrapping around the bottle's neck—reaching for wine even in death. The more we descended, the colder the cellar became and the sweeter it smelled. Aleš leaned against a barrel.

"A good winemaker is not a doctor," he said. "He is a cavalier.

He takes his fruits gently in his arm—'Please, do you want to dance with me?'—and he guides them to become wine."

"Is this the biodynamic way?" Stephany asked. Aleš was famous for his biodynamic techniques and was a proponent of slow, organic farming.

"It's frosty down here," Aleš said. "Let's have a coffee." He led us away from the cellar entrance, blowing out candles as he passed them. And when we were at our most subterranean, he opened an almost-hidden door, and we were in a lit-up winding staircase, the white walls covered in framed antique sketches of local herbs and flowers. We ascended around and around until we reached another door and emerged in the party-room kitchen, a spotless space of scrubbed-down tile and metal.

Aleš peeked out at the dining area and, seeing a collection of bearded fellows in spiffy dinner jackets swirling wine in their glasses, ducked back in. He was involved in his lecture to Stephany and didn't want to be torn away. And really, he had transformed, from the wild showman, the ballroom dancer and incorrigible flirt, into the winemaker and nothing more. He didn't want to flip into host mode.

"Let's sit in the kitchen," he said. He made us all espressos. Then he arranged his chair with some thought, placing his back against one specific wall beneath a clock and several taped-up photographs of an enlightened Slovenian guru with sleepy black eyes and an untamed dark beard. "To have the best mental energy, it's important to consider where you put your chair," he explained.

"Biodynamic is almost impossible to discuss if we don't have years," he said, crossing his legs and leaning back. "It's physics and Old World knowledge and nature and planets. But suffice it to say, to work in a biodynamic way is to mix—or dynamize—elements of the universe into each other. To raise biodynamic fruit, you take care of every element of the vineyard, from the smallest particle of earth to the worms to the trees to the air.

When there is an infected leaf, you pluck it off by hand—you don't spray everything, even that which is healthy. And you pay attention to what people before you knew. You use plant combinations. You can, for example, grow clover in an area you want to make more nitrogen-rich. You can use chamomile to repel insects. You can put animal parts in the ground to make your plants more efficient."

"Pardon?" Stephany asked.

"We put cow manure inside a cow horn and bury it for six months. And then we take it out in the spring and sprinkle a few grams per hectare and you can see an effect," Aleš said. "Why is that? Why does a cow horn hold this different type of energy? You look disbelieving. Well, let's think about something we can prove.

"If we have a group of horses in a field and one day, in order for us to protect them or make sure they don't run away, we put up a wire fence that can be electrified. Probably immediately, one horse will accidentally brush by it, he will feel a little shock, and he'll return to his horse friends. After this one horse is shocked, there is an extremely low chance that any other horse will ever touch the fence. I believe that the horses communicate, and that first horse tells the others about the danger. This means that after thirty minutes of electricity, we can shut it off and keep only the wire. Those horses, and their children, can be inside that pasture for a hundred years, *zak-zak,* and no one will try to escape.

"But if we put cows in the same fields and turn on the wire, we can see that not one cow will ever touch the line. Maybe by accident, if they're pushed or shoved, but not willingly. But after ten years, if we turn the electricity off for five minutes, all the cows will have wandered out. Why? Because cows have horns and horses don't. Cows use their horns as antennae, receptors. Thousands of years ago, someone noticed that cows use their horns in this way, to sense things, and tried different ways of capitalizing on that energy, and they found one, and I use it, too. The cow horn has energy and it helps the vineyard."

I asked Aleš if he understood the skepticism his approach invited.

"Of course," he said. "I bottle my wines according to the moon and bury cow horns. But this is knowledge I received from my parents and I see results, as did they, as did my grandparents, and so on. Sometimes I was very angry about it all, this way of making wine. When I was a child, on a perfect Saturday or Sunday, everything is okay, it's a great day to play soccer. I wake and my father comes to me and says, 'Aleš, today is a wonderful day for decantation—high pressure, perfect weather, today is the best time for this.' But I was eight years old and I said, 'Come on, please, I have a game today.' But my father always said, 'Aleš, you cannot compare the importance of your soccer game with our wine. This wine is our life and your future.'

"If you tell a psychologist this today they will say my father was wrong. When I began to work, I was sad, thinking always of how much better my friends had it. But the more work I did, the happier I became. My father knew how to make this work attractive. He showed me how to believe. He showed me how to see the result.

"So I was very young when I began to understand the moons, in part because I wanted to know in advance if I would get to play soccer on the coming weekend. I became deeply interested in the positions of the moon, the cycles, the pressure, the anti-cycles. It was common for me, and sometimes when I would speak to adults, they would be like, 'Wow!' They would be very impressed. And some people would be laughing, like, 'He's crazy, looking at the moon like it's a hundred years ago.'

"But people who think that we don't need to look at the moon anymore are deceiving themselves. Chemicals and sprays cannot correct all of our problems."

Aleš lit another skinny cigarette.

"Why do you look at a moon? Wait, where are we in the process right now?" Stephany asked. She was leaning forward in her seat, fixated.

"*Brava!* Okay, so we'll come back to the moon," Aleš said. "Now we have been patient, we have planted vines for our children and cared for the vines planted by our parents, we have controlled the bugs with natural methods, we have not killed anything in order to bring another thing life, and we have picked our fruit selectively. We have comprehended that we need fruit with the best taste to make the best wine."

"How do we find the best taste?" Stephany asked.

"It's not possible to choose fruit by measuring only sugar, pH levels, and acidity. There is no mathematic date that gives you your answer. Only by taste can you decide the exact time to pick your grapes. It is in the fall, but the day cannot be decided beforehand. You must put your grapes in your mouth and chew, and you must know how to identify the second before ripeness, because that's when the fruit is best.

"So you, having acquired the talent needed for this, decide that the fruit is ready. And then you need to be fast, very fast, because if you hang around, your grapes begin to ferment on their own, before they reach the tank, and then you need to stop that fermentation with chemicals and sulfites, and in doing this you screw yourself and ruin your wine.

"Anyway, so you need to cut all your fruit by hand and deliver it to the cellar as though you plan on selling it at a market: clean, beautiful, perfectly arranged." Aleš mimed serving his fruit on a tray.

"You de-stem the grapes and put the berries into the tank. But guess what? The tank is not empty. Because ten days before this harvest, we did a little preharvest. We picked five percent of our grapes and made them into a must and put a little bit into each tank. This isn't necessary, but it's better."

"Why?" Stephany asked.

"Think of grapes in this situation as homesteaders. You can't send a hundred people into the prairie to set everything up—that would be chaos. Instead, you send in five people to make the beds, prepare the houses, and then they can welcome their families.

"These first, bed-making grapes go into the tank as must and we keep them at the right temperature and they develop natural yeasts. They're brothers and sisters, waiting for their family to join them, fermenting. Then after ten days, when they see the new must that's just been poured in, they tell them, 'Hi, guys, we've been waiting for you! Here are the beds and this is how you do it, okay?' And that's when the good fermentation begins naturally, all the grapes working together for about a month."

"Is that how long fermentation usually takes?" Stephany asked.

"Most winemakers throw in store-bought yeasts to speed everything up and fermentation lasts only a week. They throw some powder and some sugar into some water and mix it in with their must. But really it's not a fair fight, this, because these store-bought yeasts are like yeasts on steroids. They go into your must and attack your natural yeasts and make their own fermentation, which is totally different than what your yeasts would have produced."

"Exactly why, in your opinion, is this bad?" I asked Aleš. He was into his yeast speech, which I had heard in many incarnations before (yeasts as soldiers, yeasts as boxers, yeasts as soccer players, yeasts as couch potatoes).

"What is wine?" Aleš asked himself. "Wine is a family of bacteria, which together make life. This life—in the form of thousands and billions of fermentations—takes a simple grape to a wine. In every berry, we have everything a wine needs to develop. We are cavaliers, remember? We only help the grape. We don't need to add or take away what the grape itself doesn't decide to receive or give. As man, we impact nature, so we had better be sure to impact it in a good way."

Stephany was nodding vigorously.

"Look, there are more than a thousand things you can legally add into your production process. You can add drugged-up yeasts and banana flavor if you want. And then someone can taste your wine and say, 'This wine tastes like banana!' And everyone around him will say, 'Oooh,' and 'Ahhh,' and 'Indeed, like banana and wood!' And so to them my question would be: *So what? And...?* Banana soda tastes like banana, too. Why would anyone use an aromatic yeast to make his wine turn really quickly into banana liquid? Why eradicate the taste of wine from wine in order to make it taste like something else?

"If the thing that makes a wine unique is its *terroir,* then the wine must taste like the earth from which it came. And if you add anything—anything—to corrupt that, to cause what is natural to die at the hand of what is unnatural, congratulations! You've made an alcoholic grape-based beverage, but you haven't made wine."

"So why *do* people use this stuff to make their wine turn into banana liquid?" Stephany asked.

"Because they're scared, probably," Aleš said. "They're uncomfortable with chaos and uncertainty. They don't want to lose control. They want a sure bet. Maybe the magazines are saying banana is in—they think they can get a high score with their banana powder. And maybe they don't want to be late with their deliveries—they need to be positive that their wine will be ready as soon as possible.

"I can make late deliveries and lose whole seasons of fruit to the weather. Why? Because if you work in real agriculture, things are unpredictable. You can't send your e-mail with the exact day of bottling. You can't mark things on your calendar. You can't say, 'The wine will be in the barrel for six months and in the tank for six months.' If you need to work in this chemical way, maybe you'll one day become a very important manager and all your buyers will be really happy but your wine will be soulless, and why did you become a winemaker in the first place? To tighten up your organizing skills? If you wanted to make a luxury product on deadline, you should have gone into Swiss watchmaking or joined the team at Jaguar.

"Winemakers are empaths who understand the language of nature, not business. And good winemakers are risk takers. Anyway, as I always say, 'If you don't risk, you don't fisk.'"

"Fisk? What's that?" Stephany said.

"Similar to *zak-zak*," I said.

"But now our must is only in the barrel, fermenting," Aleš went on. "What next? At the end of our slow and natural fermentation, which can take three weeks or five weeks, or anything before, after, or in between, we must move our juice from the tanks to the barrels for a long maturation. Here, we use new barrels every time."

"That seems expensive," Stephany noted.

"If you don't have the money for it, you don't have the money for it," Aleš said. "If you do, it's better, because it gives the wine, obviously, the maximum opportunity to develop herself without any influence from past wines, to show everything of herself. And really, it's polite. Think of it as a love story. You'd change the sheets for your new lover, wouldn't you?"

"I think that's the correct thing to do," Stephany said.

"But if you don't have time to change the sheets, or if you have only one set of sheets . . . well, it's not ideal, but you're not going to kick them out, are you?

"So change your sheets if you can and then you make sure you have good air coming into your cellar, because if you keep your doors closed, you hurt your wine," Aleš said. "It's gasping for breath and it gets that mildewy smell. Old-fashioned chimneys are better than small modern tubes because they keep the air humid and the barrels and wine moist. But for the most part, relax. Really, you did your work in the vineyard. The cellar is just patience, respect for the natural process. Check that everything is clean and that the barrels are full, and *basta*."

"*Basta?*" Stephany said. "*Basta?*"

"Well, *basta* until springtime," Aleš said. He reached for another cigarette.

"And then? What happens in springtime?" Stephany asked.

"One day in the spring, you wander down to your cellar and you see that the biggest barrels are having parties. The corks are jumping, the wine is dancing, everyone is psyched, party, party, party, pop, pop, pop." Aleš did a techno dance move from his chair.

"And then you bottle?" Stephany asked.

"No, they're partying. Don't interrupt their little *festa*. Instead, look around. You'll see that some barrels aren't going wild. Some barrels are completely calm. Their wine has no pressure; inside these barrels, everything is still. Everyone else was like, 'Spring is coming! Spring is here!' But these barrels are like, 'Well, it's just another spring. We've seen this before.'"

"They're no longer able to go to the clubs?" Stephany asked.

"Oh, they're *able*," Aleš said. "But they don't want to."

"They're over it," Stephany said.

"Been there, done that, no more discos for them," Aleš said. "They prefer to wear spectacles and smoke a cigar. They want to read a book and relax. They've decided they want to move on, to be bottled."

"Is this when the moon comes in?" Stephany asked.

"Exactly," Aleš said. "You always look at the moon—to plant a new plant, to harvest. But this is when you pay special attention to lunar cycles. A good wine tastes good, but an important wine has balance, stability, a long life. Wine can become clean in two ways. You can use mechanical filtration in your cellar. You push your wine, with great force, through a metal screen in order to remove from it all the 'undesirable things'—the dead yeasts, the particles, the skins, pulps, little crystallized acids—and you will have clean wine. But the wine will be dead, because you will also have taken some of the desirables, some of the yeasts that create microprocesses. And you will have hurt your wine by treating it so roughly. This wine, stripped of what naturally occurs, is only a skeleton of the wine that could have been.

"The second way that you can clean your wine is by looking back thousands of years. Mechanical filtration systems were introduced only fifty years ago, so what did people do before? They weren't drinking mugs full of sediment, so how did they work their grapes? They did it by decanting and bottling according to the moon. They didn't ask for an equation to prove to them why. They only had to look at the ocean—it moved in thirty-day cycles, with the moon. The moon moved liquid—not just teaspoons, but seas. At the beginning of the cycle, when a new moon is out, it creates atmospheric pressure that pulls all bodies of water up, wine included. So, at the start of the cycle, the wine in your barrels is cloudy, a mix of wine and residue. But as the cycle continues, the moon pushes down the residue. And after thirty days, the top of your barrel is full of clear wine. If you have ten barrels, for example, you skim the top twenty percent off each, say, and put it in a tank. But you can't leave your barrels twenty percent empty because too much oxygen will ruin your wine. So you empty one barrel into the others. Now you have nine barrels. Each cycle, the moon will push the solids down and you will skim off the top. You put it all in one tank—and after eight, nine, ten months, when you finally have all your clear liquid from this vintage, you mix it all together, bottle, and you have beautiful wine. Does it sound so outrageous?"

"Not outrageous," Stephany said. "It sounds logical."

"And by not touching the balance, we can create wines that contain small worlds. The microprocesses in these worlds aren't broken up by technology. Therefore, the bacteria in the wine keep moving and producing—building streets and houses and driving cars and having kids and holding memorial services. They slowly grow older, and they change the wine. It is still attractive and charming but maybe it is not so robust. Instead, it's wiser. Maybe it's not so powerful but has become more elegant. Maybe it doesn't laugh hard and fast but a little later. Perhaps it's not so technical but it's more spiritual. These kinds of changes can happen only to a wine in which all bacteriological life is maintained. When you use the power of *zak-zak*. And when you make a wine like this, it can last almost forever."

"For this kind of wine, you need the moon," Stephany said.

"People have stopped believing we need the moon because we now have the possibility to make everything without it," Aleš said. "But like with all new inventions, just because we can doesn't mean that we should. The key to biodynamic winemaking is to know that in the world there are some forces we can't touch, some great cosmic mysteries. We can't explain them exactly but we can see their effects. And because of this, we must have faith in their value. To me, looking at the moon is not some mystical, New Age approach. It is respecting the way things have been done for centuries. It's not trashing the oldest knowledge for a new piece of computerized metal. In my opinion, this is the highest way of farming."

"And after you bottle the wine, you store it in the cellar?" Stephany asked.

"*Zak-zak*," Aleš said. "Ten years, twenty years, fifty years, *zak-zak*. And then, when my friends come over, when we talk and we become one spirit, we drink the wine together. Come on, guys!"

Aleš put out his hand, as though we were a three-person sports team psyching ourselves up for the game. I put my hand on top of his and Stephany put her hand on top of mine.

"One spirit, three people!" Aleš said. "Wait—four people! Where is the queen of my heart? Vesna!" he bellowed. Vesna shuffled in, makeup-free, looking a little tired.

"We're one spirit, four people, V.," Aleš said.

"Okay, Aleš," Vesna said. "Lunch is ready."

"For the cosmic energy, Vesna!" Ales said, motioning her in. She gamely joined the circle and put her hand on top.

"One, two, three, and then *zak-zak* all together, okay?" Aleš said. Everyone nodded. "One, two, three . . ." he said.

"*Zak-zak!*" we all yelled, throwing our arms in the air. Then we went to the entertainment room, where Vesna had made us lunch. We ate whole wheat pasta and vegetables, home-baked brown bread, miles of just-picked dark green lettuce drenched in pumpkinseed oil made by a neighbor. And we drank a 1954 Ribolla. It was like staring at a cracked painting of a beautiful woman from long ago.

Chapter 8

PIEDMONT

───── ✬✬✬ ─────

A FEW YEARS EARLIER, as I was driving down a familiar road to the Barolo township of Serralunga d'Alba, I'd noticed something peculiar rising up from the vast stretch of foggy farmland. It was a turquoise crane. As I moved closer, a construction site wobbled into view—a partially built palatial structure made of ancient gray bricks looked out on a vista of little hills planted with vines. Then I whizzed by and made it into town in time for lunch with a friend.

Two months after my drive-by, a teenager who bore an uncanny resemblance to Prince Charles walked into my shop on East Sixteenth Street in New York.

"Hi! I am new to the industry and I would like to sell wine," he announced in Italian. He wore pressed blue jeans and a constant crooked-toothed grin. He was tall and skinny and his ears stuck out an inch from either side of his head.

"Are you a winemaker or a broker?" I asked absently. I was looking through a stack of bills.

"I, along with my mother and father, am a winemaker."

"Well, sorry," I grunted. "I don't take unscheduled meetings with producers."

"Excuse me," the boy said, still smiling, "but I am trying to sell wine in the United States."

"Yes, but I still don't take unscheduled meetings," I said.

"I am from Barolo!" he continued cheerfully, undeterred.

"Oh yeah, where in Barolo?" I asked.

"You know Barolo well?" he asked.

I did.

"Our winery is in Castello della Volta on Via San Pietro, the road from Barolo to La Morra," he said. "Perhaps you've noticed it. We plan that it will be a castle in the oldest style."

"Gray bricks?" I asked. "Blue crane?"

"Yes! That is it!" he said.

"That's *you?*" He was holding a folder and wearing designer sneakers, and he could have passed for seventeen.

"That is I," he said, extending his hand. I took from it a small cream-colored business card. "Famiglia Anselma, Barolo," it said on the front. "Dott. Maurizio Anselma."

"You're Dottore Maurizio Anselma?"

"I am. And look at the back." I turned the card over. On the back, black capital letters spelled out Dott. Maurizio Anselma's philosophy: PASSIONE PER UN GRANDE TERRITORIO.

❧

"I WAS NERVOUS that day because your store was important and you were not very nice," Maurizio reflected three years later as we stood together in the kitchen of his mother's old farmhouse.

After our week in Friuli, my family and I had planned to stop in Barolo for a few days while I made jaunts around the region, and Maurizio had offered us the simple tile-floored structure, perched at the end of a lonely dirt road, as our home base. His mother had made up the beds with flowered sheets and stocked the kitchen with a mishmash of utensils, old candles, playing cards, nonfunctioning lighters, and dishes. Maurizio was dressed in complicated designer blue jeans and an intensely patterned Missoni sweater; the matching Missoni scarf was draped over a chair. He was unloading the groceries we had bought that afternoon. He and I had decided to cook dinner.

"Are you certain you can cook rabbit?" Maurizio asked. He had no faith in Americans; he had, in his youth, watched a Midwesterner try to make gnocchi with microwaved potatoes.

"Don't you worry," I said. I had scooped a little well in the mound of flour on the counter and was methodically pouring in fifteen egg yolks. I added a pinch of salt. To go with the rabbit, we were making *tajarin,* the regional pasta—like tagliatelle but far finer.

"Sergio, you weren't nice to Maurizio the first time you met him?" my mother asked with horror. She was standing at the counter, cutting a tomato.

"He's never nice to those guys right away," Stephany said. "He can be a little bulldog."

"Sergio? Never," my mother said. She elbowed me gently out of the way and began to knead my flour and yolk mixture with her hands.

"I definitely knew that," my father said. He was reclining in his chair with the newspaper spread out in front of him.

"Is there any way to miss it?" Stephany asked. "He still refers to Maurizio as 'Princess Diana.'"

"Okay, everyone, that's enough," I announced. "Coco Chanel and I are cooking dinner, so get out of the kitchen and keep yourselves busy."

My mother continued pushing down on the dough until Stephany took her by the arm.

"He was the kindest child," my mother was saying as she looked back toward the kitchen.

Dott. Maurizio Anselma, I had learned three years previously at my shop, was not seventeen then, but rather a bashful twenty-four. It also turned out that his wine was really good and that I could help him make it even better. For this, I charged the nominal fee of being able to call him by a variety of feminine names for my own juvenile amusement; he blushed every single time, which was payment enough for me. I learned that though Maurizio may have been constructing a new castle, wine wasn't something novel for his family.

Severino Anselma, Maurizio's paternal grandfather, had owned half of the Rocche dei Manzoni estate in the 1960s, but back then Barolo was nowheresville and an owner was just a higher-paid farmer. The land held almost no value and business opportunities were rare. Plus, Severino just plain didn't like the place. "For him, it was too cold in the winter and too hot in the summer," Maurizio explained. "That kind of thing." Severino sold the land and became a merchant, buying and selling bulk wine and delivering it daily like milk.

In 1976, Maurizio's future parents married. "My father's family business was wine, but my mother came and made a revolution," said Maurizio. "She basically said to him, 'Are you able to buy me an estate?'"

Maurizio's father answered that perhaps he was. When they started to explore the possibilities, they saw that they were simultaneously lucky and unlucky.

Because of the harsh economy, most people in Barolo shipped their children off to urban areas to make a better life for themselves working in factories. In Barolo, there was no work and hardly any food. Much of the land was all but abandoned and the entire region practically collapsed. But the biggest, oldest estates survived through prestige alone; though Italians had, for the most part, no disposable income, the culture dictated that a celebration was still a celebration. When you had a party—and mass poverty never stopped Italians from throwing *una festa*—you drank good wine. Barolo, known as Italy's finest wine, was a classic Christmas gift, and it was the wine Italians liked to drink at parties. So people who had subsisted on spaghetti all year gathered up their painstakingly saved cash and bought, annually, a great bottle.

But there were also a couple of unexpected factors working to save Barolo during the lean years: big business and, in a not unconnected turn of events, Nutella. Individuals weren't the only ones handing out gift-wrapped Barolo. International companies like Fiat and Olivetti placed substantial orders and sent the recognizable wine as a present to valued clients. And then there was Ferrero, maker of the chocolate-hazelnut spread Nutella. The company built its headquarters near Alba and employed farmers in the off-season. Because of this, many people were able to avoid abandoning their land for work in a far-away city. When frost covered everything, they could still make enough money to live, and when the frost thawed, they could harvest their grapes.

But still, most people needed to sell off their vineyards. The older generation who had sent their children to the city were winding down. They were in their seventies and were often without heirs to take over the wineries. They were offering cut-rate prices; the Anselmas could get stuff cheap. The main problem was that they might well make wine that they could never sell. They went for it anyway. "It was their dream," Maurizio said.

In the process, it turned out that Maurizio's mother, Giovanna Fessia Anselma, an unassuming mousy-haired woman with a penchant for turtleneck sweaters, was a ruthless real estate maven. Just because people were selling cheap didn't mean it was easy to buy land. Barolo was an insular place, full of family feuds and secrets, so when a seller from the Morretti family had a few hectares, even if he was desperate to sell, he was likely to keep it a secret, afraid that a buyer from the long-despised rival Buia family would swoop in. Further, even those hurting for money were emotionally attached to their land.

"They wanted to sell and they didn't want to sell?" I asked. I cut the rabbit's head off at the base of its neck and then, using the hatchet, removed its legs, split open its torso, and began to whack it all into two-inch pieces. Maurizio had taken over working the dough, folding it over and pulling it back down. The air smelled of blood and flour.

"Exactly," Maurizio said. "My mother was a detective and a diplomat. She would tiptoe around, figuring out who had what, and then she and my father would go to their house the night before and talk them into letting her have the place. It probably helped that they weren't anybody's competitor." As I began cutting the rabbit into smaller cubes, he readied the other ingredients for the pasta sauce: shallots, *passato di pomodoro, peperoncino,* rosemary, thyme, garlic, white wine, sea salt, pepper, and a mix of pecorino and *parmigiano-reggiano* cheeses. "My mother took out loans, kept track of everything. She knows how to deal with these things." Her nickname was "the Train"; nothing could stop her.

In 1976, they bought Cascina Palazzo, a small vineyard in Montforte d'Alba. Then they just kept it up, eight plots in total, throughout four townships. In a period of fourteen years, they managed to accumulate forty hectares.

"People said we were crazy to keep buying land because there was a good grape market and you could just buy grapes and make wine from them," Maurizio said. I poured olive oil into a pan. "But we would have been crazy not to buy. In fact, in 1984, we could have bought the Ginestra estate for thirty-five thousand dollars, but we also kind of needed a new truck. My mother bought the truck and not the estate, and today it's worth more than three million. We still have that truck, and when my mother looks at it I can see the fury in her eyes."

In 1990, Renato and Giovanna bought their last piece of land. Now, the family of ex-farmers was the third-largest landowner in Barolo. They had for years been crafting their own wines, but their specialty was growing top-notch fruit and selling it to other wineries. "If I tell you which ones I have to kill you, but they're some of the best," Maurizio said. The pan was hot enough; I put the cubed rabbit on the oil over a medium flame. "In 1993," he continued, "we decided to concentrate only on our own label. In 1997, we decided to stop producing Dolcetto, Barbera, Chardonnay, and Nebbiolo, and to release only Barolo. That was my decision."

"Why?" I asked, watching the rabbit turn brown and shiny with caramelized fat.

"Barolo is and was our future," Maurizio said.

Throughout this time, Maurizio was studying. He attended a rigorous high school, in which he concentrated on the standard curriculum of ancient literature, music, writing, Greek and Latin language and culture, world history—"everything you'll ever need," he said. "The most open-minded approach always comes from learning the most ancient things." When he decided to buy a second motorbike, his terrified mother decided to send him abroad; he ended up in Iowa.

"I always say Iowa was the safest experience of my life because nothing happened there," he said.

"Nothing?" I asked.

"Well, I became a sporty guy, jogging a lot," he said thoughtfully. "Oh, and I decided I liked corn on the cob. I also met a dog named Seamus who you could pretend to shoot and he would pretend to be dead. Then one day he really was." He looked a little dejected.

"In a whole year?" I asked.

"The only really significant thing that happened in Iowa was that I began to see how lucky I was to be born in Barolo."

During that time, he was gathering knowledge in almost every area but wine.

"When did you have your first sip of alcohol?" I asked.

Maurizio's pale face burned a deep crimson. "You know, I also wasn't very interested in vegetables because my mother's parents were vegetable sellers." He had dumped the rabbit fat and oil from the pan and heated up some fresh oil with two cloves of garlic and a handful of chopped shallots. He was now cooking *passato di pomodoro con peperoncino,* a light, reddish-orange sauce. The kitchen was hot, and heady with meat and garlic. "I started when I was very old but I'll never reveal it."

"Ursula Andress didn't have her first drink until she was twenty-five!" I shouted.

"Sergio, stop torturing him!" Stephany shouted back.

"Yes, Sergio, stop torturing me, please," Maurizio echoed.

In the late 1990s, as a teenager, Maurizio became increasingly involved in the family business. He and his parents started to travel the world in search of fresh techniques and ideas. They hit Napa, Canada, Bordeaux, Burgundy, Spain, Germany, Switzerland. They interviewed dozens of winemakers, toured nearly a hundred facilities, investigated new styles, varietals, mechanisms. And then they returned to Italy and made a decision.

"We wanted to make Barolo like it's always been made," Maurizio said. I poured half a bottle of Bruno Giacosa's Arneis into the mix—rich but not too acidic, made from grapes grown on the same land where the rabbit ate, where the chickens laid their eggs. "If I was born in Asti or Tuscany or Gavi, or France or anywhere else, it would all be different. But I was born here, and my job now is to understand our roots." I poured us each a glass from the remaining half.

Until 1999, the Anselmas had been making wine in the basement of Renato's father's house. When they dove headfirst into Barolo's history, they decided it would be a good idea to build a castle. Not just any castle, but the physical result of an extreme fixation on their region. It was meant to be a sort of wine museum.

"This building is what Barolo is about," Maurizio liked to say when he acted serious and led tour groups through the partially finished structure. It was a monster of a project, because not only was the architecture to be historical, but the materials were as well.

"We hired hunters," Maurizio told me once. "Even if you have lots of money, it's very difficult to find old bricks. These guys go to bars all day long and sit around and wait to see who has destroyed a building or picked up some refurbished material, and then the guy has to go pick it out of big piles of knocked-down houses, and then he has to clean each piece. It's all labor-intensive. You know, we had to find twenty-two eighteenth-century doors in dark wood and they all look similar, but when you get down to it, every single one is a different size, so you have to have all these special bricks to fit them in the wall."

The place was indeed a lavish, slightly insane, and very beautiful undertaking, and Maurizio had thrown himself into it. He roamed the halls of his brainchild daily, checking that each element had been correctly integrated into the grand scheme, running his hands over the countless details on the walls and floors, which were composed of hundreds of thousands of bricks, swirling down the stairways, crawling up the walls—rectangular, square, dark, light, red, brown, cream, diamond-shaped, small and large—each laid by hand. And he was obsessed with his new cellar, too. It was a far cry from his grandfather's basement. You could look down over the main room from a viewing deck far above, but to get to the actual space, you descended the winding staircases, through the hallways punctuated with torchlike lights, and arrived in a wide, high, dimly lit room stacked with green cases full of bottles. Going farther, you emerged into the open space you'd seen from above: a big, bright room filled with fifteen steel tanks.

Maurizio worked in that room, mainly. He was not trained in the art of winemaking. At the University of Alba, he had studied mainly marketing, and that's why he'd been in my office in 2001: he'd been the family delegate traveling the world to open the markets, in England, Germany, Japan, Korea, Canada, America. He understood intuitively the importance of making a splash, of selling outside of Italy, and he understood that the castle would also differentiate them from other estates. But what he wanted to know now, more than anything, was how to make a great wine—or rather, a great Barolo.

While Giovanna worked in the vineyards, Renato and Maurizio controlled the cellar, macerating the juice for weeks, aging their wines in the cask for three years and then in the bottle underground for two years before release. They hired a new consultant every year; some were octogenarians, some up-and-comers.

"We've been trying everything, experimenting with everything," Maurizio told me. We had added water to our sauce, branches of herbs, and the dark meat of the rabbit. Then Maurizio turned the flame to low and we sat at the table with our Giacosa. "As you know, we tried, for example, barriques, but we saw that Slovenian oak interprets the region best. Piero Salvaggio once told me, 'You'll never make wine like Giacosa because you've had different experiences and you're a different age.' And I know I won't make the same wine every year. But my goal is to understand first the identity and personality of this region. I'm not trying to follow a trend; you can't with Barolo. I'm just trying to follow my own way." With flour sprinkled on the table, we flattened the pasta dough into thin sheets, folded the sheets over on themselves, and cut them into thin strands.

"So, Maurizio, what is your own way?" I asked. He was talking my language now. I remembered him in the shop, confused about his direction. He wanted to make wines in the old way but saw a market that demanded something else.

"When I was still in university, I wrote my thesis on wine and marketing, and I interviewed Angelo Gaja, Bruno Giacosa, and Bartolo Mascarello," he said, referring to Barolo's best-known threesome. "I went to Mascarello's house at ten o'clock in the morning, but he had Swiss customers there. He told me to just sit down and wait and then he talked to the other people about what they thought were banal things for three hours," said Maurizio. "For me, it was the best interview of my life! I just listened to him. He talked about what it meant to be a producer of Barolo—the deep roots, the belief in nature, the role of time.

"Later I asked him, 'Why don't you talk more to younger

people?' I had enjoyed hearing him so much. And he said, 'Maybe we haven't found the words to talk to the youth. And maybe they haven't found the ears to hear us.' So I want to do both—to talk and to listen. And then of course, above all, like it says on my business card, I want to produce a classic wine from this very specific territory."

We waited for an hour at the table as the sauce cooked in the covered pan. Then we added salt, pepper, parsley, rosemary, thyme, and a few dashes of olive oil. I put the tajarin in boiling salted water for a minute, pulled them out, added the sauce, a pat of butter, and more olive oil, and put them back in the saucepan. I tossed them over a medium flame, watching them glaze over. Maurizio was waiting for me with the *parmigiano-reggiano*, sprinkling it over at the last minute. We plated our pasta and put the rabbit aside for our second dish; then we called everyone to the table.

The wine was Maurizio's 2001 Barolo, not yet in the bottle. Before then, his wines had been good, but this was a different thing altogether—stronger, more elegant, persistent. It was the type of wine I expected from the great Barolo winemakers. It tasted of the land and of the past.

"When you make wines this great, you set yourself up for failure," I said. "You're going to be judged against a whole new standard."

"Thank you!" He was beaming.

"You better not mess it up by the time you get it in bottle," I warned. "You're a little young to be making wine like this. Are you sure you're ready to get to this level?"

Maurizio grinned as he twirled the pasta around his fork. "Yes, I think I am," he said. "Sergio, we cooked a really good rabbit."

THE VERY SPECIFIC and very great territory of Barolo had, in its recent history, hosted several masters—Giacomo Conterno, Aldo

Conterno, and Bruno Giacosa among them—but the most accomplished and misunderstood of them all was Bartolo Mascarello, the man who had allowed Maurizio to sit silently in his
office.

Bartolo Mascarello was a slim man with an impish smile
and a Roman nose, who, due to a spinal infection, had been
wheelchair-bound for twenty years. He always wore a woolen cap
and black-framed glasses. He had received me in his office many
times. The place was a sort of visual archive of his life. Generally
I drove, wrapped in Barolo's purple-gray haze, past cornfields
and vineyards, and up into his village. There, he lived and worked
in a five-hundred-year-old *borgo*.

The meeting I had with Bartolo the morning after the rabbit
feast was pretty much the same as always, at least at the beginning. I rang the doorbell and his largely silent, white-haired wife
ushered me into his office, which was clearly marked with a
black-and-white plaque: UFFICIO. Bartolo sat behind his dark
wooden desk, in front of him a vase of crimson roses. His closet
was sealed off with two ancient Japanese wooden doors decorated with paintings of geishas. Propped on the bookshelves
were pictures of Bartolo with his daughter, with his friends, at
dinners and parties. There were African elephant and zebra fig-
urines, oriental platters, a dozen glass decanters, and a sculpture
of a troll with a mass of gray hair. The walls were covered in watercolors of lakes, autumn leaves, and wine bottles, along with
framed wine labels, a black-and-white cartoon figure chugging
from a small barrel, and a poster for the 1931 French film *A Nous
la Liberté*. There were dusty old bottles of wine, sparkling new
bottles of wine, and Bartolo's two favorite self-designed Barolo
labels ever, each displayed on the bottle. The first was a pink
square filled with his imposing handwriting. It said, in thick
black ink: *No Barriques, No Berlusconi.* On an identical bottle to its
right, a length of white tape had been placed diagonally across
the pink square, and it said, again in Bartolo's script: *Censura,*

censored. At the time, Silvio Berlusconi was Italy's prime minister, a right-wing, pro-corporation billionaire-turned-politician who owned the bulk of the country's news media, and it was clear that the exceedingly liberal Bartolo did not support his policies.

Bartolo Mascarello was born in 1926, in that same house. His grandfather had nursed a two-hectare vineyard and made his own wine for years. As a result of spreading fascism, a *cantina sociale* went up and many of the individual wineries were ripped down. In 1919, Bartolo Mascarello's father, Giulio Cesare Mascarello, began to rebuild the winery. From the age of five, Bartolo worked with Giulio in the cellar. Together, they poured most of their wine into *damigiane* and then shipped it off to restaurants. But in the 1970s, while Italy struggled out of a recession, the Swiss and Germans, having hit up France and Tuscany, began to tour Piedmont. And they began to demand more Barolo.

They were a different breed, Barolo winemakers. One hundred fifty years ago in Piedmont, Barbera was literally free. If you had dinner at a restaurant, you were served, gratis, a bottle of Barbera. The abundant vineyards grew wild with the grape. Nonetheless, there were still people committed to making Barolo, a wine that was in one very important way Barbera's opposite: it cost money. But the dedicated few continued on, through poverty, war, and widespread indifference. They made it without earning a profit and they made it at a loss, but they made it for their kids and their friends to celebrate graduations, birthdays, holidays. They camped out in the middle of an area full of another, far cheaper, more plentiful, easier wine, and year after year produced something that, though it was devastatingly beautiful, could ostensibly take three decades to reach its peak.

But then a group of new winemakers came up in the 1980s, and they didn't like the reputation the wine had achieved, the idea that it was inaccessible, austere, musty. These winemakers banded together and set out to make some cash with a new marketing campaign. They decided to reinvent Barolo and to show the rest of the world that it could be young, clean, fresh. They showcased their use of temperature control, new French barriques, and selective yeasts. And Bartolo Mascarello became their example of someone who couldn't learn the new way. He was a thorn in their side, steadfastly making his wines with two-hundred-year-old methods.

Bartolo couldn't have cared less.

"You see how they're talking about Barolo," I'd said a decade earlier on one of my trips to his office.

"They'll learn," Bartolo said, his face relaxed. He preferred to spend his energy painting labels for his wines: an outstretched hand balancing a village on its palm, the hills in a rainbow of colors, a yellow flag waving in front of a *borgo*. That was what he was doing when I entered his office.

I sat on the small visitors' bench and watched him. A decade earlier, he had taught me one of the greatest lessons I'd ever learned. As always, I'd pulled up, been guided in by his wife, and sat on the bench.

❧

DURING THOSE FIRST VISITS TO MASCARELLO, I considered myself a whiz kid. I was in my early twenties, I had a full head of hair, I was friends with lots of important people, and I lived in New York City. Most important, I was working at San Domenico, being told daily that I was gifted. For an immigrant from Italy by way of Albany, it seemed like the best it could get. I was convinced that I knew everything there was to know, and possibly much more.

I never got tired, or if I did get tired, I didn't notice it. I swept through Italy like a small yet robust tornado, sometimes hitting a dozen wineries a day. My MO involved a virtual sprint through the cellar, stopping at each barrel to swirl, sniff, analyze, and impress my audience by accurately spitting back at them everything they'd ever wanted to know about their wine. Then I'd shake hands, hop in my car, and speed to my next destination, where I would repeat the process.

"So I'm just here for a few minutes," I said. "I'd love to taste whatever you think I should and then I've got to run to my next appointment."

Bartolo wasn't into it. First, it's hard to be speedy when confined to a wheelchair. Second, Bartolo belonged to a rare subspecies of human, the members of which are entirely uninfluenced by external sources of energy. His emotional state persisted despite those around him, as though he were surrounded by a force field of resolution that insulated him from all external anxiety, desire, and chaos. He saw that I was raring to go, but he clearly wasn't, and I could respond to that reality as I desired. He reached slowly behind him.

Piedmontese tradition dictates that you open a bottle of Barolo with a friend, drink two-thirds, and leave the rest for the next guest. Bartolo pulled out a magnum, one-third full of his 1978 vintage.

"I drank this with a friend two weeks ago," he said, and he poured me a glass.

The wine is probably dead, I thought. *You can't keep a wine for that long. But I'll try it.* I picked up my glass, swirled it, smelled it. *Impressive,* I thought. *Tight, well structured.* I could have told him everything about his wine right then and there—its scents, its persona, its history, every technical detail of its production. I could have said, "It smells like tar, truffles, and rose petals," because that's the easiest code in Barolo for "This is a good wine." I could recognize all the concrete elements, and I'd memorized all available information about Bartolo's methods. I was about to take a sip when I looked at the old man. He was just observing the wine. I knew it would be rude to drink before he had begun. The custom was to share the wine, and I was Neapolitan;

the need to follow my elder's lead was strong. I sat there and watched him. *This is awkward,* I thought. *Let's get a move on.*

Bartolo alternately gazed into space and gazed at the glass. He spun the wine slowly, rotated it halfway, and then sat with it for several minutes, his eyes unfocused. He smelled it, pulled it away. *Have I done something to offend him?* I wondered. He shifted. *Now we'll get down to drinking,* I thought. Instead, he twirled the glass again. Ten minutes later, he slumped in his seat. *Wait—is he falling asleep?* I had another appointment that I was already late for. I decided to motion as though I was going to drink the wine. I figured I could clue him into beginning. I brought the wine to my lips, looking at him out of the corner of my eye. He sniffed, pulled the glass back instantly, placed it on the desk. I put the glass down, defeated.

After forty-five minutes, I began to regard him with suspicion. The little old man in the wheelchair with the wine glass, his face lighting up, turning confused, uncertain, intrigued. It was as if I wasn't even there. *Wait a second,* I thought. *This guy is fucking with me!* Nobody fucked with me. I was the whiz kid! *He wants to see how long I can hold out. Well, I'm not giving in, so he can just play his sick little game. I'm waiting him out if I have to stay until midnight.* Bartolo was examining the wine's color. He moved his glass, put his nose in, pulled out. I sat stubbornly across from him, indomitable. *You got yourself a challenge, buddy,* I thought. *You're messing with the wrong guy.*

After thirty more minutes, I put the glass to my nose. An indefinite period of time followed that action. I may have stayed that way for a second, a minute, or an hour—who knows? The part of my brain monitoring such worldly concerns took a break. Abruptly, the wine was no longer what I'd first perceived. I wasn't in a world of recognizable perfumes and sensations. I was in a complex labyrinth in which nothing made sense, and whenever I would start down a path, I would hit a wall and be forced to turn back and begin again. When I was a child, wine had been a thing of emotion. Then, until that moment, it had been an analyzable product, full of characteristics that I could isolate and classify. But now it was its own fierce mystery. I stared at Bartolo. He smiled at me, just a little. I went back to my wine.

The world has its share of justifiable beauty: a supermodel, a blueblood racehorse, a prizewinning rose. You can debate their value and win—she's perfectly symmetrical, he's the finest of the species, it meets all qualifications. Nobody can successfully convince you that Christie Brinkley, in her heyday as the face of CoverGirl, wasn't beautiful. Even if California blondes weren't your cup of tea, she was, factually, a thing of physical splendor. The traits are clear for all to see at once, out in the open, obvious: the supermodel's white teeth, the horse's muscled leg, the rose's unmarred pink petal.

And then there is unjustifiable beauty. It's personal beauty, imperfection, ambiguity. It's beauty you cannot argue for because you have no material proof, only your own certainty. This was the magnificence of Bartolo's wine. It was constantly morphing, evolving, impossible to know entirely. You could experience it an infinite number of times and you would never be able to master it. This was the true beauty, the kind of great art that transcends its time and invites its admirer to continue searching within it for the answer to some unknown question. It wasn't a catchy pop song or a girl in a makeup commercial. You couldn't pin it down by saying it smelled like rose petals. That was as reductive and senseless as looking at *The Birth of Venus* and saying, "It's a painting of a girl in a shell."

As I looked at Bartolo, himself descended entirely into his own experience, I considered the nature of a great wine. Its value lies in the fact that you can never understand or master it. To begin to see even a small portion of what it is, you must smother your ego, stop trying to win at some mad game, and let yourself become completely engulfed by something bigger than you. Seeing a shape is easy, but grasping at a spirit is a life's work and then some.

I stayed in my seat for a long time. And when we'd finished the bottle, I didn't budge, but rather sat staring ahead as Bartolo read the newspaper, commented on a story, scribbled a few notes on a pad. Then I thanked him and left. The whiz kid did not come with me.

⁊

TIMES HAD CHANGED. Bartolo Mascarello no longer waited two weeks between visitors. This time, as we started in on small talk, another visitor entered—the Mascarellos' policy was to admit anyone, friend or stranger, without an appointment. The visitor was a corpulent middle-aged man with thick brown hair and a red nose.

"Signor Bartolo," he said, extending his hand. "I have made this trip from the Veneto because I wanted to meet you in person. I am forty-five years old and have just begun learning about wine. And you, Signor Bartolo, are the master of wine."

Bartolo smiled. "Is that what I am?" he said softly. "The master of wine."

"And not just a master, Signor Bartolo. You are an artist, you are Leonardo da Vinci creating the *Mona Lisa*. You are a conductor of symphonies, a poet of the most inspired verse. You are a creator, a great thinker, a true genius. When I drink your wine, I feel that I am the highest version of myself. My soul is released."

Bartolo dabbed some blue on the sky he was painting. "I see," he said.

"You have opened up my heart with your wines; you have opened up my eyes. I could never have imagined that there existed someone as talented, as brilliant, as yourself. And—"

At that point, two young Americans walked into the office, both wearing blue jeans, polo shirts, and leather jackets.

"Mr. Mascarello," said one of them, a burly blond. *"Noi sono importadores da Ohio,"* he said in mangled Italian, announcing himself and his friend as importers from Ohio. The two men gave Bartolo hearty handshakes. The blond was holding a phrase book and the illustrious *Gambero Rosso* guide to Italian wines.

"We want to understand how and why you are making good wines again," he continued in pidgin Italian.

"Non ho capito," said Bartolo, mixing together blue and yellow—I don't understand. He didn't look at me. I sat against the wall and watched.

"I speak the English," said the Italian visitor. "Maybe I can to help you with this situation."

"Great," said the other American, a lanky redhead. "Can you translate for us that we saw Mr. Mascarello in the *Tre Bicchieri* guide and we saw he got good scores but that he didn't used to get good scores and we want to know how he changed."

"Of course!" said the Italian. "He sees that you make good wine now and he wants to know why," he translated to Bartolo. Bartolo had never changed a thing in his winemaking.

"No barriques, no Berlusconi, no California," Bartolo said.

"Signor Mascarello is a good friend of mine," the Italian said. "He is the greatest winemaker in the world and he always has been."

"Did he say something about California?" the redhead asked.

"No barriques, no Berlusconi, no California," Bartolo said.

"I think he likes California," the blond said.

"Maybe he understood how to improve Barolo by studying how they do things in California," the redhead said.

Bartolo stared blankly at the wall behind his visitors.

"Signor Mascarello and I, we is almost father and son," said the Italian.

"No barriques, no Berlusconi, no California," Bartolo said, and returned to his painting.

"He is a genius, the very beautiful artist," said the Italian.

"Does he hate California?" said one of the Americans. "He said no California, I think. Is 'no' the same in Italian as in English?"

"I love California, but California must stay in California," Bartolo said in Italian. "This is Barolo."

"He stays in California sometimes," said the Italian. "But he also stays in Barolo."

"I see," the redhead said.

"*Pssst*, Sergio," said a woman's voice.

It was Bartolo's daughter, Maria Teresa, her head poking in the office. She was a wiry, diminutive woman with Bartolo's protruding Roman nose, thin lips, and strong jaw. She had cropped gray-blond hair and she wore glasses and a pair of flat brown leather boots; she projected confidence and could probably get pretty scrappy in a fistfight.

"Come with me," she said. I looked at Bartolo and slipped out. Maria Teresa's mother was at the door, telling a group of fans that they'd need to come back later as the office was too full.

"Maria Teresa, this is ridiculous," I said. "You have hordes of people."

"Oh, it's because we're trendy right now," she said nonchalantly. "But we don't care. We never forget who stuck with us in hard times. We never forget who spit on us because they thought we were the source of their misery. Shall we go taste some wines?"

"Of course," I said. Maria Teresa led me out of the back of the house and into the connected *cantina*. She ran the parts of the business that her father couldn't from his wheelchair. She was poised to take over everything when he died.

"My father always says that our operation is so little that even a small girl could run it," she told me as we walked through the hallway and briefly outside, past a sleepy yellow Labrador, and into the cellar, which was lined with six small oak casks and metal crates full of bottles thick with dust, a small chalkboard attached to each one: *Barolo 1986; Barolo 1964; Barolo 1958.*

"Did you always want this?" I asked.

"Usually, when you're born into these families, you either hate wine or you love wine," she said. She spoke quickly and furrowed her brow. "I refused to drink it, I refused to work here, and I refused to show any interest in it. I lived in a state of refusal, and my parents were respectful of that. They never pressured me."

Maria Teresa instead studied French literature at the University of Turin and intended to become a teacher. But when she was twenty-six years old, she realized that though she had never had so much as a drop of wine, she was curious about it; her friends were increasingly holding tasting parties and her mother always encouraged her to try some at dinner. When Maria Teresa gave in, the first wine she tasted was Château d'Yquem, the world's finest dessert wine. She realized what she'd been missing.

"But my desire to work here was more emotional," she went on, lightly motioning toward her heart. "I am an only child and if I didn't work here, this would all be over. How could I close this story to work in a school?" She glanced around the room. "I realized that I wanted to bring my family forward."

Of course, I thought. *Maria Teresa could never have really left this place.* I thought of her with her father, their identical bespectacled faces. She had lived in this house with him until she turned thirty-six, and then she moved two blocks away. They were similarly rigorous in their work, and she was equally unwilling to waver from her principles, which were, uncoincidentally, also his principles. Both of them searched relentlessly for perfection.

"He never told me what to do. He just always stayed with me, in the office, down here. Today we're in the era of consultants; I consider my father my exclusive consultant." Maria Teresa motioned me into the next room, a *cantina* with several twenty-foot-high wooden *botti*. She pulled a ladder up to one and scrambled up the shaky steps. When she reached the top, she hopped off, crouched down, and inserted a wine thief—a long glass siphon used to remove wine from a cask. She sucked the liquid into the cylinder, let the wine out into the glass, and presented it down to me. I climbed nervously up four steps, afraid that the ladder would break, leaving me injured and her stranded, took my wine, and hurried back to safety. The wine was a rusty-rose color. I inhaled.

"What do you think?" she called down from her perch.

I inhaled again. "Mascarello Barolo," I said.

"My father always says that he isn't embarrassed of our land," Maria Teresa said. "He said we had to let the wine taste like where it came from. You can't violate your environment, you can't make it something it's not."

"People wonder if you'll change any methods when you take over," I said.

"I don't want to be closed to things," she said. "I am not unwilling to make alterations. But above all, I need to be aware of my history. I think we can adjust quality but we can never adjust taste. My father isn't some conservative; he's a traditionalist, tied to his past." She paused, still squatting on the barrel. "Then again, the wine my father makes is good, so why would we change it?"

"But people are always trying to make you change," I said. I was thinking of the negative reviews they sometimes received.

Maria Teresa grinned. "Journalists don't know what they want. Now indigenous varietals are hot, right? The same media that bashed them before now rave about them. Once I had some American wine people here and they were shocked that my wine was so light. They said it was no good. 'But this is the color of Nebbiolo,' I told them. 'This is how Barolo is made, and this is how it tastes.' They told me that good wine in the United States is black. And then I understood why everyone is always giving us bad marks and trying to correct our wine: they want what we grow in the heart of this little town to taste the same as what they grow in Napa."

What Maria Teresa wasn't mentioning was that the media tended to react to her family's wine like rejected children—petulantly and aggressively. The fact was, the Mascarellos not only refused to pander to the media, they actively offended the media. Following the do-the-opposite-of-what-the-industrials-are-doing philosophy, they declined to send out bottles for tastings. The Mascarellos had always figured that if, say, *Wine Spectator* wanted some wine, its reviewers could very well take a plane to Barolo and stop by for a glass.

"They could come over and we could talk," Maria Teresa said innocently.

Therefore, reviewers, accustomed to the fawning winemaker, the desperate winemaker, the corporate winemaker—all of whom gladly sent free wine and more, and right away—had to go to the store like normal people and purchase their bottle. This made them a little edgy when they started their reviews.

Maria Teresa shrugged. "We could have a drink together," she said.

After we'd tasted, we went back into Bartolo's office. His visitors had left and he was putting the finishing touches on a woman's face on the label he was painting.

"Should we try some wines?" Bartolo suggested. Maria Teresa adjusted him slightly in his chair and took a bottle off the shelf. As she did so, I noticed that behind her hung three black-and-white photographs. The first was of her great-grandfather dressed in military garb, his dark hair parted and combed neatly back. The second was of her grandfather, a disheveled tie loose around his neck, bald-headed and sporting an enormous mustache. The third was of Bartolo, standing when he could still walk, wearing an apron and deep in concentration as he plunged a corkscrew into one of his bottles. She plunged in a corkscrew, too, mirroring, almost exactly, her father's image.

We talked a little and waited for the wine to settle down. I liked tasting wine with Bartolo—if he spoke, he made only the simplest remarks: "This wine needs to go longer." "This wine is perfect." "This wine fascinates me."

After we'd finished our glasses, he took out a fresh sheet of paper and a clean brush, and Maria Teresa left the room to get him a cup of water. I didn't say anything; I was thinking about his wine. The only thing that kept running through my mind was: *tastes like Piedmont.* Bartolo picked up his brush, dipped it in a brilliant green, and painted the outline of a Barolo hill.

Chapter 9

MONTALCINO

❦

SEVERAL DAYS AFTER MY TIME in Barolo, I headed toward Montalcino, in Tuscany. It occurred to me that the last time I had made this dreary drive to Montalcino, I'd been in the company of the fervent, possibly nuts, modernist Luca Maroni. For me, Maroni has always conjured up images of poultry. Tall and bony, he resembles a fresh-plucked chicken, and his bald head looks a lot like an egg with a goatee. He wears fantastically elegant clothes, heavy on the silk and cashmere, and has an impressive command of the Italian language—so lyrical is his spoken prose, in fact, that I have, many times, surrendered in an argument only because I could not match his poetry.

Maroni suffered from *astemia* due to alcohol from his adolescence until 1984. Of course, all Italians have something perpetually wrong with them—some suffer from chronic headaches, others from car sickness; many are allergic to chocolate, some can't be within twenty yards of a glass of milk. Thousands can't eat flour and, at any given second in the day, at least twenty thousand Italians worldwide are saying, "I think I have a fever." And another two hundred thousand are saying, "I think *you* have a fever." For their problems, they usually need rest, some powdered medicine, an injection, or their mothers. One day, I asked how it was possible that every day, after working for three hours, my apparently robust Italian friend had either searing back pain, a stomach problem, or something weird happening to a place on his arm. "You don't understand your own people," he said. "I just want a little attention." The point is, *astemia* is a widespread condition in Italy, and its sufferers don't drink wine because they don't like wine. Or maybe, as another friend said, they "feel very hot and get pimples."

So Maroni wasn't into wine. Then one day he met a woman who owned land in Montalcino; she gave him a bottle of wine as a gift and, careful not to perish from his self-diagnosed *astemia*, he tasted it. He didn't like it, it seems—he loved it. He saw what wine could be, and wanted then to know how he could isolate the errors in most wines and thereby help improve the entire species of the beverage. He bought a guide to Italian wines by the American journalist Burton Anderson, picked fifty bottles that Anderson had approved of, and began trying to figure out where, in his opinion, these bottles went wrong. Over time, he decided that the problem with wine was that it was too damn old.

Today, Maroni is the leading proponent of completely banishing aging requirements for wine. In short, he wants wine to taste like fruit or bubblegum. He argues that in order for the industry to attract youth—kids who have been raised on Coca-Cola—it must give young consumers easy wines that are immediately and obviously yummy, and can be drunk like juice. He has begun a movement to make it so. He invests his own money, writes a monthly magazine column and a weekly newspaper column, has authored multiple volumes of his yearly wine guide, *Annuario dei Migliori Vini Italiani*, and travels the country judging wines. So there we were in the back of a friend's car, a couple of ideological opposites engaged in a two-hour debate on the direction in which the wine world should be heading.

Maroni had invented an esoteric, mathematical, and, frankly, really weird system for assessing wines. In his obsessively researched annual 924-page review book, he judged wines using a rating scale he explained in mathematical terms:

Quality = pleasantness = fruit

"The fruitiness of a wine," he was saying, "is directly proportional to consistency, balance, and the integrity of taste." Thus:

Quality / pleasantness / fruitiness = consistency + balance + integrity

Or, to be more economical:

$Q/P/F = C + B + I$

After everything has been assigned a number through painstaking algebraic equations—each category must be separately understood through its own equation and calculated using the conversion table that Maroni provides in his preface—a wine can, in its maker's wildest dreams, achieve a score of 99, by gaining 33 points each in consistency, balance, and integrity.

I wanted to see him in action, if only to understand how, exactly, he employed his system. Maroni and I arrived at the Montalcino wine consortium, a group that included as members nearly all the winemakers in the region. We were ushered respectfully into the basement, a dank stone room that resembled a torture chamber. The windows had been sealed with black plastic and it was very cold. The lone light hung wanly over Maroni's seat, which was placed in the middle of the room. I was to sit at a separate table off-center; clearly, I was not the honored guest. A long table holding about four hundred bottles of wine hugged one wall. Three nervous young men—consortium interns, I supposed—stood to the side, glancing at Maroni as he made himself comfortable. He sat at the table and arranged his notebook and pen. Then he frowned.

"Sergio, do you mind tasting in the dark?" he asked me. "This light would really bother me."

"Of course," I said.

And then: black, with only a sliver of yellow sneaking in from under the door. When my eyes adjusted, I could make out the figures of the interns, who had placed a half-dozen glasses in front of Maroni. They'd distractedly put some on my table, too.

"Everybody, quiet for the maestro!" one announced, and the other two began to silently pour the first six wines.

I squinted. I could hear Maroni swirling each glass, smelling it. He put the last one down and there was a moment of silence. Then he began to yell.

"SS1! SS3! P47!" He took a sip and spit it out. "SS24173! Next!" The interns scurried back and forth.

When he finished the six, he picked a top two and took a taste of them. He tapped each glass dramatically. "P4, P7, 29, 27, 21, 26, 25! Next! Next!"

The interns began, despite the dark, to navigate swiftly around one another, putting the top choices away and bringing out the next six drinks.

"SS1!" he yelled. "SS2, SS3, 28, 99, 0, SS9!" I had become too nervous to taste my wines, and I couldn't think fast enough to follow the codes. Suddenly, he held a glass in the air. *"Tappo! Tappo! Tappo!"* he screamed—Cork! Cork! Cork!—indicating that the wine was, indeed, corked. The kids began to run.

"Away, away!" Maroni bellowed.

An intern smelled the glass. "The maestro is right!" he shrieked. "Get it out of here! Now!"

Maroni was poured a new glass of the same wine from a different bottle. "It's better, but SS4!" he said. "SS4!"

This continued for at least an hour, during which I sat, dumbfounded, at my rickety table.

"SS3," he said. "*Si*, yes!" The interns gasped.

At the end, they brought Maroni his twenty finalists, which he would then compare. Then they crouched next to him and, scarcely breathing, watched him as though watching a world chess champ decide his next move.

"S2," he said with distaste. "S3, S1, SS587."

And then he was down to ten finalists.

"S1, but a tiny hint of S4," he said.

And then the top five, the top three, the top two. Though the room was cold, I could see, by the minuscule sliver of light, beads of sweat forming on the brows of the interns.

Maroni sat back for a minute. Then he lightly tapped one bottle. "Thirty-two," he said. And immediately the next: "Thirty-one."

The interns exhaled. "Maroni's finished!" one announced, like a 1950s television announcer. "Top wine out of sixty-one, he gave sixty-four!" Everyone clapped loudly. *What the hell*, I thought, and I clapped, too. After all, bottle 32 had been awarded an SS87 and was the top of sixty-one, receiving a 64. If that didn't deserve a good cheer, what did?

❧

ACROSS TOWN LIVED A MAN named Franco Biondi Santi, who essentially represented all that Maroni railed against. This day, a year after my journey into the bizarro world of radical modernism, Franco was waiting for me. He was at the center of a local-cum-international controversy about aging requirements and the integrity of Brunello di Montalcino, and I wanted to check in.

I drove through his imposing gates and down the manicured white stone drive, which was lined on both sides with skinny cypress trees. The property stretched over hundreds of acres and several vineyards, and included lush gardens and a litter of bright white retriever puppies lounging on the lawn.

At the end of the drive sat an open garage containing three Mercedeses and a sweeping dark wood villa covered in ivy and so perfectly maintained that several times tourists had wandered in, convinced that the place was a historical museum.

Franco's American assistant Olivia shook my hand.

"*Il Dottore* is waiting," she said.

Just inside the door stood Franco himself. At eighty-two, he remained erect and elegant, with bright blue eyes and a head of thick silver hair. He was tall and exceedingly slender. He wore cashmere slacks, a cream shirt with a collar that curved like wings at his throat, and a maroon and green jacket accented by the red paisley handkerchief folded precisely in the breast pocket.

"Sergio," he said, shaking my hand, "please make yourself comfortable." His manner was gentle and open; despite his grandiose estate and impressive lineage, he remained warm and relaxed. His study was a sunny room with a pair of glass doors overlooking the emerald green lawn, a marble fountain, and pink and yellow rose bushes. I sat down on one of the couches and surveyed the floor-to-ceiling bookshelves stuffed with atlases, wine guides, encyclopedias, and new and ancient volumes of history. The walls were covered with pictures framed in gold: maps of the world and sketches of buildings and churches, pencil drawings of faces. As we settled down to speak, surrounded by such ancient splendor, an electronic jingle rang out.

"Please excuse me," Franco said. He retrieved from his pocket a slim silver cell phone. "*Pronto!*"

Franco Biondi Santi was the fourth generation of one of the most important winemaking families in the world. His great-grandfather Clemente Santi had begun by growing Sangiovese. His grandfather Ferruccio Biondi Santi had single-handedly isolated the Sangiovese clone that would go on to make Brunello. And his father, Tancredi, had discovered how to improve and market it and had then gone on to create dozens of Italy's most famous wines. Together, the three of them had made Italian wine a global commodity, and Franco was carrying the torch.

In the nineteenth century, Clemente Santi cared for his little plot of land, Il Greppo. He grew and harvested the local Sangiovese grape and taught his son, Ferruccio, the tools of the trade. By the late 1860s, vines throughout Italy had suffered a series of ailments, culminating in the European plague of the mite phylloxera, which so destroyed plants that all the growers had to pull their vines out of the land and start fresh. Ferruccio noticed that one of the replanted Sangiovese vines was different from anything he'd seen. It was brown and produced clusters of small, purply brown grapes that made a totally new wine—reserved, highly structured, impenetrable in its youth, and extremely long-aging. In 1870, Ferruccio nicknamed the clone Brunello, "little dark one," and decided to dedicate a good deal of space to it in his vineyards.

"How do you think he knew that it was the right thing to do?" I asked.

"It was just an intuition," Franco said. "There were many red varietals at that time, but he just knew this one would make fantastic wine. But he never wrote about why or how he knew. He was more of an artist. He preferred to paint."

It would have been pretty simple, then, for Brunello to remain an obscurity, its inventor dabbing oil on canvas in the middle of his isolated estate in an unrecognized wine region. But then came Ferruccio's son Tancredi, and he changed everything.

After Ferruccio died in 1917, his one-hectare estate was divided among his three children: Tancredi, Caterina, and Gontrano. Caterina took some war bonds and Tancredi and Gontrano split the land. In 1922, Tancredi took out a loan and bought out his brother. He had big plans.

Tancredi had studied enology in the Veneto and had then

moved on to the University of Pisa to take up agronomy and forestry. He understood the science of the vine and was dedicated to comprehending the smallest details of his wine. While his father had been more of a farmer, using any spare space in his vineyard for olive trees and grain—getting the land to yield as much as possible—Tancredi was interested exclusively in the wine. He hoped to pick only the finest grapes, and forget everything else. He was, to put it mildly, fixated.

"I didn't discover my father's passion so much as know it," said Franco. His hands were long and graceful, accented by a gold wedding band, frail with age. "I call Brunello my brother. I loved it all, too, really. I started working when I was five just because it was fun, crushing the grapes with my feet. That sensation—how viscous the must is against the plant."

"Your father was your boss, then, from a very young age," I said. "Did he command you?"

"Yes, and once, long ago, kids listened to their fathers," Franco said. "But honestly, it was stupendous to work with my father because he gave directions so obliquely. 'If it were me, I might do it this way,' and so on. He was very *umano*, you know. We were very united as a family. To tell you how united my family was, a journalist once came to write about our wine. He was here only a few days, and he wrote of my father and mother that it was very gratifying to see this couple aging well together."

Franco was, in addition to being a genuinely positive fellow, a born marketer. Though he liked to say that winemaking was in his DNA, I was sure that public relations was, too. Because his father did not just make great Brunello; he *made* Brunello. He made Brunello into what it is today: Italy's most internationally beloved wine.

Before Tancredi, there was just his father's plot of land and a bunch of bottles of a wine no one else had made or heard of. The dusty village of Montalcino was an agricultural nowhere, the poorest town in all of Tuscany.

"This was the most communist town in the most communist area in the most communist region in the most communist zone of communist Italy," said Franco. "People didn't want to make more than cheap table wine, and they wanted to drink it themselves."

In 1920, Tancredi asked himself a question: If he had such a glorious product, why was everyone—even rich Italians—drinking French wines? The answer was that everyone knew about French wines, and nobody knew about the other stuff. Why was that? Was it because French wine is inherently better than Italian wine? Or was it because, rather, the French had figured out how to get their drinks into the cellars of the kind of people who *had* cellars? Tancredi was certain that if people could just taste the wines, they would become devotees. He also knew that no American wineseller was going to drive up to his door and ask for a glass.

So, then, what techniques did the French use? First and foremost, they did one thing the Italians never thought of: They marketed their wines. They understood that a wine could be conceived of as a sort of blue-chip stock, but you had to prove to consumers that this bottle of purple fluid was an investment. The purchasers could sell it for a lot of cash after a long time and it still would be great wine—or, even better, they could keep it in their collection and hand it down to their children. And if they weren't interested in all that, they could drink it.

Tancredi decided to hold vintage tastings, a novelty in Italy but standard practice in France. While Gontrano had drunk all of his old wine, as Italians tended to do, Tancredi had saved his up. He had wanted to see what would happen to the wines, their capability to age, their evolution, their perfumes.

"He felt it would be a sin to drink them without showing them off," said Franco.

Tancredi was a world-class organizer. He invited opinion makers to his estate, regaled them with the particular beauty of Tuscany. He traveled the world with suitcases full of bottles. He served fifty-year-old Brunello to international experts, journalists, and buyers. He courted the media and stubbornly pursued an official regional appellation so that only wine made in Montalcino could bear the Brunello name. Soon enough, magazines were touting the beauty of this newly discovered red; industry insiders constantly discussed the Biondi Santi estate, and Brunello, thanks to Tancredi's campaigning, scored its own *Denominazione di Origine Controllata e Garantita*, or DOCG, a term that not only guarantees that all wine bearing the area's name has been produced under strict regulations, but that it has also been analyzed by a panel of government agents to ensure its quality. Sellers from Japan and New York were requesting cases by the hundreds.

Tancredi wasn't just a brilliant businessman, he was also an accomplished agronomist who understood the intricacies of his vines and soil, and, as such, was hired as Italy's first wine consultant. He traveled Italy, making his mark in almost every region. He championed indigenous varietals, helped plant the first French varietals, and, most important, taught producers how to care for their vines. He helped an obsessive prince create one of Italy's most hard-to-find and long-aging whites at his tiny farm on the outskirts of Rome. He visited the estate of an old university friend in Lombardy and planted Trebbiano to create Trebbiano di Lugana. At the Sassicaia estate, where no great wine had ever been produced, using grapes that had never grown in such a climate, Tancredi collaborated with Mario Incisa della Rocchetta to create Italy's most prized modern wine, Sassicaia, the red that launched Tuscan wines from obscurity to international fame. After Sassicaia came a cascade of blended wines from the region, and the combination of their near-simultaneous emergence on the market and their massive popularity came to be known as the Super Tuscans movement.

For his entire life, Tancredi bounced from place to place, inspiring many of today's most influential winemakers, tasters, consultants—Maurizio Castelli and master taster Giulio Gambelli among them. Tancredi was an outspoken proponent of long-aging wines.

"When you taste old wines, it's quite touching because they're so complex," said Franco, squinting into the sunlight. "This is what my father was interested in—a complicated wine, something that changed with time, becoming deeper, finer. He didn't care much for the table wines people were making around here, but he understood the concept: the farmers just needed something to drink at home."

"Did he think the wines had any other merit?" I asked.

"No"—Franco paused—"he thought they were bad. Then again, the farmers didn't like him much either. When they started making money and formed a consortium, we didn't join. My father had discovered Brunello and he understood exactly what made it Brunello. He pushed for aging requirements from outside the group. He wanted Brunello aged for four years in the barrel. Of course, nobody else in the area wanted this because you can't make fast money like that. You know, at first they tried to call our regional Sangiovese 'Rosso di Brunello,' but my father thought it was too dishonest. Technically it wasn't Brunello in the wine. So we called it Rosso di Montalcino eventually. If there was one thing my father taught me above all else, it was to be honest. Did I mention how close we were?"

"Franco and Sergio, please join me for lunch," his wife said. She stood in the doorway, a clear blond beauty in her seventies, a green silk scarf tied around her neck.

The dining room was connected to the kitchen, a room half filled with an imposing copper and stone fireplace, upon which various pots were steaming. To one side, the mansion stretched out, a succession of staircases and antique furniture. To the other, smoky bright light streamed through a window. A decorative clay sink held large, leafy plants. The walls were covered with antique plates. A Sri Lankan chef in a low-collared red shirt was the cook and server. He had prepared the greatest rarity in all of Italy: a vegetarian lunch. We had thick bread-and-bean soup, a saffron risotto with curry and raisins, a platter of braised wild fennel, and frothy chestnut pudding. Set before us were a 1975 Brunello, a 1985 Brunello, and a 1995 Brunello.

"So they're trying to ban aging requirements, then?" I asked. The Brunello consortium had been trying to push through a new law that entailed aging Brunello for two years, as opposed to the current four. Almost everyone was for the idea, but just as voting time neared, Franco broke Biondi Santi's decades-long aversion to the consortium and joined. The other winemakers were too ashamed to go against the institution responsible for their livelihood.

"You know the journalist Luigi Veronelli?" asked Franco. I nodded. "Really, he was more a wandering poet. Anyway, he said that Biondi Santi is like a magnificent, budding flower that you'll never know just when to pick because it only improves and transforms." He looked at his wife. "He said of an 1891 once: 'I drank it alone, all of it, and enjoyed it much like a great wedding to the very end.'"

❦

THERE WAS ONE more person to see in town, a former industrial insurance broker from Milan who was widely considered the single best producer of Brunello di Montalcino in the world. The stated plan was that in midafternoon I would stop by his place for a tasting of his latest Brunellos. But I'd left the rest of my schedule that day blank. I was already fairly sure that the same thing would happen that always happened: I would tour his land, drink wine drawn from the barrels in his cold little cellar, and when I started up my car to leave, he would ease himself into the passenger seat and direct me to a local restaurant, where he would torment the chef and waiter, complain about the food, expand on his many philosophies, and advise me on life in general. And, comfortingly, it happened pretty much like that.

Gianfranco Soldera seemed like your average retiree—a little grumpy and very hunched. He was short, with a substantial nose and belly, tufts of white hair around his ears, a mustache, and a pair of enormously messy gray eyebrows that gave him a consistently sympathetic expression. When he was outside, he wore big black sunglasses and a black woolen beret. When he met me at his Case Basse estate, he was in hiking boots, corduroys, a pink sweater, and a checkered shirt, with a paisley ascot tied around his neck. He gave me a firm handshake, put his hands behind his back, and began to stroll through his property. I followed behind. The Case Basse estate wasn't manicured like Biondi Santi's Il Greppo. In fact, it wasn't like any place I'd ever seen.

"Really, it's a botanical garden," Soldera began. When he was sufficiently fond of you, he was able to talk endlessly without receiving any response; he required only your physical presence. "My wife has planted over fifteen hundred types of roses here." His wife, Graziella Felicità, was standing on a ladder over a sloped rose trellis, pruning back leaves; her face was bare, her short brown hair pushed back, and her most notable accessory was a green canvas apron that held her shears. "This garden is truly a feat of attention," Soldera said, regarding Graziella. We ambled on.

The botanical garden began at Soldera's ivy-covered stone house and office and continued past a single rose plant the size of a sprawling tree, past the leaf-covered pool bordered by bushes, a fountain full of fish, a small garden restricted to white flowers—"For nocturnal pollination," Soldera remarked—a pond covered with lily pads.

"Painters come here and tell me we have a special, clean light," Soldera said. "Professors come here to study, to experiment with the earth. Just these last two weeks I had visits from a

Florentine microbiology professor, an Australian expert on vine leaves, a Friulian teacher of vegetable pathology, a professor of viticulture from Piacenza, and a German professor of climatic mutations. They understand that it's not enough to stay in the lab, that they must develop a rapport with the land that can endure over time. If you don't do this, you can't do anything, because it's not only what's in the glass but also how the vine and earth operate. If you ask me, students should be paying farmers to teach them about biology."

We walked down the rocky paths thick with moss under a silver midday moon, by a basketball court obscured by vines, a honeysuckle plant covered in bumblebees, a small clay bench, a slender, humid creek, a man-made pond. A nightingale flew by. The air was buzzing with insects.

"To create a biosystem, you need to give animals not only bugs and plants to eat, but also water to drink," Soldera said as he gazed into the murky water.

We continued down a series of small paths lined with cabbages, birch trees, and hydrangea plants, past putrid compost bins and irises. We finally arrived at the vineyards. There, two crinkly old men were moving together as a team, pruning each vine; one controlled the clippers while the other located branches and held them in position. They had been working for a day and still had covered no more than a hundred vines.

"You missed a spot," Soldera said immediately, pointing to a lone leaf on an obscured vine in the middle of the plot.

"Where?" said one man. "We did?"

Soldera, in his sixties and fairly stiff, threw himself under the wire holding up a row of vines, rolled over the hay-covered ground, and sprang up.

"Here," he said. He motioned for the clippers and removed the errant leaf. Then he rolled back under the wire, put his hands behind his back, and strolled a few more yards to his winery, a newly constructed stone facility that overlooked the vineyards.

Soldera shook his head. "It's never, ever completed. When I buy a door handle, I still need to buy a toilet cover. When I get the toilet cover, we need a table." He sighed.

We entered through the back door into a vast sunny room filled with cases full of bottles and glasses and bordered by potted lemon trees. We walked down the grated metal steps and into the small, freezing cellar, which contained a bottling room, a sink, three wood fermentation tanks, and six *botti*, each of which was marked in chalk. One, in addition to being labeled by year, was also decorated with a series of pictures: a messy heart, a smiling whale, a one-eyed stick figure in a fancy dress, a pair of big lips, and two ships.

"Grandchildren," Soldera noted.

"And what do they think of your wine?" I asked. I thought of my son, Sal, and how much he loved a sip.

"Nothing at all," Soldera said. "In my family, you can't have wine until you're fifteen. The alcohol is bad for children." He shook his head.

The room had been built beneath the earth and was contained by walls of big, gray stones, set one meter thick and held together loosely within a sort of floor-to-ceiling metal fence. The floor, too, was made of stones, and it was soaking wet. The echo of every drip reverberated throughout.

"It's almost as if this *cantina* was no more than a literal hole in the ground," Soldera said. He began siphoning wine into a glass and passed it on to me.

"How did you find your vineyards?" I asked.

"I was in Milan, selling insurance, and I wrote to my partners to give them fair warning, and I said, 'If I find a great piece of land in the next year, I'm making the best wine in the world.' My uncle Giovanni told me about this place and I bought it. And then I made the best wine in the world, just like I'd promised."

I put my nose deep into the glass. It would be hard to argue with him. Soldera, too, closed his eyes and smelled. Then he opened them abruptly.

"No spitting in my cellar," he directed.

"Why?" I asked.

"Because wine is good and if you don't like it, I won't let you drink it," he said.

I nodded, but I hadn't needed him to tell me his rule; nobody with a heart would spit out Soldera's wine. Other wines out of the barrel were murky; they assaulted your mouth and stripped your tongue, and the first time I'd ever done a barrel tasting I'd wanted to quit the business. But Soldera's wine, at only three months old, was sweet, fresh, and ruby red. I sniffed again. Soldera did the same. He began to nod intermittently. His wine was so layered and alive that it was impossible to smell the same thing twice. It had a hypnotic effect. We went silent.

"*Perché è così,*" Soldera said every once in a while. Because it's like that.

We tasted his 2000, 2001, 2002, and 2003 Brunellis. When he got lost in his wine, a wide smile took him over, and he looked as if he was about to laugh.

"*Perché è così,*" he said. "*Perché è così.*"

Each vintage was full of baritone voices and higher pitches, rises and falls, rushes and lulls.

"This one I was worried about because the vintage was difficult, but in fact it's grand," he said when we reached his 2002. "Wine can be like a premature baby. It has its issues at birth but you don't know its future. It could become extraordinary."

After an hour or so, Soldera was finished. My hands were nearly frozen but my face was perfectly warm.

"What did you like best?" he asked.

"The 2001," I said.

"As I always say, some people have the ability to taste and some people don't," he said approvingly. "I have a brother who might as well not have a palate at all. Can't smell a thing. Once, my father got an ulcer and he could eat only rice. I was in the military at the time, so it was only my rice-eating father and my no-sense-of-smell brother at home. When I returned, my mother had a party. She said, 'Thank God! Now I can finally cook again, for someone who can really eat!'"

Soldera shuffled over to the lights and turned them all off. Then we walked back through the garden and to my car.

"Now I'm taking you to dinner," he said, as he lowered himself into the passenger seat.

"Just direct me on the way," I said. We made our way down the dirt path leading back to the main road, and then down the curving pitch-black streets, by dark fields, to a honeycomb Tuscan town, a maze of stone buildings rising upward. At the top was a relatively modern square, and set down from the street three steps was a small white restaurant.

"Here we are," said Soldera. He motioned me to the restaurant, taking each step slowly. At the door stood a black-haired man wearing a crisp white shirt and apron. In under one second, upon his seeing Soldera, his features descended into pure despair and then regained their gracious expression.

"Signor Soldera," he said.

Soldera smiled briefly and strode to the corner table at which he always sat. Across the restaurant, which seated no more than twenty, seven young men were getting drunk on red wine and eating voraciously. Behind us sat a family of three, mother, father, and baby girl.

Soldera sat down and pushed the menu away. "We'll take the roasted vegetables, the fritto misto, the prosciutto, the beef with truffles, and the breaded lamb," he said. "And my 1999 Brunello. And Ettore, tell your cousin not to serve me any crap."

The waiter cracked a weak smile.

"Natural or sparkling water?" Soldera asked me.

"Whatever you're having," I said.

"I'm complicated," he said. "I like half-and-half."

Ettore brought out the wine. Soldera stuck his nose in his glass; I did the same with mine.

"It's really unfortunate that your brother is related to a great winemaker and can't smell a thing," I said. It seemed like a minor tragedy.

Soldera put his palms up and shrugged. *"È così,"* he said. "It's not the right of everyone to have taste. It's not true that there's a lot of good wine. Not everyone can taste beauty. Not everyone can climb Mount Everest. Not everyone can write a masterpiece. Many people can put pen to paper, but how many people are great? The Greeks invented theater and the Romans sat around for a thousand years and they didn't do a thing but make war. How can you say it's all for all?

"You had Aristotle, Homer, Sophocles, Euripides, Shakespeare, Molière, Brecht, Chekhov, Ibsen, Goldoni, Pirandello, Goethe, Svevo. Many wrote plays in the world, but if we speak of the greats, *those* were the greats. And how many is that? In all the world, in three thousand years, no more than ten. Or say we go with novelists: Dante, Virgil, Proust, Cervantes. I'm speaking only of the Western world because I don't know much about Africa and Asia, but still, in all of the Western world, in three millennia, there can't be more than fifty. And what does this say? This says that excellence is small. That the most magnificent things are only for the few."

Ettore delivered the roasted vegetables—sliced zucchini, carrots, purple onions, and potatoes, crunchy and caramelized on the outside and soft, deep, concentrated on the inside—on a porcelain platter.

"Nothing just happens," Soldera continued, filling my plate with food. "When you make something elevated, you don't make it by chance."

"How do you make it?"

"You make it by being always in discussion. You must always

confront. You must try always to know more. We need people who have the courage to motivate us, to question us, to tell us what we need to know, to open windows for us. *È così.*"

But how did he, the son of a Milanese farmer, who left school at fourteen to work in an office when his father fell ill, come to make one of the best wines in the world?

"You don't need to have been born in the country to have taste. What you need is a culture of food in the family. In my family, we ate natural foods, with flavor, without preservatives. I learned then how to understand, and I have taste memory; the smell of something arrives in a particular part of my brain. If you don't start with this culture, if you eat only fake, manufactured food, you can never make up for that.

"You must be able to comprehend what is the perfect steak, the true delicacy of a fresh fish. You need the ability to smell a tomato, to open up its perfume, to know something fantastic. The perfume must be something from your childhood, though, something deep inside you. If the family gives a big importance to food, to *la materia prima,* then children will grow up with an idea of what food means and will pass it on to their children. If everything is hot dogs, refrigerated vegetables, hormone-filled fruits, then you'll never be able to differentiate.

"For people these days it's difficult, especially for people in a city. But if you decide to bring children onto this earth, you must force them to understand *la materia prima.* That is your work, your obligation. What is man if he is not his culture? He is nothing if not his past."

The baby at the table nearby let out a shriek. Her parents looked at Soldera apologetically.

"Pardon us," the father said.

"But why?" Soldera asked. "A baby *must* cry, *must* make noise, so that we know she is there." He waved at the baby. The baby giggled. "Now she is content," he said.

"Sergio," Soldera said, "you need to work extra hard with

your children, especially in New York City. They need to see where food comes from. And you must also make sure that they grow up well. You know what they say: If they come out right, it's because of the mother. And if they don't, it's the father's fault."

Suddenly I felt a tightness in my chest. I missed Sal and Lili terribly.

"Every day," Soldera went on, "I sit with my children at dinner, without the television, and I look in their faces—when you look in their faces you can see every problem they have—and I eat with them and we talk to each other. We sit at the table and we transmit our culture. And wine and food are a significant culture." Soldera paused and looked at his wine, then back at me.

Ettore returned with the fritto misto and placed it gingerly on the table. Soldera began to shovel the bits of salty, lightly battered vegetables into his mouth by hand. "Eating with your hands is the way to really get the flavor," he said. He picked up an artichoke.

"Remember that my wine is the only wine in the world that goes with artichoke," he said. "What other producer will order artichoke for you?" He took a sip. I followed suit. Indeed, his wine, unlike virtually every other wine in the world, was not affected by the pungency of an artichoke.

"My wine is *Italian* wine, and further, it's true wine. California wines are the same as hormonal cows. You have people who eat big, strange, manufactured blackberries and then you give them a wild blackberry and they say, 'What is this?' Well, I prefer wild blackberries."

"A great wine is a wild blackberry," I said.

"A great wine . . . let's see. A great wine has harmony, elegance, and complexity. And moreover, it tastes natural. And even more important, it has medicinal effects."

"From when I was a child, my mother gave me a bit of wine to make me better if I felt sick," I said.

"Well, your mother gave you wine much too early, but it does give you a sense of well-being. It's good for you. You feel good when you drink it. You make new friends. You are satisfied in your brain, in your heart, and in your stomach."

Ettore carefully placed on the table a plate of beef—nearly raw, sliced thin, and covered in delicate shavings of black truffles.

"A black truffle is nothing compared to a white truffle," said Soldera, glaring at the plate. "Sometimes I like to eat a black truffle just to remind myself that the French don't know a damn thing about food." He cut himself a bite and let out a satisfied chortle. *"Che schifo,"* he said. Disgusting.

Ettore was back by the door, trying to avert his eyes.

"Ettore, I asked you to tell your cousin to cut this out," said Soldera loudly. "Black truffles are good for nothing."

Ettore sighed. "I'll tell him, Signore," he said.

Soldera leaned in to me. "Being different from everyone else is the ability to exercise your right to criticize what your nose and palate tell you is bad."

He poured himself some more wine. "To have harmony, a wine needs to be proportionate. It needs equilibrium. Without that it will collapse. And what is elegance? You know it when you drink it. It's a wine with finesse. And complexity, as anyone knows, is the multiple sensations you get when you drink it: fragrances, tastes, pleasures. To make something natural, you need to make it with clean, ripe grapes and nothing else.

"What is wine? Wine is only the transformation of sugars by yeast from sweetness to wine. I take great grapes and I squeeze them. We cultivate the vineyards by hand. I have twelve people helping me to make every one of my fourteen thousand bottles—that's almost one person per thousand bottles in a year."

"But the ability to do this," I said, holding up my glass, "doesn't come just from your childhood, but also from your capacities."

"Well, clearly," said Soldera, "if you don't have a nose, you can have all the customs in the world and you still won't know a thing about food. You need a nose with a memory. But it's much harder now than ever to have a nose. We're losing our sense of smell.

"Our nose was once the most important way we could survive. Man could smell danger before he could see it. He could tell when food was bad. With his nose, he selected the person with whom he wanted to reproduce. In the 1700s, they used to cover odors, but now we're eliminating them. Pollution is killing our olfactory sense and then we're finishing off the job with deodorants, shower gels, perfumed soaps. Your brain can no longer decipher what real smells are, what's natural. You can't sterilize yourself and think there won't be consequences."

Ettore brought a platter piled high with breaded pieces of lamb. Soldera and I both dug our hands in this time. The lamb was tender.

"Beautiful," he said, licking his fingers. "These lambs are raised free, on the hills over there, feeding on the purest grass. You'll never find lamb like this anywhere else in the world.

"You know, eating and drinking are the best ways to know people. I've had many people at my table—writers, political people, artists, businesspeople—and when they are at the table and you're all feeling physically well, that's the moment when you learn the most."

He plowed through his lamb and sat back contentedly, an enormous cat licking his whiskers.

"With wine, you need typicity," he said. "In a true wine there needs to lie the possibility for you to recognize the microterritory where the wine was born. Can't you taste the Case Basse in my wines? But typicity leads me to uniqueness. A great wine cannot be replaced. It's literally impossible for another producer to make a wine like my Brunello. It's never been done and it will never be done because my wine is a combination of so many things that are impossible to replicate, including myself."

He wasn't especially modest, but he was certainly correct. Soldera did with his wines what only a master can do: He made them personal. He knew how to insert into his wine an aspect of himself; in this way, the wine was nearly human. It could evoke in you an emotional reaction—in fact, it was intended to do so. His wine was like music, like a great story, like sex. It was an exercise in tension and release, which was why you had to keep smelling it. In a song, when a drummer skips a beat, you realize the tension inherent in the melody; in Soldera's wines, you could also feel the stress and satisfaction. But this wasn't just from his grapes and his techniques. It came from something innate within him. You could give another artist Michelangelo's materials and his training, but this artist wouldn't be able to make the *Pietà*. Michelangelo put himself into his paintings and that was what made the difference.

"And last, I place value on rarity and longevity," said Soldera. "You can't make the highest-quality product for the masses. It doesn't work like that. And by the way, I don't *want* the masses to drink my wine. They wouldn't understand it. I only want the right people taking a bottle of Soldera home. Not the rich, but those who know."

"And longevity?" I asked.

"Wine must improve over the years and it must offer different sensations over time," he said. "Wine is man's only natural product that can last longer than man's own life." With that, he finished his last glass. "And by the way, if you don't miss a wine after you've drunk it, don't ever drink it again."

Ettore approached again. "Sir, would you like some grappa?" he asked.

"Grappa is poison!" Soldera announced, still leaning back. "You can use that stuff on your wounds, but if you drink it, it'll burn through your insides. You want to give me poison?"

"Of course not, Signore," said Ettore. Soldera patted his belly and took a coffee. The child from the next table toddled outside when she saw a scruffy dog prance by.

"La storia, la famiglia, il cibo, il vino. Questa è la vita dell'uomo," said Soldera. History, family, food, wine. This is the life of man. "And that's all I'll say on that."

Chapter 10

CHIANCIANO TERME

⸙

THE LANDLOCKED TOURIST TOWN of Chianciano Terme is a little like Las Vegas, but instead of gambling, they have mineral water. The area, smack in the middle of a Tuscan nowhere, caters to an entirely Italian crowd of water enthusiasts who flock to the spot's spas to indulge in water cures, which involve, generally, drinking water. They can also bathe in water, swim in water, sit near water, shower in water, and be massaged with water. The main attractions are several water parks, enormous grounds featuring old trees and sculptures, swimming pools, wading pools, and dipping pools, all protected by buildings of concrete. In the high season, the place is filled with families, most of them consisting of the older demographic. Its wide streets are lined with 1960s-style grand hotels—L'Ambassadore, Best Western Majestic—and 1980s-style regular hotels, and its brightly lit restaurants are completely booked. We were in Chianciano Terme to spend Easter with my father's family, a group composed mostly of retirees who had committed to spending two weeks watering themselves down.

"I don't understand," Stephany kept muttering as we drove through the town. "They're spas, but you can't get pedicures?"

"No, *bella,*" my father said.

"A manicure?" she asked. "A scrub?"

"You can take a dip in the pool," my mother offered.

"But it says it's a *spa*," Stephany said dejectedly.

The Espositos, once crammed together in that little apartment near the Naples train station, had scattered—my father to America; his sisters Rita and Rosario to Puglia and Caserta, respectively; and his twin brother, Antonio, to Bologna. Their mother, their father, and their sister Carmela had passed away years ago. My father hadn't celebrated Easter with the remaining bunch in over three decades, and my mother had spent months organizing his reunion, especially with Tonino, which is how Antonio was referred to.

The family was set up at a combination hotel and religious retreat, which offered a church, daily Mass, bedrooms, and a veal-and-ravioli dinner for one low price. My parents would be staying with us at an *agriturismo* outside of town, but our first stop was the retreat. It consisted of two buildings: a pale yellow 1960s-style church, and a convention center that also provided lodging. The latter was a three-story building, tile-floored, with a long white and yellow dining hall and a few recreation rooms. On every spare ledge sat a small sculpture of Jesus and Mary. We found the Neapolitans and their spouses firmly ensconced in a room filled with faux leather couches and a shiny grand piano upon which one of my cousins, a concert pianist, was playing a repertoire of classics and southern folk songs. Except for a couple playing cards, the rest of the relatives were dancing. When they saw us, they reacted with screaming and hugging, thereby demonstrating the kind of southern Italian emotion that makes you feel that you're the most loved human in the world. Then we all ate broiled fish and played poker and argued politics.

"Yes, I voted for Berlusconi," my lone conservative cousin was saying, "and I'd do it again."

"Ma perché? Perché?" his brother was asking. But why? Why?

"Perché sì," my uncle said. Because yes.

"Oh," his brother said. "I see." Everybody nodded understandingly.

"Babbo, Lili has an upset stomach, so we're going to go back to the hotel for a bit," I told my father. "I take it you want to stay here."

"Well, you'll be back by dinner anyhow," my mother said.

Our *agriturismo* was Palazzo Bandino, on the edge of town. We navigated our way through the streets of Chianciano, turned onto a main road, and took a left into a wooded area. There, a man named Gabriele lived with his twenty-year-old daughter and his eighty-year-old father, whom we spotted, as we drove down the drive, tottering perilously on the top of a six-foot ladder, pruning his olive trees.

Gabriele was a soft-spoken, recently divorced winemaker who annually made five thousand bottles of an honest Chianti that I sold in my store for $11. He had a thin handlebar mustache, rough skin, and soft eyes, and he had refurbished Palazzo Bandino himself. A large beige stucco house, covered with flowers, it was all antique doors and dark wooden shutters. He had planted pine trees around the entrance and placed pots of miniature palms leading up the stairs.

"Welcome, Sergio," Gabriele said, taking my hand. "You have made it to our home. It is not grand or spectacular, but for us, it is important."

He led us to our apartment, a couple of rooms named La Noce, "the nut," and so marked with a hand-painted sign depicting walnuts. It was a simple space: a double bed made up with a delicate flowered spread, a spotless kitchenette, windows covered with white lace curtains. I lugged our suitcases in and looked at my family. Stephany was cradling Lili in her arms as Sal climbed on a dresser.

"She's tired," Stephany said, putting Lili on the bed. She lay down next to her—a couple of girls with matching brown eyes, yawning in unison. "We need a nap." She motioned toward Sal, who had begun to attempt a cartwheel in the enclosed space.

"In that case," I said, looking out the window, "I think Sal and I can find something to do." The grounds were covered with apple and cherry trees, lettuce beds, olive trees. There may have been a man-made pond, and I was fairly sure that I had seen a frog. "Toad alert," I said. Sal repressed a squeal, pulled manically on my hand, and we were off.

With Lili and Stephany snoozing in "La Noce," we ran through the orchards in search of the frog, stopping occasionally to inspect a bug, a rotting apple, a murky puddle. When we'd made our way down the fields, we reached a thicket in which a pair of rabbits were chasing each other. We pushed our way through and found ourselves in a pine forest, the ground blanketed with ferns and wet leaves. We collected nine worms and named them before setting them free. When we emerged from the forest, we found ourselves on a slippery mud road shaded by a canopy of trees.

As we trudged through the mud, which splattered my pant legs and gradually covered roughly half of Sal's body, we came to a clearing. To one side of the road was a small vineyard of gnarled old vines; to the other, bunches of ancient oak trees wound thick with ivy. With every step, we discovered new bushes of fruit—blueberries, strawberries, raspberries, all small, wild, and packed tight with flavor. We used Sal's T-shirt as a basket and picked a bunch. Then we sat by a baby pine and ate them by the handful; my son, previously mud brown, was now also blue and magenta.

"Your mother's going to be thrilled," I said. Sal mushed a berry into his hair.

After acquiring the appropriate pair of walking staffs, we persisted down the path. As we neared the end, Sal saw, in the distance, a horse chewing on a mouthful of hay in the middle of a small pasture.

"Can we pet it?" he asked. "Please, Papà?"

The horse's pasture was near a one-story stone house; a rusty tractor in a nearby field served as a bed for two cats. The horse, bright white with a pink muzzle and thick black eyelashes, regarded us and looked away, unimpressed. It was a mare, a little long in the tooth, and it might not have been ridden in a decade, but to Sal it was a prize stallion. I lifted him up. He put one small hand on the horse's nose.

"You should go find her an apple," I said. "I think she'd appreciate it."

As I was letting Sal down, a man and a teenage boy curved around from the back of the house. "Hi there," the man said in accented Italian. "Her name is Lunetta." The man was an old hippie farmer, tall and lean, with straggly gray hair and leather sandals. His son was similarly built, with sandy-blond hair.

"I hope we're not bothering you," I said. "My boy just saw this horse while we were taking a walk and wanted to pet her."

"Absolutely not," the man said. "We're always happy to have visitors. I'm Jens and this is my son, Mauro."

"Sergio Esposito," I said. Sal took off to locate the apple, and I began to talk with Jens. He was Swiss, it turned out, and lived with his wife on the farm, their return to nature. They slaughtered their own meat, put up their own preserves, pressed their own olive oil, grew their own vegetables.

"The idea is to be self-sustaining," he said. "We were sick of consuming so much." They also, he mentioned, made their own wine. When I told him about my work, he invited me down to the cellar. I looked over at Sal, who was gathering fallen fruit with Mauro.

"Why not?" I said. "Sal, I'm going in. Want to come?" He gave me a dismissive shake of the head. "I'll be inside if you need me," I said, and followed Jens into the house. He led me through his living room, stuffed full of knickknacks, hand-sewn blankets, books, and photographs, and down below to his *cantina,* a cool underground room that also housed jars of peaches, yellow peppers, and sun-dried tomatoes; vats of olive oil; cartons of onions and potatoes; and a hanging proscuitto shank. We sat down in a minuscule tasting room with one rickety table, with a few glasses of wine taken from some of the barrels that filled the *cantina*.

"I brought some antipasti for our guest," said a woman, descending the stairs. She was Julie, Jens's wife, a woman with short black hair and a long Indian skirt. She set down a platter of strong black olives; sweet, fatty salami; and sharp sheep's milk cheese. Then we began tasting the wine.

"What do you think?" Jens asked. "We're pretty new at this."

Julie and Jens were facing a common challenge for producers in their area: the challenge of making wine in Chianti.

❧

CHIANTI IS AN OVAL that starts south of Florence and north of Siena. From the center, it's a straight shot to the shipping port of Livorno. For hundreds of years, Chianti was a vacation destination for wealthy Sienese and Florentines, who kept country houses out in the lush hills. They hunted rabbits, pigeons, and wild boar on the weekends, and didn't stick around for more than two or three months a year. This lack of deep roots meant that little attention was devoted to the process of winemaking. Marketing, however, was another story.

Florence is a banking city, and thus houses a population that understands business. The Florentines came up with the idea of bottling Chianti in immediately distinguishable straw flasks, and they shipped it around the world. This combination of market savvy and wine ignorance meant that Chianti was soon the most recognizable wine in the world, but that it was also associated with low cost and low quality, with checkered tablecloths and spaghetti-and-meatballs meals. Everyone finally knew that Italy made wine, but everyone thought that Italian wine was kind of gross.

When Chianti began to falter, another wave of nonlocals swooped in to save it. The South Africans, the British, the Swiss, the Germans, the Americans—everyone wanted to have a pretty Tuscan plot, and to redeem Chianti. They all went about buying up properties and hiring expensive consultants. They whipped up wines using French techniques, German techniques, Californian techniques, and a lot of blending. The new establishment came up with wines that were popular and well received, but that lacked history and typicity. The wines were made in Chianti, they were called Chianti, but they weren't really Chianti.

True Chianti, or original Chianti, was made by mixing Sangiovese with red Canaiolo, white Trebbiano, and white Malvasia. Today, virtually nobody produces such a drink, and only two estates—Castell'in Villa and Montevertine—focus on an apt expression of Sangiovese, something that brings out the taste of Tuscany. The others don't even seem to bother.

In the early 1990s, owing to market economics, the regional consortium decided to allow Chianti makers to omit the two white varietals. By the late 1990s, the only restriction on Chianti was that it had to be 85 percent Sangiovese; the rest was up to the vintner. Then again, the loosening of the rules probably didn't matter much anyway; to save time, energy, and money—and because American critics had developed a taste for richer California drinks—wineries had been illegally blending Aglianico and Primitivo into their Chianti for years.

This sort of mutation of the wine was especially hurtful because of the nature of Chianti. This particular Sangiovese is such a gentle grape—grown on rolling, sweeping hills and calmed by constant cool breezes—that even 5 percent of a strong grape like Cabernet impacts the wine intensely. I watched dolefully as these wines that tasted like Napa Valley Syrah got high scores and pulled in wads of cash. They may have been decent, but they sure weren't pure, and they certainly didn't taste like Tuscany.

❧

JULIE AND JENS HAD FOUND their perfect piece of land, and they had set out to do everything in as natural a way as possible. But when I tasted their wines, I sensed a mask—the wine seemed camouflaged. There was something covering the Sangiovese.

"It's the Merlot," Julie said.

"And the Syrah," Jens said.

"Why did you add them?" I asked.

"We were doing just plain Sangiovese," Julie said. "But then our friends told us no one would buy it. They said we should add in the French grapes. You think we don't need them?"

"Sangiovese should be a high note," I said. "The grapes sing. Merlot and Syrah are low, deep. They strip the energy and character from the Sangiovese."

They both looked at me. They had never made wine before and were depending on some friends to advise them, and they were stuck in quite a quandary. They weighed their options: the insecurity and risk of making the wine they'd once sought to make, in all its light-colored, market-unfriendly glory, or the relative security of keeping in the more popular varietals. They would, ultimately, choose the latter. But back then, they were still considering the scarier possibility.

Every half hour or so, Sal would come rushing down the stairs, help himself to an olive, take a quick sip of wine, nod approvingly, and run back to his games. "Yummy," he said. I always said I didn't care what Sal wanted to do with his life as long as he was happy, but I was lying. I wanted him to really love wine. I was willing to stay in that *cantina* forever, watching him run up and down, and talking with Julie and Jens. And I did stay there as the sky grew dark. Then we wandered up to their kitchen and looked out at the setting sun.

"What a beautiful day," I said.

"That's for sure," said Julie. "What a perfect day for Easter."

My pride-filled heart dropped to my very full stomach. *"Porca miseria!"* I said. "What time is it?"

"Nine-thirty," said Jens.

"I have to go right now," I said. "I was supposed to have dinner with my wife and parents two hours ago." I gave them my card, thanked them for a wonderful time, grabbed Sal by the arm, and we left running.

"I did good today, didn't I, Papà?" Sal asked as he made his way through the woods.

"You did great," I said. "But Papà spaced out. I think Nonna and Nonno may be a little mad at me."

"They should be happy that we had the best day in the world," he said.

"You know what would make this day even better?" I said. "It would be even better if it was our secret day."

Sal considered the option. "Okay," he said. "Pinky swear." He offered me his pinky. We wrapped our fingers together and made the promise.

"Excellent," I said. *"Andiamo."*

❧

WE LOCATED STEPHANY in the *agriturismo* restaurant, a tavern outfitted with dark wood tables and walls lined with grappa bottles. She was bouncing Lili on her lap and sharing Easter dinner with Gabriele. She looked a little glum.

"What happened to you guys?" she asked. "Why is Sal purple?"

"I'm really sorry," I said. "We went for a walk and then we found this little winery. I lost track of time."

"Oh, right," she said. "Work. I was worried."

She was the most admirably even-tempered woman I'd ever met, a little annoyed but certainly not all-out angry when her husband skipped Easter dinner without so much as a phone call and returned hours later with a violet three-year-old. I noticed she was wearing a pair of elaborate lace-up heels—I knew she had planned their unveiling for the family dinner. I began silently plotting ways to make it up to her.

"Well, I hope you don't mind, but Gabriele was eating alone, so we figured we'd just eat together," she said.

"Please join us," Gabriele said.

"I'd love to," I said, though the option presented an even greater problem: Gabriele and Stephany were only on the soup course and he was alone, his daughter having gone to spend Easter with her mother, and his father, presumably, still off clipping the olive trees somewhere. I certainly couldn't tear my wife away and leave Gabriele to a solitary holiday meal as we met my large family. I sat down; I was definitely going to get in trouble with my mom. Would it be better or worse than that time when I was ten and accidentally exploded a can of red paint on my face, causing her to briefly believe I was covered in blood? The answer was unclear. I stayed where I was.

Dinner was Tuscan food, a generally heavy cuisine usually referred to as "brown food." This evening, it was brown and green food. First, *minestra*, a mixed soup of white cannelli beans in a clear chicken stock, loaded with leafy vegetables—chard, kale, escarole. Then we had boiled eggs topped with sea salt and a *salsa verde* made of basil, parsley, and olive oil. We ate pecorino-and-ricotta ravioli cooked in brown butter and sage, and *capretto,* baby goat roasted with potatoes and sprigs of rosemary, served with crunchy, lightly fried baby artichokes.

At the end of the meal, Gabriele offered us dessert. "We're already so late," I said. "I'm so sorry, but we should go get my parents."

"But of course," Gabriele said graciously. "I understand."

At eleven, we slunk guiltily over to Chianciano Terme. My parents were back in the recreation room where we had left them nine hours earlier. The family was drinking tiny cups of after-dinner liqueurs—brandy and syrupy brown nocino—as my cousin played "Funiculì, Funiculà" on the piano.

"Sergio, where on earth did you go?" my mother asked. "What happened?"

"I'm sorry," I said. "Lili got sick."

"That's too bad," she said. She'd been boogying and speaking Neapolitan all night, which meant she was definitely less furious than during the red-paint incident of 1978. I vowed to also make it up to her. "A drink?"

Stephany and I had some limoncello and then danced to a few old standards. My parents played Bingo. Sal passed out on the couch next to Lili.

"But it's *Pasqua*," my mother said in the car. "How could you miss *Pasqua*?"

"*Ho sbagliato*," I said. I made a mistake. "I'm sorry about tonight but I have a plan for tomorrow. Pack your stuff because we're leaving early."

෧

WHEN EVERYONE WAS IN BED, I went outside and made a call.

"Sergio Esposito!" shrieked the voice on the other end.

"Andrea Carelli," I said.

"I hope this call means that you are coming immediately to see me," he said.

"I screwed up today," I said. "What do you think about getting together for tomorrow?" In Italy, the day after Easter Sunday is called *Lunedì di Pasqua*, or Easter Monday. Most Italians have a picnic with friends and family. It was the perfect opportunity for redemption, and Andrea Carelli was the overorganized, well-connected man for the job.

"I have prepared a fish feast on the seashore," he said. "I will expand it to include your family. I expect to see you tomorrow morning at half-past eleven. Meet me at the market." Then the line went dead.

Chapter 11

ANCONA

———— ✦ ————

I MET ANDREA at his office, where he was doing what no sane Italian would do on a holiday: tying up some loose ends. He was manic like that; sometimes I thought of him as a high-strung purebred, all sinewy limbs, perpetually in nervous, dutiful motion. He worked above his eponymous supermarket, a flat industrial structure with his name mounted across the front in bright green block letters. When I found him, he was flitting around in beige designer sneakers, black pants, and a perfectly ironed, very tucked-in blue shirt. In the background, I noted two young employees dressed identically to him, each with gelled hair and snug trousers. The open space itself, full of light wood and bright, geometric furniture, looked like a Copenhagen architectural firm, with Andrea as its metrosexual head. If he hadn't had such a prominent nose, he could have been mistaken for a Dane himself.

"Late, late as usual," he said as he tapped his watch. He then grabbed my face, kissed me hard on both cheeks, and embraced me. "Well, hasn't somebody gained weight," he said loudly, holding me at arm's length. "Always fatter, Sergio! Tsk-tsk!"

"Thanks, Andrea," I said. "Ready to go?"

"I'll race you down the stairs," he said. He grabbed his backpack and took off down the hall.

"Not fair!" I protested, and sprinted after him.

When I reached the street, breathing heavily, I found Andrea leaning smugly on my car. "You *must* do sports more often," he said. He had, in his youth, been a semiprofessional motocross racer, and his idea of a great Sunday was windsurfing for eight hours with his two hyper and perfectly formed young sons. "Want to race around the parking lot?"

"No, Andrea, let's go," I said. "Everyone is waiting for us at the restaurant."

"Want to take my scooter?" he asked. "You sit on the back!"

"No, I don't want to ride on your scooter with you," I said. "Let's take my car."

"Race me around the parking lot first," he said.

"No," I said. It wasn't fair anyway. He woke up in the dark every morning to run ten miles. I popped an Ambien after staring at my computer until 4 a.m.

"Race me!" he said. He stood on a divider.

"I'm not racing you," I said. "We're adults."

"Three, two, one," he said, and I was off as fast as I could go. Twenty seconds later, I had lost.

"Exercise is a necessity, not a luxury," he said, regarding my stomach and shaking his head.

"Can we just get in the car?" I asked.

"Only if we can listen to Ooh-two," he said.

"What's Ooh-two?" I asked.

"You don't know Ooh-two? Very famous. My favorite band. I jog to them every morning." He slipped into the passenger seat, pulled a U2 CD out of his backpack, and popped it into the stereo. He then began dancing in his seat and inaccurately mouthing lyrics to "Pride (In the Name of Love)." I pulled out of the lot and onto the main road.

"Go slow! Go slow!" Andrea shouted. I sped up. "*Porca puttana!* You're going to make me vomit." He opened the windows, closed them, danced a little more. "You think you're Flash Gordon," he said. He opened the windows again. "I'll die of this heat!"

"You're an idiot," I said. "Did you know that?"

"No, *you're* an idiot," he said. "Slow down!"

The street out of the business center was an impersonal mini-highway lined with strip malls. It led into the city center, a clean, modern succession of avenues that circled around a main point: Andrea's house. Situated behind a large stone fountain made up of cherubs and ponies, it was the only building in the town square. It was a sun-flooded five-story pink and yellow brick building the size of several brownstones. The bottom floor was a pharmacy and the middle three floors were rented out and relatively bare. On the top floor, below the large clock attached to the roof, Andrea lived with his wife, Christina, and their children. The balconies dripped with red flowers; the windows were covered with long white curtains. From behind those curtains you could see Andrea's café a block over—a bustling coffee-and-sandwich shop his grandfather had founded in 1923. It was from this mansion that he scooted to work every day.

"There's no city more beautiful than my Ancona," he said, his voice breaking. Like all Italians, he was a slave to nostalgia, hopelessly devoted to his birthplace, convinced that it couldn't be rivaled by any other worldly spot. *Che bellezza!*

We continued through the city, past the grubby port, the run-down hotels for sailors, the wooden ships, chipped and colorful, swaying indolently. We went on as the buildings thinned out and the hills rose up, blanketed with jade green trees. The air turned salty. The roads curved toward Portonovo and the beach, and the blue of the water intermittently poked through the trees. Finally we pulled up into a drive made of crushed shells and packed with cars, all shielded from the sun by bamboo canopies. The restaurant, Da Emilia, a one-story white stucco building, was overflowing with people, a line winding out of the polished wood doors and into the lot. Andrea rolled up his sleeves and un-buttoned a button on his shirt, and we pushed our way past the crowd.

Inside, Da Emilia was a sort of historical museum, a place that, upon its walls, displayed evidence of every relevant happening since its founding over six decades ago: pictures of Nonna Emilia herself back in the 1950s, her fat bare arms poking out of a muumuu, toasting the camera with a glass of red wine, a mural of a shell decorated with her name framing her head; Emilia wearing a kerchief, shaking hands with a young Prince Charles; a smudged black-and-white shot of Emilia in her early kitchen, a live fish in hand; Emilia in front of a little shack with her name on it, next to a young waitress in hot pants holding two plates of steaming mussels; the whole family posed on the sand, daughters stretched out languidly, Emilia with her hands on her hips; white-haired, apron-wearing Emilia deep in conversation with a button-nosed, caftan-clad 1960s movie star; Emilia at the center of a long table, holding hands with a dignified man in a dark suit as dinner-goers applaud. In addition to the photographic documentation of Emilia's life, there were also paintings of sunflowers, pictures of fishermen, bits of coral reef preserved in lighted glass boxes, handmade miniature wooden boats, silvery shell collages, ancient mariners' bells, rusty navy clocks, framed magazine articles, intricately drawn catalogs of nautical knots, and straw hats wrapped with ribbons.

The Nonna Emilia recorded on every inch of wall space was now dead, but what she'd done for Portonovo carried on in every facet of its being. She had, in effect, single-handedly created the area as we know it. Before Emilia, this place, now overrun each summer by fish-hungry hordes, had been an overlooked stretch of rock and water. Then Emilia, almost accidentally, wandered down from the hills, nailed together a hut, and established an entirely new food culture.

Ancona-born Emilia had once made herself a little business

cooking meat for workers from her village. But in 1929 she ventured down to take a look at a nearby waterfall. She noticed that there were bunches of tourists who had traveled miles to see the cascade.

I bet they're hungry, she thought. She made a small shelter, stocked it with ingredients, set up several benches on the sand, and offered her services. She whipped up antipasti and *panini,* sold bottles of water and little nut cookies, and, if the customer preferred, wrapped it all up to go. She ran the place alone, looking out at the smooth water, down the empty shore.

The beach was small, and in the days before central heating and electricity, it didn't make sense to have a waterfront view—you'd be at the mercy of the bitter winter and the pounding rain. The people who lived near the sea huddled inland. They didn't tend to go especially close to the shore for most of the year, and perhaps for this reason, they had never developed fish-based cuisine. Instead, in their houses a half mile from the salt water, they ate the mountain game that they slaughtered. For centuries, the bonds of tradition had prohibited them from breaking out of what they knew—if your grandmother and great-grandmother had been experts in preparing lamb, how, exactly, were you supposed to go about preparing clams? And even if you were a clam-curious insurgent, if your husband was a hunter, how, exactly, were you supposed to obtain said clams?

Around the time that Emilia began her sandwich business, some entrepreneurial radicals had noticed that there were tons of calamari and mussels relatively near the shore. They began to take their wobbly boats out, pick up the mussels, and sell them to the villagers. The enterprise was new and might have been inconsequential had it not been for the kids. Emilia's clients were often priests who led families on camping trips; they prayed at dusk and then came to eat at her shack. The children, while swimming during the day, followed the fishermen's lead, and plucked off their own mussels.

"I'll cook those for you," Emilia would say when they arrived bearing baskets full of tiny black mollusks. If the kids had done all the work, the least she could do was figure out the best way to steam a shellfish. And so she began to serve the groups her spaghetti with pork fat along with bowls of the shiny mussels that the children had gathered.

The mussels, it turned out, were unusually sweet and tender. People told their friends about them and Emilia gained a cult following. She stopped relying on children and sent local fishermen out for more. The sheer mass of business grew too much for her to handle, and village people who had come to help her in the kitchen eventually opened their own shacks, serving the abundant mussels and calamari, and branching out into any other seafood they could manage to hook.

"The more restaurants we open, the more people will come," Emilia said happily of her competition.

Then, in 1961, a French travel association, Club Méditerranée, got word of Portonovo. It loaded its members on a bus from Paris and drove them to Emilia's, where they ate everything she had to offer. After that, seafood-hungry troops of Italians and foreigners began to flood the place.

Despite the ever-growing popularity of the beach, there remained an element of humility to Portonovo, an obscurity and an absence of the aggressive glamour found in every inch of vacation towns like Portofino. There were no helicopter pads or $3,000-a-night hotels, and you were unlikely to see a mass of Russian billionaires draped in YSL carousing in the streets. The prices at Portonovo weren't prohibitive, and the people serving up the food were blessedly normal—for example, there was Marina.

Marina was Emilia's daughter, who now ran the restaurant. She cooked whatever her husband, a squinty-eyed old fisherman named Franco, brought in from the deep throughout the day.

Marina greeted us as we squeezed past the line. She was short and sturdy like her mother. She wore her light hair in a kind of accidental mullet, and her round face was accented by a pair of wire-rim glasses. She sported heavy beige pumps and an apologetic air, and had known Andrea since he was a child.

"He's crazy like a horse, but a fantastic person," she whispered to me upon introduction.

Marina had worked at Da Emilia since she was twelve, long enough to have witnessed the rise of the area and all the repeat customers, the devotees who flocked to her no-frills place, rendering it a sort of foodie mecca. Recently, a man of fifty had come into the restaurant, she told us, and she had recognized him as a member of one of the first families she'd ever served. He had been a child, running around on the beach, and she'd been a preteen, balancing a tray, nervous about doing well by her mother.

"Is your name Piero Pioceci?" she'd asked when he entered, gray-haired, with his own wife and grown children. "Did you come here forty years ago with your two sisters and your parents?" She described what he'd worn and how he'd scampered along the beach as his mother and father drank cocktails in lounge chairs. The man had burst into tears.

Now Marina led us out to our families on the back porch, a long structure supported by turquoise beams, its outdoor space so close to the water that, at high tide, the waves lapped the floor. Waiting for us were Paolo, my importer friend and former owner of the beloved-by-models restaurants; his wife, Allison, with her bangs and miniskirt; and Andrea's friend Simone—a resident ice-cream seller—and his blond Swedish wife. There were my parents next to Paolo's mother; Andrea's wife, Christina; and Stephany. The children—Paolo's three-year-old, Kika; Simone's Nordic brood of four; our Sal; Andrea's pair of Olympic swimming hopefuls, the absurdly athletic six-year-old Giorgio and eight-year-old Luca—were out on the sand, integrated into a larger mass of other people's children, involved in an incomprehensible game that involved raucous giggling and lots of running. They were all covered in a thin layer of salt and sand, and many of their sweaters had been abandoned in a damp pile. Lili, dressed all in lilac, sat silently in her chair, sucking on a pacifier and gazing out at them and wondering, I guess, when she would be able to join the party.

It was technically too early in the season to open the outer porch, but Marina had agreed to do so for Andrea. We were the only people outside, and our rickety white wooden table was set with overflowing platters: rough white Atlantic oysters; marinated swordfish topped with pink peppercorns; oily octopus languidly outstretched on a bed of pale green celery and small roasted potatoes; rosy, lightly cooked salmon; and warm, thinly sliced potatoes mixed with coarse rocks of sea salt—the world's best chip. Stephany, in gold peep-toe sandals and a white cotton shift, against which her skin glowed a deep brown, was talking to Christina, an aristocratic middle-aged woman with Byzantine features and chestnut hair. Christina was wearing a silk shirt-dress. They were drinking sparkling wine. Andrea rushed over to his stately wife and demanded a kiss. She allowed him one; he regarded her gratefully.

"She is my queen," he said dreamily, taking her hand. *"La mia regina."* Andrea had met his wife when she was sixteen, courted her for fourteen years, and married her twelve years ago—a wedding during which he might as well have been the blushing bride. He had been obsessed with her every step of the way. He had the habit, when he thought of her, of shamelessly sniffling as his eyes turned wet and glassy. "She has a wonderful smile, the skin of an Asian, and she smells sweet, like candy," he once said to a group of strangers. I put my head in my hands.

"Andrea darling, please," she said gently, and continued her conversation with Stephany.

"Of course," he said, stepping away. "I am the luckiest man in the world," he announced to no one in particular.

After an hour spent finishing off the spread, we sat down. The children were far down the shore, their foreheads furrowed, faces close to the ground, amassing, it seemed, shiny, valuable objects. The beach stretched out from the table. Portonovo sat nestled into a mountain that was clothed in fir trees at its peak, and descended into simple gray stone on its way to the clear, azure sea. The coast itself was a vast assortment of pebbles, sanded bright white over time.

"This could be the most beautiful place I've ever been," Stephany said.

"You see!" Andrea said. He had recently begun to take English lessons. "The best wonderful things only with me! Even if you hate me!"

"How could I hate you, Andrea?" Stephany said.

"It is not possible," Andrea said.

The waiter brought us the mussels, smooth and blue-black, steamed with lemon and parsley, with baby tomatoes and wild fennel, gathered a few hours ago, a few yards away, by squinty-eyed Franco. We ordered a Sartarelli white, the 2002 Verdicchio dei Castelli di Jesi.

We pulled out the mussels' orange bodies with small forks and popped them in our mouths, frenzied, immediately addicted, uncharacteristically silent. Occasionally a child, or a group of children, would approach, take several mussels, pull the meat out, gulp it down, and saunter off. Sal, his hair sticking out in all directions, cupped my wine glass in both hands and took a tiny sip. Then he emptied his pockets, depositing a pile of blue, pink, and green sea glass on the table.

"Got to get back to work," he said.

Then came a platter of *canocchie,* steamed, like the mussels, with lemon, oil, and parsley. They were crustaceans, orange and white, more primitive than shrimp and almost insectlike in appearance. They tasted only of flesh and ocean. We cracked them open and scraped out the substance. Andrea sucked audibly on a shell.

"*Shhh,*" Christina said.

"Good God, Andrea, keep it down," I said.

"What fun is it to eat quietly?" Andrea asked.

I looked to Paolo and Simone. "You guys grew up with him," I said. "How did you take it? So many years?"

"He was worse when he was young," Paolo said. "He wasn't getting laid. Can you imagine the nervous energy he had?"

"I was maybe getting laid," Andrea protested softly, angling his words away from Christina.

"You didn't get laid until you were at least twenty-eight," I said. "If it weren't for those two kids over there who look exactly like you, I'd guess you were still a virgin."

"Not true!" Andrea screeched. "Women love me."

Simone rolled his eyes.

"How do you do it, Simone?" I asked. "How do you live near this guy?"

"The ice cream keeps me sane," Simone said. "I take breaks."

Then came broiled razor clams, long silver and black jewels, sprinkled with bread crumbs. We ordered more Sartarelli, a Verdicchio Superiore "Tralivio" 2001.

"You wouldn't care to try something else?" asked the waiter. We all shook our heads.

"You really can't drink anything but Sartarelli here," Paolo said, looking at his glass, which held a clear, pastel yellow liquid.

Paolo was correct. For some reason—simplicity, sweetness, geographical closeness—Sartarelli wines were the only thing that seemed right.

Like the region's seafood culture, its wine culture had long been undiscovered. Sartarelli wines were made only from the indigenous Verdicchio grape, grown inland in nearby vineyards. The varietal had been considered an irrelevant, low-quality drink, relegated to cheesy fish-shaped bottles. The story of its rise to international success was the story of many country wines, otherwise known as *vini di campagna*.

Ninety percent of the wine made in Italy is country wine—simple, nondescript alcoholic grape-juice-in-a-jug that is either purchased by city dwellers twice a year or made by and drunk by farmers. Italians are, in many ways, economically and ideologically attached to their country wine. For city people, country wine offers the communist dream: mediocre stuff at low prices for everyone. And if you want to mix your Sangiovese with a little fizzy water just to get a taste to complement your pasta, it works perfectly. For country people, it's pure tradition. If their fathers made wine from the grapes that grow on the land, they want to make wine, too. Moreover, their physical and emotional connection with the drink renders them unable to discern its quality. Maybe an average person will be struck down with a splitting headache from Uncle Renato's wine, but Uncle Renato is convinced that the sour, slightly bubbly mixture is ambrosia—ambrosia that he made by hand with his family's ancient fruit. On the whole, this is the attitude that allows Italians from all walks of life to casually throw together a seven-course meal and drink their wine out of regular glasses: it's all in a day's work, nothing exceptional here.

Or at least that's the way it had always been. Recently, vintners who provided wine for themselves and the trattoria in their two-hundred-person village have set their sights on America. While the wines are cheap and plentiful, their biggest obstacle remains that they present an intimidating amount of diversity to Americans who are confused when they regard a shelf full of foreign, unpronounceable names: Lacrima di Morro d'Alba, Cirò, Lagrein, Falanghina. If not well made and correctly and aggressively marketed, these wines blend together into a forgettable blur. Sartarelli is an example of a producer who successfully made the trip across the Atlantic.

Verdicchio grapes have long thrived in the Castelli di Jesi and Matelica appellations of Le Marche. The Etruscans, Greeks, and Romans made wines from them. As Verdicchio grew more regionally beloved in the 1950s, many lazy winemakers dismissed quality and went for quantity. In an unwise publicity ploy, they began churning out thick fish-shaped bottles full of the stuff; as with the cursed Chianti flask, the idea backfired. The fish was easily distinguishable, all right, and just as easily interpreted as code for "crap."

In the early 1970s, the Sartarelli family, based in the village of Poggio San Marcello, were grape-sellers who had collaborated for years with a popular *cantina sociale,* where people filled up their jugs. In the middle of the decade, the family decided to try bottling its wine. Verdicchio was a difficult grape to control: it developed in close clusters, required an abundance of air, grew moldy in humidity. For almost a decade, the Sartarellis tinkered with their methods, selling only loose liquid to locals. Then, in 1980, they managed their first bottling.

The wine was good and word of mouth spread. Restaurants in Le Marche placed orders. By 1990, the *cantina* was sending out ten thousand bottles a year. That was when a baker named Patrizio Chiacchierini entered the picture. He was the conservative, gray-haired husband of the heiress apparent, Donatella Sartarelli, a robust, glossy-lipped bottle blonde. Patrizio had been helping his father-in-law in the cellar for years, but he decided it was time to focus less on bread and more on wine. He gave up his bakery, took to the vineyards, and, with his wife, expanded their land. Patrizio wanted the vines handled artisanally. He suggested, moreover, that they employ sophisticated pruning techniques, that they implement green harvesting, that they expertly manicure the vines and continually retaste the wines. He proposed a new aesthetic with which they could break away from the grape's embarrassing fish-bottle past: a tall, thin, dark green bottle with a white label bearing only the family name.

"We put 'Verdicchio' on the back so that we didn't scare people," Patrizio once told me. "When we took it to tastings we would just tell people, 'This is a Sartarelli white.'"

With Patrizio and Donatella at the helm, the estate acquired sixty hectares. They developed three types of Verdicchio: their simple "Classico"; their single-vineyard, highly structured "Tralivio"; and their single-vineyard, late-harvest, long-aged "Balciana." They cultivated their grapes in order to acquire the French-style "noble rot"—a mold that allowed them to make sweeter, lighter wines. They extended their reach past Le Marche and into the other areas of the country. The highly acclaimed Italian wine guidebook *Gambero Rosso* took note. In 1994, the family attended Vinitaly, and by 1995 they had opened the American market. Soon they were in Germany, Norway, Japan. They were pumping out bottles—300,000 a year—but they wanted to go bigger. Agents were pressuring them for tons more wine, so they were scooping up more land, hoping to hit 700,000 bottles—or 690,000 more than what once seemed beyond reasonable. They had risen nearly in tandem with the area's new seafood cuisine, and perhaps because of this they had become inextricably linked with it, undeniably complementary.

This achievement was never more evident to me than when I watched Andrea eating his razor clams with a glass of Verdicchio. He was displaying two of his most distinctive qualities: insatiability and unexpected modesty. When it came to wine, Andrea was a secret expert with an imposing palate, but he never said a thing about it. Since he was a middleman, he thought it would be out of place for him to comment on wines, and he lacked all pretense when smelling and tasting them. He was quiet only, it seemed, when he drank wine. He had plunged his big nose into the glass and was contentedly sniffing. He had also managed to eat at least one-third of all the mussels, and only good manners had stopped him from consuming the rest. It was a combination, perhaps, of his metabolism, his energy level, and the amount of sheer physical activity in which he engaged, but he had a phenomenal ability to eat. Also, I sometimes thought he just wanted to show off.

"Does anyone want the rest?" he asked as he scoured our plates, hitting each one with his fork and polishing off all leftovers. I thought of his splendid pink and yellow manor and his worldwide business as I watched him, giggling, steal Stephany's potato chips while she was speaking to Paolo.

As I observed my friend consuming the better part of an aquatic ecosystem, I saw a local beekeeper approach him. Andrea was, to farmers, a sort of hero; they knew him by sight even if he didn't know them, and they all wanted him to carry their merchandise. Andrea was the man to know if you were in the food business. He was famously committed, knowledgeable, connected, and reliable. Maybe it was due to the inexplicable Nordic aspect of his character, but one reason he had cornered the area wine market was that he arrived at estates bearing a check—a sight so rare that many producers, accustomed to waiting a year to get paid, sank to their knees in shock and gratitude. Now Andrea temporarily abandoned his spread and considered the man seriously, offering feedback on his ideas. His posture straightened and he pushed his plate to the side.

"You need to have realistic market expectations," he said.

"But he's so professional," Stephany said with wonder.

"He may be literally unbalanced," I said.

Andrea turned at an angle so that the beekeeper couldn't see and blew me a kiss.

"We'll need to come up with new concepts on packaging," he continued. "Contemporary consumers go for a different aesthetic."

I remembered Andrea's niece telling me that before he married, he lived at home. Every morning, he woke up at five to jog, returned at six, and blared salsa music for an hour. For her entire childhood, the niece never got a good night's sleep.

"For this, I am so happy," she said sardonically.

Andrea accepted the beekeeper's business card and shook his hand.

We were presented with *spaccasassi* mixed with poached seaweed, olive oil, and white vinegar. There were shining sardines, sliced opened and salted; chilled raw scampi with translucent skin; small, fried fish over thin-sliced zucchini; two types of sea snails, *crocette* and *bombi*, both cooked in a concentrated paste of tomato mixed with strong fennel and *peperoncino*. We sucked out the *crocette*, and picked out the *bombi* with toothpicks. There was more Sartarelli, this time the 2000 vintage of "Tralivio"—a bold, muscular expression.

Marina herself arrived at around three o'clock, bearing a scratched steel pot full of tagliolini pasta and scampi and a bowl of spaghetti and mussels. At four, we managed to make our way through gnocchi dumplings, calamari, and a lush risotto containing many different morsels that Franco had discovered.

For some time, Andrea's boys flanked him, eating. They were all arms and legs and they considered him their personal idol. When they took off, he stroked his wife's arm.

"Andrea, that's enough," Christina said tenderly.

"You love her more than she loves you," I whispered.

"That's not true!" he said. "She loves me madly."

"Who loves who more?" I asked Simone.

"Actually," Simone said thoughtfully, "I think she loves him more because she puts up with him."

"Then again," Andrea said, "maybe I do love her more. Do you remember that trip to the Caribbean? She wanted two rooms but there was only one available, so she slept in the bed with the children and made me sleep outside on the porch."

"Andrea, there wasn't space," Christina said.

"I woke up every day at dawn and rode my bicycle around the island with Giorgio in the basket because he didn't like to sleep," said Andrea.

"You did return one morning covered in blood," reflected Christina.

"The bicycle fell over," he said. "I had to catch Giorgio. I couldn't really break my fall."

"That's the definition of a father," Paolo said.

"I'd say we love each other equally," Christina said. She ate a gnocco and patted her mouth with her napkin.

"Do you want the rest of that?" Andrea asked. She pushed her plate toward him and he cleaned it in one minute flat. Then he took out his camera and tried to take glamorous photographs as Christina covered her face.

"Cheese!" he shouted. After his wife rebuffed him, he summoned his sons and Sal.

"Supermodel!" he called out. "Villain! Monkey!" The children assumed their poses quickly.

At five o'clock, Marina delivered *rombo al forno*, a turbot roasted in a foil-covered deep pan with olive oil, white wine, and sea salt; it was white and moist, and it had taken in the oil. We ate it with mounds of crispy fried artichokes on the side and several bottles of the Sartarelli Verdicchio "Balciana" 1999.

"I don't know if I can do any more," Stephany said. Lili was slung over one of her shoulders, fast asleep.

"*Basta?*" my father said pleadingly. *Basta*—"That's enough"— is usually a declaration, but my father phrased it as a question. He may have lived in the States for many decades, but he still knew that a woman like Marina wasn't interested in moderation.

Indeed, Marina was deaf to the cries for mercy. She had one last fish dish, a *coda di rospo in puttacchio*—monkfish cooked in

olive oil with garlic, tomatoes, and branches of fragrant rosemary, and caramelized over a burner.

"Maybe just a little taste," Stephany said when she saw it.

Six hours after we'd begun, we were granted a reprieve. Marina, in a show of benevolence, came by with plates of *colomba,* a
fluffy dove-shaped cake topped with hardened dark chocolate,
and cups of espresso *sorbetto,* strong and frothy.

Lili needed to go home, it was clear, so I joined Sal on the
beach. Before we left, he took me on a short tour of his findings:
a certain rock that housed a small guppy pool, an area rich in
shiny pebbles, a fish skeleton, a crab shell.

"Impressive, Sali," I said. He hooked his hand in mine and we
returned to the table to say our good-byes. There were a few
knocked-out kids slumped on the benches, and all my friends
finishing up with slices of fresh pineapple.

"I will see you very soon," Andrea said as we hugged.

"No you won't," I said.

"Oh, yes I will," he said forebodingly. "Just you wait."

We drove off the sandy drive, past weather-worn wooden
fences, out onto a narrow main road, around the hills—jungle-
thick with plants—and up to our hotel. Called, appropriately,
Hotel Bellissima, it was a rose-colored building on the top of the
small mountain. The owner's young daughter and corpulent
mother were watching TV in the marbled lobby, sprawled contentedly on the couch together, while the skinny owner and his
spikey-haired wife raced back and forth between the dining
room and the front desk. They handed us our keys and we
walked to our room, a tile-floored double with a wall of windows.

"Sergio, I think I can see where we just were," Stephany said,
after putting Lili in her crib. Sal was organizing his treasures on
the floor.

We wandered out onto the terrace—wide and planted with
yellow flowers—and peered over the forest that stretched down.

Dusk had begun and the violet sky was filled with shocks of fluorescent pink.

"Is it there?" she asked, pointing. Far down, past the hotel's gardens and the circling streets, where the green of the mountain stopped and the blue of the sea began, the land curved slightly, just enough to create the rocky little inlet where Emilia had built her shack.

Chapter 12

NAPLES

━━━━━━━━━◦⟨⟩◦━━━━━━━━━

AFTER ALL THOSE YEARS as the children of *signori,* dreaming of their abandoned cliff-top home, their grandfather's seized antiques, the shiny valuables taken in pawn by the government, the Tschantrets had graciously admitted defeat. They were now entrenched in Barra, having purchased apartments in different corners of the projects. And Barra itself, I noticed as we drove down its plain streets, was neither the colorful, bustling neighborhood of my childhood nor the drug-addled, trash-strewn wasteland I remembered from my subsequent visits.

But the maze of buildings looked the same: that mass of communist structures, architecturally irrelevant rectangles with green shutters and balconies strewn with drying clothes, all connected by small, identical one-way streets crowded with dingy parked cars. I noticed that in the better building clusters, a bored and unarmed young man dressed in navy sat in a little guardhouse; there were also more plants and trees, and every single window boasted an unwieldy white satellite dish. Open areas were filled with dark-haired teenagers pressed together, deep in conversation or trying to insert their whole bodies into each other's mouths. They promoted a universal style: baggy blue jeans, elaborate belts, tight T-shirts covered with English slogans—*Rich Princess; Unmarried and Happy*—and shiny white sneakers. The boys had aggressively manipulated their hair, gelled it into inch-high spikes rising from their pimply fore-heads, while the girls had chosen to spend their precurfew time applying gobs of black liquid eyeliner.

I saw, superimposed on the scene, my long-ago teenage cousins pushed up against the same buildings, standing on the same gum-sticky pavement, making out just as fervently, but outfitted in their makeshift 1970s wear, long hair combed and parted, or rising up in an Italian Afro. And I saw myself down the street, grabbing the hand of my mother and carrying toward our building the loads of fish and vegetables we'd bought at the winding street market.

We rolled up to a bunch of buildings labeled SECTION E and rang the bell marked "Tschantret." Margherita, my childhood partner in crime, answered the door. Now thirty-six years old, and poured into a sheer turquoise shirt and long flouncy skirt, she had blond hair, cropped short, and blue eyes, lined with cobalt pencil. She tried to embrace my entire family but managed to fit only my parents and Sal in her arms. Then Margherita passed them behind her to her waiting sisters and greeted me. She was my first best friend—really, the only close female friend I've ever had—and she always cried when she saw me.

"How I've missed you!" she said, and threw her entire body on mine. "Why don't you come back and live here with us?"

Stephany stood in the hallway in her new yellow patent leather pumps, holding Lili and smiling widely to conceal her nervousness. She tended to be shy in new situations, and she'd never met this part of the family, so different from her own re-served Alaskan parents who greeted people with a firm hand-shake. And then, within twenty seconds, she was all but lifted up by three of my female relatives, deposited on a couch, and fawned over so forcefully, in a mixture of broken English and Italian, that when I looked back a moment later, I saw my wife, her hands intertwined with my cousin Cinzia's, engaged in a highly enthusiastic and personal conversation as my cousin Daniela cradled Lili. This was not a place that suffered the timid.

After the initial greetings, we walked across the parking lot, over the narrow asphalt divider, around the building, and up four flights to the apartment of Zio Oscar and Zia Maria Tarallo—the two-bedroom, one-bathroom place that housed Oscar; Maria; cousins Daniela and Sandra, thirty-one and thirty-three years old, respectively; and, while their house was being renovated, Cousin Gino; his wife, Luisa; and their towheaded baby, Anna. The home was relatively spacious, if you considered that Zio Oscar and Zia Maria had raised seven children there.

"Yes, sometimes I would prefer some more privacy," I heard Daniela say to Stephany, who was looking at the bed that Daniela slept on, which pulled out from under the bed Sandra slept in and occupied entirely the tiny family computer room. "*È così.*" She shrugged.

My relatives came in droves. There was, of course, Daniela, with her mass of brown curls, her large green eyes behind glasses, her cupid lips. There was Sandra, petite and smart, a law student and part-time journalist who attended church three times a week. There was Zia Maria Tarallo, age sixty-four, in her stockings and floral dress, concocting an eight-course feast in her cramped kitchen, and there was gray-haired Zio Oscar, the once-temperamental boss of the house, now struck down by a heart attack, nearly deaf. There were portly Gino and Luisa; powerful Margherita; her mild, bearded dentist husband, Claudio; her two girls—dark, forceful, eleven-year-old Maria and the perpetually grinning nine-year-old Valeria, who had adopted Sal as a sort of living doll and had already dressed him in a red knit cap and scarf. There was Tonia, a mother of three, her brown hair in a bob, and there was Stephany's newest obsession: my cousin Cinzia, the most Neapolitan of the bunch—overtly sexual, with thick eyebrows, green eyes, and the habit of saying whatever she wanted, whenever she wanted, however inappropriate. She was wearing skintight white jeans and had both of her hands on Stephany's knees as she leaned in close, her cleavage immediately visible in her low-cut shirt, mumbling all sorts of family secrets. Cousin Anna and her husband, Arturo, two portly math teachers, had arrived bearing homemade *taralli*, dense pretzels with fennel seeds. There was Zio Boris, with his fedora and boxer's nose, leaning on his cane and fishing a blue and gold bracelet out of his pocket. And there was Zia Liliana, the perpetually elegant, multilingual matriarch, sitting erect even on the couch, dressed in a purple wrap dress, her hair, still fiery red, piled in that same beehive, with the same ringlets framing her face.

The air, smelling of fish and tomatoes and cooking steam and cigarette smoke, was freshened by a cool breeze coming through the balcony window. My mother had gravitated to the kitchen. This was the kitchen she'd cooked in many times in her life, a tiny room she'd sat in every day until October 24, 1974. This was where she'd canoodled with my father when she was sixteen years old, a place where they'd come to dance with their friends and drink sweet liquor.

"But I wasn't allowed to talk to him for the first year," she once told me. "My older sister was my chaperone, and she was a hawk."

My mother and Zia Maria spoke fast Neapolitan, barely pausing for breath, as they chopped tomatoes, washed squid, stirred the contents of pots and pans. For perhaps the first time in twenty-five years, when my father walked through without his sweater on, my mother didn't seem to notice.

The table was crammed with chairs and overflowing with Falanghina and Aglianico wines brought from the countryside and siphoned into empty San Pellegrino bottles, and with pitchers of water, plastic cups, paper plates, and the best silverware, newly polished. Zia Maria beckoned us to the table and she, my mother, Daniela, and Sandra began serving us your average

Neapolitan Sunday lunch. We would finish when the sky went dark.

First, antipasti, arranged on long white platters, to be passed around: chunks of *caciocavallo*, a soft, tart cheese; hard, salty ricotta salata, white and crumbling; small, fatty *salamini*, sausage links; *scamorza*, smoked mozzarella, brown and leathery on the outside and burnt yellow inside; pink slices of mortadella; heaps of headcheese, that grand jellied sausage incorporating pieces of skin from the pig's head; *prosciutto cotto*, prosciutto made of cooked ham; big green olives marinated in brine; greasy silver anchovies lined up in obedient rows; *melanzane sott'olio*, slabs of skinned eggplant topped with bright *peperoncino* flakes and garlic, set for a month under oil, eaten on a slice of bread; and *giardiniera*, a jumble of carrots, cauliflower, and celery pickled in white wine vinegar.

"How is he at work?" Margherita was asking Stephany from her left side. "Is he tough but generous? Do they love him or hate him?"

"Margherita has girls who work for her, too," Sandra was saying to Stephany from her right side. Sandra was practicing her English. Margherita ran a small publicity company.

"Well, what kind of boss is Margherita?" Stephany asked.

"She is—how you say?—always talking, talking, talking," said Sandra.

Second came perhaps the most classic regional pasta dish of all time, which was called, ironically, *paccheri di Pasta Gragnano alla genovese*. *Pasta alla genovese* evolved, like many great dishes, from poverty—the poverty of Genovese immigrant merchants who sold their wares in the bustling ports of eighteenth-century Naples. The Genovese could afford onions and pasta, and scraps of fatty beef that the butcher would give to them practically for free. They diced masses of onions, sautéed them, added the meat, a few tomatoes, and some herbs, and cooked it all for six hours, until the bits of meat disappeared into the mix. At the end of the process, al dente pasta was swirled in. The result was what we were eating today—a sweet, beefy stew, with large tubular pasta, a food that defined *scarpetta*. *Scarpetta* is a single word that means: "That dish I just ate was so tasty that I must wipe the plate clean with my bread in order to consume every bit of juice." It's the ultimate compliment to an Italian cook.

"I'm watching my form," Margherita said. "I don't want any." She patted the tops of her thighs and moaned.

"Me, too," Daniela said.

"Absolutely ridiculous," my mother and Zia Maria admonished, and Daniela and Margherita finished everything that was served to them.

"I'll take a second helping," said Gino, who must have been close to three hundred pounds.

"You have a very excellent figure," Daniela said to Stephany. "How?" The women at the table looked at her expectantly.

My mother had taken over the fish portion of the meal, and had battered and fried up first a fritto misto of baby artichokes and zucchini blossoms. Then there was *triglia fritta,* fried red mullet, along with fried calamari; pinky-finger-sized bait fish that you ate whole, head and spine included; and baby sole, flat and white. We even ate the bits of plain crispy dough left on the platter, and managed to get most of the meat off the bones of the sole.

"For you," Zio Boris said, passing me the bracelet he'd taken from his pocket earlier. He always gave me jewelry when I visited. If I didn't warn him that I was coming, he took the watch off his wrist and pressed it into my hand.

"Zio, thank you," I said, "but I can accept this only if you eat lunch with me at the proper time one day before I go."

Zio Boris shook his head. He ate his breakfast of three butter cookies at four in the morning and he ate his lunch at ten in the morning.

"But we could all eat together, you, me, my family, and Zia Liliana," I said.

"No can do," he said. "Why don't you all come at ten? Or we'll have dinner."

Zia Liliana didn't pay attention to the argument. She had been cooking her brother a morning lunch ever since his wife died two years earlier and she wasn't going to complain. At eighty, she woke, went to the market, returned home with pasta, vegetables, and fish, and prepared his meal. She ate her pastry, drank her cappuccino, and waited for his arrival, at which point she served him, sat with him, talked with him, said good-bye to him, packed up the remainder of food, and put it away, and then reheated it for herself in the afternoon.

"Doesn't it drive you crazy, Zia?" I said. "Cooking for a madman so early?"

"He's got to eat," she said nonchalantly. "If his body needs lunch at ten, his body needs lunch at ten." He was still her little brother. "So I make lunch at ten. *È così.*"

Zio Boris, his cane balanced on the back of his chair, nodded. "I must be fed at ten, and that's that," he said.

Zia Maria emerged from the kitchen bearing *salsiccia e friarelli,* the midday meal of workers throughout the south: sweet, fatty sausage grilled with bitter greens and garlic in a pan and pressed, oily and dripping, onto a slice of bread. Behind her, Daniela bore our side dishes: *crocchette di patate,* croquettes of mashed potatoes mixed with mozzarella and chunks of prosciutto; and carrots and cauliflower, served side by side, each boiled, blanched, and covered in olive oil, white wine vinegar, and loads of red pepper flakes.

We had *filetto di bufala alla pizzaiola,* fillets from the gentle *bufala* (water buffalo cow): a dark, lean meat, cut into medallions and covered in a sauce of fresh tomatoes, garlic chunks, and oregano. We paired it with *parmigiana di melanzane,* quickly fried eggplant topped with mozzarella and *parmigiano-reggiano; peperoni gratinati*—skinned red and yellow peppers burnt over an open fire, stripped of their charred skin, sautéed with garlic, black olives, and capers, and finally mixed with bread crumbs; and *ragù alla cocuzella di Napoli*, small zucchini cooked in a broth with onions, white wine, and mint and other herbs.

"Zi'," Cinzia shouted to my dad across the table, "still getting it up?"

My father turned to look behind him, hoping to find another *zio*.

"Yeah, you," said Cinzia. "I hope so, because you grabbed yourself a real woman and you had better keep her satisfied."

"Oh, don't worry, *cara*, he's up to the task," my mother said. "Always has been, this one."

My father looked like he might be briefly missing Tucson. Cinzia lit a long, thin cigarette and took a drag.

"So how is law school?" my father asked Sandra. "Are you enjoying it? When do you plan to graduate?"

After cigarettes had been smoked, dessert was delivered to the table. There was *budino di limone,* a light vanilla cake topped with lemon pudding and shaved bits of lemon peel, and *babà,* an airy pastry soaked in a mixture of sugar, water, and rum until it becomes heavy and deeply sweet. We ate *zeppole di San Giuseppe*—little sweet dough morsels fried and topped with vanilla cream and grape preserves—and slices of *cassata napoletana,* a layered tart filled with fresh ricotta and candied fruits.

Finally, we retired to the couches with our liqueurs—my aunt's homemade limoncello, *liquore al caffè,* and the inimitable, indescribable, and really weird Strega, the fluorescent-yellow liquid made in a nearby town and packaged in a two-foot-high bottle.

Margherita cradled Liliana. "Sergio, you chose such Neapolitan names for your kids," she said as we watched Valeria comb Sal's hair. "Why?"

In fact, Salvatore and Liliana were so named not only because of my aunt and my brother, but also because those names were some of the most classic southern Italian names available.

"He wants them to remember where they're from," Stephany said.

"That's right," said Zio Boris, rubbing my arm. "You don't run from our history, not like so many people. We have nothing to be ashamed of." He sang a note from Pino Daniele's classic song "Napule è": *"Napule è tutto 'nu suonno e 'a sape tutti o' munno ma nun sanno a veritá!"* Naples is just a dream, and the whole world knows it, but they don't know the truth.

Chapter 13

THE TWO SICILIES

❧❧❧

THE NEXT DAY at the crack of dawn I slipped through Margherita's apartment, down the marble steps, and out into the wide parking lot, where the security guard was fast asleep at his desk. I was going to be spending the next four days on a trip arranged for me by a man named Teodoro Nadei. Teodoro, considered by wine people as "the man to know in the south," had, at my request, arranged a series of appointments through the regions of Puglia, Basilicata, Calabria, and Campania. I had wanted to see the newest developments in the area.

For years, the south had been largely overlooked by journalists and wine enthusiasts. Bulk wine accounted for half of Italy's total wine production, and the south churned out about 60 percent of that bulk wine, but after the southern farmers had grown, pressed, and aged their grapes, they shipped them off to Piedmont, Tuscany, and France, where the wine was mixed in with other wine, bottled, and sold under other names. Recently, however, I had noticed some changes taking place in the south: more up-and-comers, more farmers bottling wine made from their own fruit, more hope, and, along with it, more mistakes. I was curious to see firsthand what was happening down at the tip of the boot.

My tour included small, two-person operations and enormous companies. I met up with Piero Mastroberardino, the current head of the two-hundred-year-old Mastroberardino winery, at his industrial operation off a main stretch of asphalt in Atripalda. In Avellino, I passed through the shiny new cellars of Feudi di San Gregorio, the hi-tech, impeccably maintained estate supported by the owners of the Banca di Roma. A few miles inland from Salerno, I tasted cult wines at the Montevetrano estate, where a photographer named Silvia Imparato and her friend, the consulting enologist Riccardo Cotarella, had released their blend of Cabernet, Merlot, and Aglianico in 1991 and watched as their previously unheard-of estate was dubbed Italy's Château Lafite. In Castel Campagnano, I sampled lush, velvety wines made with the ancient Casavecchia grape, which had been rediscovered in a defunct vineyard by a mustachioed attorney named Peppe Mancini. In Melfi, I toured cellars built into the foot of Mount Vulture by an introverted prince who was both a licensed architect and a winemaker. I visited at least a dozen other estates. There were dignified, world-traveled producers in designer wear, who welcomed me into their mansions, and there were businesspeople dedicated to grasping the art of contemporary winemaking. There was one 15-person family in a 120-person village in the Calabrian hills that gathered around me as though I were a member of another species entirely. The men were all dressed in nylon suits and the women in housedresses or tight miniskirts, depending on their generation. They huddled together to peer at me, whispered among themselves, loaded me up with wine, handed me a homemade brochure printed on lightweight paper, and sent me on my way. I imagine they didn't get many visitors.

By the end of the many dealings, I was exhausted, a little bloated, and anxious to get back to Barra. But on my way, I wanted to meet up with the man who'd set everything up for me: Teodoro Nadei. I grabbed my cell phone, pulled his business card from my wallet, and gazed at the image beneath the script announcing his name and profession. Behold, the magic of Photoshop: there was

Teodoro, his thin, dark hair pulled into a sad little ponytail, emerging bare-chested from a barrel and holding out a bunch of grapes.

"Would you like to have dinner?" I asked, desperately pushing the image out of my mind. "You choose the place. I'm coming back through."

"I know just the restaurant," he said. "Meet me tonight at eight-thirty."

"I'll be there," I said. "And I'm programming your number into my phone so I never have to look at this picture of you again."

"I assume you have the wine barrel one, then," he said. "I have one in which I'm literally an egg. I should have given you that one."

❧

I MET TEODORO where he met everyone: the Novotel parking lot on a commercial stretch just off the A1. He was always punctual, and his ponytail was always pulled back tight, highlighting a chubby, bespectacled face that was generally arranged in a pleasant expression. He had planned our dinner at a restaurant in his neighborhood in the small, ancient city called Capua, most famous for its gladiator-training amphitheater and for its position as the starting point of the slave Spartacus's revolt against the empire. Despite the fact that he lived in Capua, Teodoro had no intention of taking two cars. This was classically Italian. We would drive fifteen minutes down the highway together in my car in order to arrive at a place approximately two blocks away from his house, and then after dinner we would drive fifteen minutes back to deposit him in the Novotel parking lot, where he would pick up his car in order to drive fifteen minutes down the highway again to his house. To an Italian, it was not wasted time—it was more time in the company of a friend.

And so we did. Teodoro plunked himself down in my car, lit up a cigarette, and directed me back onto the Autostrada. We exited onto a long, gloomy street lit sporadically by tall lamps and drove past some forlorn farmland at dusk, past garbage bags piled against walls and topped by hungry cats, and into a cobblestone-paved town. There, tucked into a shopping center, the only bright spot in the black mass of buildings, was a small trattoria, empty but for one short, exceptionally fat man by the door. His name was Antonio and he was the owner. He kissed Teodoro on both cheeks.

"Well?" he said, motioning toward his ample midsection. "What do you think?" He shuffled a bit and managed a full turn.

"You look fantastic," Teodoro said. He turned to me. "Antonio lost over one hundred pounds this year," he said.

It was difficult to imagine Antonio—or any human, for that matter—surviving at one hundred pounds over his current weight, so I was as impressed that he had done so as I was that he had lost the weight. I offered him hearty congratulations and he offered us *spumante* and our choice of any of the tables.

A restaurant that is well set up but lacking in clients is a red flag in the United States. If you're walking through a deserted area on the north side of Boston and see, say, a sparkling red-upholstered bistro with all its lights on and nobody eating, you're smart to keep on walking. But in Italy, a shortage of clients doesn't really reflect on the quality of the food. I'd done it many times: asked a local for a good place and arrived to find a fifteen-table establishment, with violet tablecloths, enormous bouquets of fake lilacs, mauve fabric-covered seats, and the owners' collection of blues paraphernalia tacked over every inch of the wall. Initially I'd been wary, but in every case I'd enjoyed an amazing meal prepared by a passionate, kooky individual who had managed to keep his own historical food society alive because he loved what he did, not because he hoped to make money. Lots of people, like Antonio, had fallen on hard times—Capua had recently been hit by an outbreak of Mafia warfare, which was never great for business. Others had never done enough market research to figure out if they'd have customers at all, and they usually didn't seem to care—like the couple in Chianti whose two-diners-on-a-Saturday-night osteria ran a movie-screen-sized slide show of their life together throughout dinner. The point was that now, when I saw a place like Antonio's, I knew I was sure to be lavished with attention and served all of the chef's specialties. The *spumante*, as always, prepared my stomach for what was to come.

Antonio called out to his son, who had been milling around with some other young guys in the kitchen, and together they decided what we would be eating tonight. As they conferred, Teodoro and I dipped bread from the basket into strong, spicy olive oil. I wanted to talk to Teodoro because he was all-knowing when it came to the area. He was born and raised there, and he had never strayed.

Teodoro was the youngest son of a teacher and a housewife, and he had grown up next to Naples's famous Teatro di San Carlo. To appease his father, he'd studied medicine at the University of Naples, and then, in a move that did just the opposite of appeasing his father, he'd gone on to make a lot of money selling photocopiers for the local 3M Italia company. But it was the weekends Teodoro always looked forward to. That was when he pursued his collecting hobby, touring Italy, fresh *mozzarella di bufala* balanced on his passenger seat, and knocking on winemakers' doors.

"I dangled it in front of their faces because I knew they wanted it," he said. He toured the country, up to the Swiss border and back down. He met Mascarello, Gravner, Soldera—all the greats. When he knocked, unannounced, at a producer's door, professed his devotion, and offered up the cheese, even the steeliest reserves melted. Teodoro, with his humble charm and earnest wine obsession, was admitted everywhere, allowed into cellars, poured samples. He talked to the winemakers, questioned them, bought from them, and amassed a personal collection that nearly put him in debt. "My motto is, 'Mozzarella opens doors,'" he liked to say.

After Teodoro left 3M in the late 1980s, he turned his weekend pastime into a real job, using the American marketing and sales skills he'd acquired to land a job as a representative for the Tuscan powerhouse winery Antinori. He covered the entire south, selling to restaurants and wineshops. Soon after, he was selling for Villa Matilda, northern Campania's leading winery, and Regaleali, Sicily's leading winery.

By 1996, Teodoro had picked up the accounts of Mastroberardino and the Venetian winery Santa Margherita, and was thus responsible for some of the strongest brands in all of Italy. Around that time, the acclaimed journalist Luigi Veronelli, hearing about the south's rise, made a trip down from Bergamo and asked Teodoro to show him the ropes. Teodoro did so, traveling for a week with Veronelli in his passenger seat. When the trip was done, Veronelli bestowed upon Teodoro the title of "Campania Correspondent," and that was what Teodoro remained, officially and unofficially.

Antonio delivered platters of antipasto. There were folds of prosciutto; a tomato bruschetta with roasted mortadella; a large white scallop shell filled with sliced *seppie,* raw scallions, crunchy peppers, *rucola,* and radicchio; two balls of milky *mozzarella di bufala,* breaded, fried, and topped with tomato sauce and soft ricotta; and deep, fatty slabs of wild boar sausage. Teodoro plucked a piece of sausage with his fingers and popped it in his mouth.

"So, how did it go this week?" he asked.

"Everyone is looking for the next new thing," I said. "They're going so modern, so new."

"Everyone thinks *he's* the next new thing," Teodoro said.

"I guess I was most surprised that Mastroberardino is making the best wines around again," I said. "I feel like they circled back, but they'll never admit it."

"They have always aged extraordinarily," Piero Mastroberardino had said to me from behind his large wooden desk when I'd mentioned how much better the wines were then compared to those made ten years earlier. He had to have been aware that his wines, once made for a king, had taken a turn for the worse in the 1980s, when an internal dispute distracted the family members. And he had to know that now that the company had begun to concentrate on making wines with an eye on history, they'd reclaimed their excellence. But he was in constant public-relations mode.

"To be honest with you," I said to Teodoro, "it's all a little confusing. Everyone I met is really sold on this idea that they have to make ultramodern wines or they'll never sell their stuff."

"The scourge of consulting enologists," Teodoro muttered. He ate a fried mozzarella ball. "Antonio, let's have a bottle of Alois Pallagrello Bianco."

"It's like a gold rush out here," I said. Ever since the wild success of Casavecchia and Montevetrano, farmers had been more intent on making wine, each convinced that he could be a grand success. This was good because it meant that previously marginalized people were taking the initiative, and bad because they usually had no idea what they were doing. Consulting enologists, their ears pricking up at the rustle of new business, came along to help the inexperienced but gung-ho masses, offering their services, pushing products, promising big returns. Like most naive people who are aching to start businesses, the farmers were gullible, which accounted for a lot. Most enologists don't benefit much from encouraging people to concentrate on raising good grapes; it's easier and more profitable to sell yeasts and machines, to introduce first-time producers to newfangled devices that change their wine in drastic ways, to pound in the idea that only international-style modern wines—full of chemicals, processed to death, supersweet—sell around the world.

"I've never seen a place get more muddled up by new techniques," Teodoro said, shaking his head. He was the one tasting 500 new wines a year now, and he was the one spitting out 350 with a grimace on his face. "If they would just try to make a simple wine!" He curled his fist and took a sip of the lush Pallagrello. "I had a professor who once said, 'Shoot first and then go get your catch.' A lot of these guys buy land, build a winery, plant vineyards, hire this smooth-operator enologist, bottle their wine, pay a graphic designer to make a beautiful label, stick it on the bottle, and then sit down. They look at their bottles and say, '*E adesso, che cazzo faccio?*'" Now, what the dick do I do?

Teodoro sighed. "I think they were under the impression that someone magical would just appear and buy the wine," he said. "Quite simply, they forgot about that whole marketing-and-selling aspect.

"A lot of these guys haven't traveled and have no experience with wine outside of their own," Teodoro continued. "They're convinced that their wine is good, and *basta*. I have tasted wines that were literally vinegar, and the producer was grinning and he said, 'So, how much can I sell it for?' I say to these guys, 'Why do you need to sell it? You want to hurt someone?'"

Antonio came by with plates of thick pappardelle with pheasant *ragù*. Teodoro dove in, childlike in his delight.

"So, how do you think these poor guys will fare in the American market?" he asked, twirling the pappardelle around his fork. "Sink or swim?"

"Call me a conspiracy theorist, but I swear there's some hidden prejudice here," I said between bites. "Everyone's always rooting for the south. I read a dozen or so magazine and newspaper articles a year about its awesome potential. But in their brains, they've filed the south under 'cheap wine.' I invite these same journalists in, give them a great wine, watch their faces light up, and when I tell them the price, they get all grumpy. They say, 'This is too much.' Too much for a *southern* wine is what they mean, because they'll pay three times the amount for a Super Tuscan."

"Unfortunately, good wine costs money to make," Teodoro said. "Yeah, I'd like an Armani suit for two euros, too, but it doesn't work that way."

Antonio proudly presented a silver dish of short ribs in sweet tomato sauce, and *soffritto*, that classic Campanian mixture of savage-tasting pork innards and spicy tomato sauce.

"I want to say, 'Hey, what do you want? Better wines that cost more or the same crappy cheap stuff?'" I got fired up at times like this. Teodoro nodded enthusiastically and continued tearing into the *soffritto* with joy. "'Make up your minds!'"

"It's hard to change a person's mentality," Teodoro said. "The worst part is this, Sergio: Southerners themselves can't even really grasp their own potential. They're so beaten down."

Here was a big part of the barrier the south was facing: a collective anti-southern sentiment. Most Italians unabashedly criticized the southerner, in ways both acceptable—"You're always late"; "You just want to get laid" (both largely true)—and unacceptable—"You're lazy"; "You're thieves"; "You're murderers." It had eroded the collective self-esteem of the region's citizens; they had, as marginalized people do, internalized the message. Whenever a bloody crime committed in Puglia, Naples, or Calabria was splashed across the news, Lazians and Umbrians and Tuscans sighed and pronounced, *"Sono violenti per natura."* They're naturally violent—it's in their DNA.

It was nonsense. There was nothing criminal in our DNA.

But most people, wracked by poverty and undereducated, didn't know that only 150 years earlier, while farmers starved in northern Italy, the south had been its own nation, known as the Two Sicilies, with Naples as its capital. It had risen to become the third-largest world power, after England and France. The Two Sicilies contained renowned theaters, galleries, architectural masterpieces, palaces that rivaled Versailles. There was Pompeii, that city of dust at the foot of Mount Vesuvius. Naples was the center of Italian culture and commerce, its people famous for building ships and guns, for making silk, for their rich public libraries, agricultural equipment factories, technical schools, operas, comedies, central roads, railways, volcanic observatories, international scientific conferences. The south once held almost all of Italy's wealth.

So the contemporary southern situation couldn't well be a result of any innate tendencies—it was, at least initially, about politics. In 1860, Giuseppe Garibaldi, the gray-bearded general from Nice celebrated in piazzas across Italy, sought to unite the country and free it from all foreign rule. He and his revolutionary comrades, under Victor Emmanuel II of Sardinia, headed down south and conquered Sicily and Naples. Soon after the victory, Garibaldi left the region. Mysteriously, banks in the south were wiped out, and within months everything in the area ground to a halt. The once-gleaming trains sat forlornly in their stations, the factories closed their doors, and the people were hungry. Many fled to America, hopping ship and sneaking en masse into the larger cities, where they would take any work they could get.

While the north quickly fashioned itself into a streamlined industrial powerhouse, the south descended into chaos. Local thugs—the Mafia—took power and fostered a new order based on terror. They made themselves known as leaders through bloody fights, and they instituted a cash-for-life system, in which business owners, such as shopkeepers, were charged a flat fee to be allowed to exist. The shopkeepers paid, even when they hadn't made a penny that month, and in exchange they were not beaten to death or shot through the heart. Mafia members managed to become the new police captains and mayors. The situation wasn't ideal for starting new enterprises, for learning new skills, for feeling good about where you came from, or for dreaming up possibilities.

"It comes down to politics and economics," Teodoro mused. "I guess like everything."

I saw Antonio moving toward us. He may have been smack-dab in the middle of Mafia-run Capua, trying to support his family in the gorgeous but besieged region, but he wasn't thinking about any of that right now. He was, instead, smiling widely as he set down a plate of sheep's milk cheese—soft, white, salty young pieces and yellow, tart, crumbly aged pieces. He then shuffled back to the kitchen and returned with Mastroberardino's "Naturalis Historia," liquid proof that Mastroberardino was going back to tradition: the elegant and classic wine was named after Pliny the Elder's most famous work, and was made beautifully and simply, in an attempt to pay homage to the region's past.

Antonio opened the bottle and poured us each a glass. We looked at each other and toasted.

"Well, let's move away from the heavy stuff and enjoy this for a second," Teodoro said.

We decided to quit and concentrate instead on how remarkable it is that the same cheese, aged for different amounts of time, can deliver such different tastes. When we had finished ruminating on the cheese, we moved on to dessert: *torta caprese*—a chocolate and almond pie first made on the island of Capri—and a bottle of sparkling Asprinio Bianco. Then, slightly heavier than when we had entered, we thanked Antonio profusely, got back in my car, and drove our fifteen minutes back to the Novotel parking lot.

As we cut through the night, I considered our situation. Here we were, two wine experts, who could go anywhere and do anything, so devoted to this troubled region. Were we just loyal fools, stuck to our birthplace, unwilling to see the truth?

"I know we said we'd move away from this subject, but I can't help asking: What do you honestly think is the future of the south?" I looked at Teodoro.

He turned to me. "Honestly? In the next six or seven years, I estimate that about thirty-five percent of producers will no longer exist," he said. "We have maybe ten great estates now, right? I think, soon enough, we're going to end up with fifty or sixty spectacular wineries."

I looked out the window to see the hills speeding past, lit by the moon. These hills were famous. Italy was considered by the ancients Greeks to be the land of wine, the near-mythical Enotria. It was the most perfect place on earth for growing grapes—so many varied exposures, so much sunlight, so much air flowing from coast to coast. The ancient Romans had their pick of any wine around, and they picked Falernium, a sweet, dark, highly alcoholic wine made from grapes grown on the slopes of Mount Falernus in Campania. They practically worshipped the wine, paying homage to it in their literature. When, during Naples's boom in the late 1700s, Pompeii was excavated, archaeologists found what seemed to be a part of an ancient bar: marked on the wall were the prices for wine, categorized as "normal," "good," and "excellent." And then there was Falernium, priced three times higher than the most excellent wine.

We may have been on a slick highway, and Mount Falernus may have been surrounded by little brick houses with buzzing dishwashers, but this was the same *terra*—the same geography, the same spot. The history of the south was long, the legacy great. Perhaps at this particular moment, we were emerging from only a comparatively minor rough patch. What had come before us was truly grand, and that was why Teodoro and I kept searching for a sign of it, for things to circle back around. How could we, in good conscience, ignore such a dazzling past?

Chapter 14

THE PRINCE

POSITANO: THE PEARL OF THE AMALFI COAST is tucked like a jewel in the half ring of the mountain's inward curve, a village that seems to be carved entirely from pale, sharp rock—the world's largest and most intricate, shining sculpture. We'd driven on the snaky roads, cut through small, sunny towns, all of the buildings tight together, houses cloaked in ivy, gardens filled with orange and lemon trees. We'd climbed, in the car, past the mossy stone walls, grass pushing through every crack; the church with the peeling blue and gold mural of Jesus and Mary; the overflowing gelato shops and fish restaurants; the cobblestoned main streets lined with shops. We'd looked up at the highest peak, where a wooden cross had been planted before the two-mile straight drop down into the turquoise water. And we'd made it to our last Italian home for the spring, a white stucco hotel, nestled in the midst of the town, its balconies dripping with bougainvillea. I was drinking a Campari and soda, looking at the ocean. Stephany and Liliana were lying on a lounge chair and Sal was occupied with his toy cars. Before me stretched the endless Mediterranean, punctuated by shabby fishing boats and immaculate sailboats. I wouldn't be working anymore, I thought, and we would spend our final week here together. It was about time, after two and a half months of travel. Midway through my contemplation, I felt my phone buzz in my pocket.

"Sergio, you need to come back to Ancona *immediately*," Andrea said. "These guys want us to taste some vintage Malvasia made in the seventies by a crazy prince."

"You're a funny guy," I said. "Would it be foolish of me to ask if you've lost your mind?"

"Don't argue with me about this, Esposito," Andrea said. "This prince was a mad nut! He was a verifiable genius! You should be honored!"

"First of all, a prince? Second of all, vintage Malvasia? Are you a complete moron?"

In addition to the fact that I was now officially on vacation, I was not interested in wines made by unbalanced royals—especially ones so unbalanced that they aged wines made with the famously low-quality Malvasia. Malvasia was known as a *pagadebit*—pay a debt—grape, the fruit you grow to cover the bills. You harvested it, squished it, waited a few months, drank it at the table or sold it to a local and made a little cash. You didn't make Malvasia wines in the 1970s and drink them thirty years later, especially if you didn't have a taste for extra-sour vinegar. Plus, even I had to admit that Italy had not produced very many long-aging whites.

"I remain only fifty percent moron," Andrea said. "I am also fifty percent very important businessman and that half is talking now. I promise, you'll like this stuff. The tasting is in three days, so prepare yourself."

"I'm not working anymore," I said. "I'm with my kids."

"You're coming, kids or no kids," Andrea said. "Tough luck."

"No, I'm not," I said, and hung up.

That night, for the first time in almost three months, I fell into a deep sleep. Eleven hours later, I woke to a chorus of birds. Stephany brought me a cappuccino in bed, and Sal sat next to me as I drank it in our bright room. As I put down my cup, the phone rang.

"Andrea, seriously," I said. "I'm on vacation and I don't want to talk about work."

"Okay, I understand," Andrea said. "Let me just tell you the details so you can arrange transportation and lodging."

"I'm not coming," I said. "Accept it."

"How can I accept it? This is the chance of a lifetime," he said.

"No, *this* is the chance of a lifetime," I said. "To be here in Positano, away from you and all that lunacy."

"Would you come if I told you that there will be a celebrity there?" he asked.

"What celebrity?"

"Filippo Polidori!"

"Who?"

"Filippo Polidori, the deejay and MTV veejay!"

"Andrea—"

"Now he runs his family's restaurant and we're tasting the outrageous vintage Malvasias there."

"You, a veejay, and an old white table wine?" I asked. "Why don't I leave my wife, in her string bikini, and speed right over?"

"Yes, perfect," he said. "Monday."

"I'm not going to raise my voice with my son here next to me," I said. "But I am turning off my phone now." I pushed the power button and listened to the lovely fading of the electronic jingle.

The next day, Sal and I wandered over to the main street for a gelato with whipped cream on top. Stephany and my parents were in a nearby shop buying Lili a cotton dress, and my son and I were sharing a cone when I felt the buzz. I hoped it was someone at my New York office, informing me of some administrative disaster. But it wasn't.

"Changed your mind?" Andrea asked.

"What is wrong with you?" I answered.

"Fine," he said. "I didn't want to tell you because I know you get weird about things like this, but this is not a regular tasting."

"I gathered that," I said.

"Luigi Veronelli has organized this tasting for us," Andrea said. "He asked specifically that you come."

I licked the gelato thoughtfully. Sal, out of concern, put his hand on my arm. I was totally conquered. How, exactly, was I supposed to back out of a tasting arranged by *the* Luigi "Gino" Veronelli, forefather of the Italian quality-wine movement; the man responsible, at least in part, for my livelihood; someone I'd spoken about hundreds, maybe thousands of times, whose works I'd read; who had, without ever meeting me, taught me an immeasurable amount about my life's work? Indeed, it appeared that the great journalist had fallen on hard times, especially if he was subjecting me, a complete stranger, to this bizarre farce of a tasting. But then there was the real kryptonite: Veronelli was almost eighty, and a Neapolitan never says no to an elder.

"So you see why I have no choice?" I said to my family, who had gathered around in the cobblestoned piazza. "I don't want to but he's really old. I'm so, so sorry."

"Well, as we say in Naples: Respect your elders, especially the ones you have respect for," my mother said.

⁊

TWO DAYS LATER, we all drove north to Umbria, the green heart of Italy, a lush central farmland full of grazing sheep and olive groves. I had, as a way to make amends, booked my family in an ancient castle in a village near the hilltop town of Todi, a two-hour drive from Rome. While they stayed by the pool, I would take off for Ancona. And when I returned, we would leave for the airport.

Medieval Castello di Todi, gray and imposing, rested at the top of a small slope, the drive surrounded by uneven cypress trees. A small pack of deer was said to roam the property, but due to the torrential rainstorms that had swept the area, the animals were nowhere in sight. I could make out only, far in the distance, a couple of hearty pink pigs sleeping in the mud.

The castle gates opened automatically and we slithered onto the dirt lane, which had turned into a mustard-colored river of rock, water, and earth. The rain had begun to fall harder, pummeling the land. As the car listed to one side, Sal giggled.

"Want to see something cool, Sali?" I asked. I hit the gas and we began to bump along. He laughed harder. "Want to see something even cooler?" I hit the gas again and the car jumped up the hill, listing. A few seconds later, as the car landed after another hop, I heard a loud crack. Several seconds after that, a repetitive clanging commenced. I peered into the rearview mirror: behind us, an oil slick fanned out. As we reached the castle, the car let out a death rattle and sputtered to a stop.

Stephany looked behind us at the stream of goo exiting the car. "That doesn't seem right," she said.

Who was I to deny the clear existence of a cosmic sign? I called Andrea.

"Game's over," I said.

"Oh, really?" he said. "Let's see."

An hour later, my phone rang. It was Filippo Polidori. "Please forgive me for intruding in this matter," he said. "I hope I'm not disturbing you."

"Not at all," I said.

"We've never met, and I know you are having a difficult time getting here," he said. "Please, let me know if I can do anything to help—really, anything."

"I would sincerely love to come," I said, "but I'm afraid I simply can't."

"Right," Filippo said. There was a brief silence. "Gino is almost seventy-eight and nearly blind," he continued. "He's not well. He gave his word to a friend that he would show these wines to the right people, and Gino is always true to his word. Anyway,

I wouldn't do this if I didn't have to, but what I'm saying, really, is that you need to come. For Gino Veronelli. And I'll do whatever it takes to get you here, so just say the word."

"My car's broken down," I said. "I apologize, but there's no way I can get it fixed by tomorrow."

"Gino is quite weak, but is nonetheless driving almost four hours from Bergamo to meet you, specifically. There will be only you and Andrea there with us. If you couldn't come, it would be quite a shame for Gino."

"That would be a shame," I said.

"Gino has had his eye on you for a long time," Filippo said. "He is committed to seeing you, despite all the obstacles he must overcome, his health being the greatest. Since your obstacle is a car, could I send someone out there to drive you here? You seem like a man who makes things happen. Do you have any other solutions?"

"Don't worry then, Filippo," I said, pressing on my temples with one hand. "I'll figure it out."

"I can't tell you how much I appreciate this," he said. "Gino will be so happy. You have no idea."

The game, as Andrea had known, was not over, not until the old-timer called it.

"I'll see you soon, then," I said.

"I am so looking forward to it," Filippo said.

When we hung up, I started looking for repair shops.

❧

THE NEXT MORNING, I met Andrea in the flat concrete office park outside his market. His hair, as always, was held expertly in place, and his shirt collar was extremely stiff. We climbed into his car and we took off for the Apennines. We were meeting Filippo and Veronelli in a small village in the heart of the mountain range.

"I hope you're happy," I said. "Do you know how impossible it is to get someone to repair a busted oil pan on a Sunday? I spent hours begging people. Begging!"

"Sergio, Sergio, Sergio," Andrea said, shaking his head. "You don't know it now, but you are going to thank me for this one."

We passed stone houses with closed green shutters, rocky tilled farmland, a level field with a lone crow flying above, pastures and forests, and kept going up and up. Eventually the slope was nearly vertical, the bending roads blasted into it, the mountain walls craggy and covered in metal netting to prevent boulders from falling. When we emerged, after an hour of winding around, we came to a relatively smooth area, a succession of towns settled in the middle of the range, punctuated with squares of bright white wheat fields. Below was a massive lake, flat, with pebbly shores, weaving off into the vague distance. Finally we reached the sign for Sassocorvaro, the town in which Filippo resided. If we made it to lunch in twenty minutes, I figured, we'd be done by three, and I could get back to Umbria by nightfall. Andrea pulled off sharply to the side.

"Hungry?" he asked.

"Aren't we on our way to lunch?"

"Well, then, let's get a coffee," he said, and hopped out.

"This is rude," I said. "Veronelli is waiting for us."

"Nothing is quicker than a coffee," he said, and ran into a one-level building with blinking letters above it: BAR. I followed, pushing through the strings of beads hanging in the doorway, and entered the main room, a combination arcade and café. A cluster of teenage boys dressed like Bronx-born rappers were playing darts while at least two dozen old men wearing caps and button-down shirts played cards. Andrea passed by the main counter, where a couple were drinking their coffees, and headed to the back.

"Andrea, if I'm late to meet Veronelli, I'll murder you," I said. "We get our drinks up front."

"Signora!" Andrea said to a stout woman with a bun of silver hair and a crisp pink apron. "Is that a roast pig I see?" Indeed, behind the woman a baby pig was resting in a large open oven. The woman stared impassively at Andrea. "Then cut us up a slice," Andrea said. "That is, if it's not too dry."

"*Dry?*" the woman gasped. "My pigs are never dry. What? You think I bought this beauty at the market? No, we raise them ourselves." She grabbed Andrea's arm firmly and led him to the window. "Right there." Four small pigs, surrounded by a fence, munched on feed in a makeshift farm.

"Well, I'll have to taste it to believe it," Andrea said. "Let's see some proof."

The woman drew a carving knife out of a drawer, approached the pig, stopped it midturn, and sliced off a thick white piece topped with a square of crispy, caramel-colored skin.

"Delicious," said Andrea, plucking it from the knife. "Now, make us up a kilo, would you?"

"*Deficiente,*" I said. "*Stupido.*"

"You said you wanted a coffee!" Andrea said. "A coffee doesn't taste good without some pork!"

"Pork and coffee?" I said. "Plus, lunch is now in fifteen minutes."

"You have a point," Andrea said. He turned to the bald man with thick glasses and thick arm hair next to the woman. "Signore, do you have some wine? Something simple, red, discreet. A communist wine—not like the stuff you sell to the tourists."

Andrea, having dedicated his life to regional cuisine, understood precisely to whom he was speaking. We were in a communist hub, there in Emilia-Romagna—a place in which most people, out of principle, didn't care for cash or luxury. The idea of a fancy and prohibitively expensive wine was outrageous, unethical, and bourgeois, and furthermore, the wine itself was probably disgusting. The good stuff was made by the peasants, for the peasants, and its existence was proof of the widely held belief that access to fine, cheap wine was an unalienable right.

The man pulled a brown ceramic jug out from under the counter. "This," he said, tapping the jug. "I made it last November from my Sangiovese. Thirty-five years, those vines have. Hey, come take a look." He grabbed Andrea's arm as firmly as his wife had and led him to a different window. He motioned to a peak thick with gnarled plants and swung Andrea back around. "Now, taste this," he said, returning to his counter and pouring three glasses, including one for himself.

"*Complimenti,*" Andrea said. "This is excellent."

"A Tuscan once offered me a blank check for my grapes," the man said, leaning closer. "You know what I told him?"

Andrea shook his head.

"I told him to shove his check up his ass! I could have chased the jerk all the way back to Tuscany."

"Those boorish city dwellers," Andrea said.

As I'd already begun drinking the wine—juicy, wet, bright, and delicious—I figured it couldn't hurt to have some pork, too. And while I was at it, I'd taste the salami the *signora* had set out for us. Andrea had the car keys and the directions. As far as hostage situations went, mine was not entirely unpleasant.

"How did you make this amazing stuff?" I asked the couple as I tasted my first piece of salami. It was delicate, fatty, a little soft: perfect.

"If you know how to care for your pigs and how to kill them, you don't need anything else," the man said. "You feed them fresh food, not grains, and when you slaughter them, you sneak up from behind with a gun. They never know what hit them, and they don't have the chance to let out that final blast of adrenaline that toughens the flesh. I put in salt, a clove of garlic, and a splash of white wine. More, and I wouldn't give it to my family." He looked us up and down, and, having decided that we were a worthy audience, leaned closer again. "But I'm really famous for my cheese," he said in a hushed tone. He reached beneath the counter and pulled out a white, waxy hunk. "I make it after the cows give birth, when their milk is richest and fattiest."

"And the calves?" Andrea asked, his napkin tucked into his collar. "What do they drink?"

"The calves?" the man said, handing us each a bit of wax paper spread with the smooth cheese. "Soon enough, they're veal."

❧

A HALF HOUR LATER, we arrived at Ristorante 2000, a white concrete building just off a road curving around the compact mountain town of Sassocorvaro. Its name, in black capital letters, was attached above the entrance arch. Inside, the restaurant was vast and simply decorated. The lobby housed three blue leather armchairs, a potted tree, and a coffee table, and the rest of the decor consisted of white curtains, white tablecloths, a brick-colored marble floor, and pale orange marble columns. Every spot was taken—the place was packed with about a hundred people, all trying to speak over one another, the sound rising in a lunchtime crescendo. There was soup and pasta and meat, bottles of wine, and purses hung on the backs of chairs. And the strangest part was that although everyone was eating, there appeared to be almost no staff, just two waitresses in blue jeans to serve the entire crowd.

Filippo came through a side door. He was in his late twenties, with gelled black hair, a small goatee, and a wide, white smile. He wore tight designer jeans and a red shirt. He threw his hand out to me.

"A very nice spot you have here," I said, gesturing around Ristorante 2000. "How do you do it with so few people?" I imagined a Manhattan lunch joint at this hour, with almost as many servers as customers.

"You haven't seen anything yet," said Filippo. He led me to

the kitchen and opened the door. Inside, two dark-haired women in chef's whites raced around the shining, spotless counters.

"My aunt and mom," said Filippo. "They do everything, including desserts and cleaning. They make the pasta fresh every day, too." In a New York kitchen, a hundred-person clientele required at least a chef, a sous-chef, two dishwashers, two line cooks, one salad maker, and a pastry chef. "Anyway, let's go to my pet project." We left the kitchen and Filippo ushered us out of the main room and through a side door. "This is La Vineria," he said.

La Vineria was Filippo's clear fixation and a labor of love; upon entering, I did not get the impression that Filippo hoped to make a profit off the place. Though it was connected to Ristorante 2000, its external walls were differentiated by color and care. Where the white of Ristorante 2000 ended, the pale yellow of La Vineria began, its name daintily hand-painted on a wooden sign against a lilac-and-leaf motif. Its windows were covered in climbing ivy; its door was flanked by antique barrels. La Vineria was a one-room, one-table establishment that pretended to be a dining area when it was clearly a shrine to wine. Every inch of the walls, illuminated by candelabra and chandeliers and painted a rosy Nebbiolo red, was covered in paraphernalia that Filippo rotated according to his mood: a portrait of Bacchus, god of wine; a hundred wooden labels cut from cartons. There were several colorful framed watercolors by the Piedmontese winemaker Romano Levi, who was famous for his depictions of the round-faced women with braids whom he called *donne selvaggie*, "savage women." There were oil paintings of women draped in leafy emerald vines, of men drinking from pitchers; there was a large collage made of corks, a poster of grapes, a sculpture of a drunken cherub, and a photo of the pope. In one corner, Filippo had placed one of the ancient clay urns that Josko Gravner preferred, and in another he had hung a laminated letter from Veronelli and an overblown black-and-white photograph of them together. The ceiling was tiled with renderings of a gleaming glass of red wine gazed at from above, and every available opening was used to display a bottle: empty bottles fastened to the walls, bottles in glass cases, on shelf after shelf, on counters and side tables.

Filippo had not always been so obsessed. Though his family had owned Ristorante 2000 since 1969, he'd had no interest in wine until he turned eighteen. While working as a veejay in his early twenties, he was approached to host a television show about wine, for young people. While hosting his program, he wrote Veronelli a fan letter. A few weeks later, Veronelli called him.

"*Ciao,*" he said. "When can we get together?"

"Now we're like brothers," Filippo said. "Even though he's almost sixty years older. We talk about women, clothes, all that. We've even gone white-water rafting in Piedmont. He's my best friend. He even once told me he would come live with me but he didn't want to be a burden because he's going blind."

Veronelli was on his way; Andrea had lied to me about the time because he wanted that *porchetta.*

"Why do you think you get along so well?" I asked Filippo.

"Curiosity is our commonality," Filippo said. "He invented a whole new world of thought in this country. He has a degree in philosophy, you know, and he's a poet. I wrote him in the first place because he talks about wine in such a personal way. 'This wine could confront you,' he says. And here he is!" Filippo raced to the door. "The great Gino has arrived," he announced with a talk-show host's boom and vigor.

Veronelli entered, supported on the arm of his assistant, a silent young man with a bowl cut. Veronelli was thin and elderly, and his deep brown eyes searched in vain for a focus point. He had a sympathetic face, a little gaunt in the cheeks, and thinning gray hair. He wore gray slacks and a green button-down shirt, open at the collar.

"Signor Veronelli," I said, "it is an absolute honor to make your acquaintance."

"Come closer to me, Sergio," Veronelli said. I stepped toward him and he grabbed my hand and cupped it in his. "Thank you for coming all this way," he said, his face near mine. "You must call me Gino." He held my hand for a long moment and then we sat down.

As we drank a glass of *spumante,* Veronelli complained about the A1, the pesky and notoriously standstill stretch of road he'd been stuck on for hours. We all nodded, and I thought about my wife stretched out on that lounge chair, holding the baby. I held my neck straight to stop myself from looking at my watch.

Filippo began the formal introductions, Italian style. That means: adequately elaborate. An Italian would say, "John is responsible for the safety and health of our city's inhabitants and also personally helps the tourist economy by providing adequate care of not only our individual but also our collective need to maintain an above-par standard of living." An American would say, "John is a garbage collector."

Therefore, Veronelli, father of the Italian wine renaissance and the most influential wine journalist of our time, had single-handedly carried the torch for quality Italian wines while inventing a language of inimitable poetry and lifting up from the depths many producers of indigenous and obscure drinks. Andrea was a major entrepreneur who responsibly and unfailingly sold the finest supplies to every appropriate restaurant on the Adriatic coast and helped wineries across the country succeed in their mission of producing beautiful products. I was America's most important Italian wine merchant with a client list that included the who's who of both East and West coasts, and I had very kindly made a great journey for this special occasion. And the young man helping Veronelli was a loyal student devoted to the old man's work.

"And the reason we are here," Filippo said, "is to honor a

genius winemaker: Prince Alberico Boncompagni Ludovisi, Prince of Venosa."

"Hey, Filippo, do you have that *brodo* your mother makes?" Veronelli asked.

"The *cappelletti in brodo* my mother makes," Filippo said to me and Andrea. *"Ti spaccano la testa!"*—they split your head open.

"Bravo!" said Veronelli, with a clap of his hands.

"The Prince had an estate outside of Rome," said Filippo. "There, he tilled his own land, without help from any outsiders. He was royal, but he loved nature."

"Is the broth coming?" Veronelli asked. "God, that broth is good."

"Absolutely, Gino," Filippo said, motioning to the waiter. "Soon. So this Prince, he wasn't a normal aristocrat. He was more than a wine enthusiast—"

"Sometimes I like to take a bite of cheese and then eat my cappelletti," Veronelli said.

"Before we taste the wines, let me tell you the story of the Prince," said Filippo.

Call me jaded—Veronelli may have been a great journalist, but he appeared to have gone senile. Had I really abandoned my one vacation in five years to listen to an old man talk about soup? Did I have to suffer some kid's long story only to drink those weird, acidic wines? I sat back and, internally, threw my hands in the air.

"I will begin again," said Filippo. The room grew silent; Veronelli was breaking off some bits of *parmigiano-reggiano*. "In a land not so far from here lives Prince Alberico Boncompagni Ludovisi, the descendant of a thousand-year line of Italian royalty, one that produced two of our popes—Gregory XIII and Gregory XV. The Prince is now confined to a bed, unable to eat or drink much. But he was once one of the world's most gifted winemakers." As the waitress began pouring the wine, Filippo told us the true tale, and it went like this:

When Prince Alberico was a young man, he inherited the family estate, Fiorano, a working farm on the hills outside of Rome. He helped with the harvest of wheat and vegetables, and people in nearby towns purchased the friendly country wine he made. The Prince kept mostly to himself, spending his days alone on his property, behind tall metal gates.

The Prince loved food and wine and devoted much of his time to amassing and tasting great old wines. One day, not long after moving to Fiorano, he tried the most glorious wine he had ever had: a 1946 Biondi Santi Brunello di Montalcino made from grapes grown at Il Greppo. Inspired and exhilarated, the Prince promptly sent a letter to Tancredi Biondi Santi, praising the achievement: "I would describe the wine, in my own way, as a majestic red: severe, masculine, medieval—a *primitivo senese,* to compare it with the school of art from the same region. I hope that a passion for this noblest of wines passes down through your family line forever!"

Flattered, Tancredi, then at the top of his field, visited the Prince, and helped him plant some new vines of his own. The Prince had decided to plant some French varietals on his land, and for that he also requested Tancredi's aid. For the next ten years, until his death, Tancredi assisted the Prince in tending to his vineyards. The Prince set plantings in the dry, windy terrain, forcing the vines to send roots deep into the earth to draw on the salty, mineral-rich volcanic layer below, and every few months, Tancredi traveled to Fiorano to trade tips on caring for the grapes and their juice. They schooled each other in the most complex and intricate techniques of winemaking, and after Tancredi died in 1970, the Prince continued to follow these methods, almost religiously. For his own enjoyment, he made three wines: a red Bordeaux blend; a pure Sémillon, dry in the "Graves" style; and a Malvasia di Candia from indigenous vines he'd preserved on his property.

Thirty years ago, Veronelli had been working on a story about the wines of Lazio. As he was driving through the countryside, he passed a vineyard full of gorgeous, high-quality vines. Curious, he pulled his car over, snuck through the unlocked gates, and was headed toward the bounty to investigate when the Prince, on horseback, a rifle slung over his shoulder, intercepted him.

Veronelli smiled widely. "Gino Veronelli," he said, his hand stretched out. "I was just admiring your plants."

Soon enough, the two were sharing a bottle of the Prince's white wine on the balcony. Though Veronelli had expected something good to drink, he was blown away by what he discovered. "To obtain the Prince's *crus* is practically impossible," he wrote in 1982. "If I lived in Rome, I'd beg for them at his door every morning."

Indeed, prospective buyers weren't exactly dealing with an eager seller. A buyer had to be approved by the Prince personally, yet since the Prince refused to see people face-to-face, his secretary handled everything. The lucky few would be given a specific time to show up at the estate and an exact price—no change would be returned. When the meeting day came, the secretary would show buyers into a cavernous, ancient library, its shelves stuffed with textbooks on farming, agronomy, and enology, light flowing in from tall windows. Then, her shoes tapping on the marble floor, she would exit the room and lock the door from the outside. Buyers, trapped in the room for hours, were forced to thumb through some books on agriculture as they waited. When the secretary returned, the buyers would be escorted to the doorstep, where the wines sat, boxed up and ready to go. The buyers had to load the crates into their cars themselves.

During those years, the only thing that could rival the Prince's love of his wines was his love of his daughter, Francesca. When Francesca got engaged to one of Italy's most successful wine merchants, a man named Piero Antinori—who was in part responsible for the Super Tuscans Solaia and Tignanello—the Prince was devastated, but not because Antinori was merely a *marchese*. "Antinori is an opportunist," he would say despairingly. "*I* am a true winemaker." The couple married on the estate grounds. The Prince shook his head throughout the ceremony; he didn't want Antinori near his grapes. "He's madly in love with his estate," Antinori once delicately observed. "Sometimes when you are so in love, you are also a bit jealous."

After his daughter's wedding, the Prince became even more reclusive. For years, few people in town saw him, and his wines became almost completely unavailable. Once, a villager claimed to have spotted the Prince cutting the grass himself, a straw hat shielding his face from the sun. Rumors that his health was failing circulated around town.

One day in 1998, Veronelli paid the Prince a visit. As he made his way up the drive, he noticed that the once-lush vineyards were now barren plots, the flora ripped from the ground. How had this happened, he asked the Prince. All those practically primeval vines, gone forever.

"I destroyed them myself," the elderly Prince said, his face blank and stoic. "I could not bear the thought that another might mistreat them."

Veronelli returned to Bergamo empty-handed and heart-broken. A few years later he wondered: Perhaps the Prince had just one or two bottles lying around? He needed to experience those wines again. It was worth a try. He asked his young friend Filippo to drive to Fiorano, and to ask if any wine remained. Veronelli gave Filippo a specific set of instructions on how to negotiate with the Prince (Don't take no for an answer; stress that the wines are for Gino Veronelli; and no matter what they say, wait it out), and Filippo set off.

When Filippo arrived at the address he'd been given, he was confused. He seemed to have stumbled upon an abandoned home, a grand crumbling estate, the surrounding land an immense, lonely, windswept plot, alternately overgrown with weeds and pounded down to bare dirt and pebbles. Filippo knocked on the door nonetheless. After several minutes, he heard the sound of shoes on the floor. A woman opened the thick wooden door. To Filippo, she looked like a German *dottoressa,* corpulent, with short black hair, and about seventy years old.

"The Prince is very sick," she said. "He isn't receiving visitors."

"Gino Veronelli sent me," Filippo said. "He's an old friend of the Prince and a great admirer. He's wondering if the Prince might have just a case or two of that Malvasia that he could have."

"As I said, the Prince is sick," the *dottoressa* said. "And the wine is gone, not a bit left."

"Would you please relay the message to him anyhow, then?" Filippo asked. "Gino Veronelli just wants a few bottles to remember the times the two had shared years earlier. I can wait."

"You'd do better to come back tomorrow," the *dottoressa* said. "But don't expect any wine, because there isn't any."

Filippo spent the night in a hotel near the airport in Rome; its curtains stank of cigarette smoke. At the crack of dawn, he navigated the long outer-city streets, past the transvestite prostitutes and Gypsy towns, and traveled out into the countryside, back to Fiorano.

The *dottoressa* appeared again at the door. She led him silently into an antechamber and asked him to take a seat. She then took a seat opposite him and observed him carefully. "I spoke to the Prince," she said. "You cannot have a few bottles."

Filippo slumped in his seat. He had so wanted to do this for Veronelli.

"You can, however, have all of the cases," she said.

"Pardon?" Filippo said.

"You can have no bottles or you can take everything in the cellar," she said. "These are the Prince's orders."

"Can I take a look?" Filippo asked.

"All or none," she said. "You have to decide."

Filippo considered the proposition.

"Mr. Veronelli would have to swear to the Prince that the wines would go to the right people," she added. She presented Filippo with six bottles to bring back to Veronelli and wished him a safe trip.

Filippo traveled back to Bergamo with the half-dozen Fiorano Malvasias in dusty, unmarked, clear bottles. On his way, he stopped to see an old friend in Tuscany. He opened a Fiorano and they tasted it together.

"Oxidized," Filippo said. "Unusual, lacks fruit, way too old."

"Don't waste your time with this stuff," his friend, the owner of an estate, said.

Disappointed, Filippo continued north, past Milan, into the center of Lombardi, and on to Bergamo, where Veronelli was waiting. Filippo carried the five bottles into Veronelli's house and they sat down.

"Open them," Veronelli directed. "Let's taste."

Filippo obliged, but he wasn't too enthusiastic. Veronelli could see it. They began with a '75. Veronelli closed his eyes, and his face glowed. "I'm sorry, but it's just so old," Filippo said. "I'm not getting it."

Veronelli looked at him. "Filippo," he said, "if you find a person of ninety with great culture, who has lived a remarkable life but has trouble speaking, or forgets often because of his age, would you judge the person for that?

"If you drank a '71 Brunello today, not knowing anything of that noble vintage, you would send it back because it has so many defects. Today, we have a crisis because people are searching for perfection, but those who work the earth cannot possibly find perfection. This is the limit of modernity—the conception of wine as something like a car, like a computer. When you use technicalities, when you analyze the wine only to pick it apart, you destroy it. Wine is not water, it's not survival. It's a long tale. You have to search for it."

Filippo sat back. During that evening, Veronelli taught Filippo to transform his ideas. Filippo saw, soon enough, that these wines were some of the best he'd ever had.

"I was struck by the impeccable acidity, the remarkable minerality," Filippo recalled. "They had seemed simple, but when I looked deeper, I saw that they had huge personalities."

The next day, Veronelli accepted the Prince's offer. The two discussed the details of the deal. The ailing Prince explained he could not survive the thought that his wines might be consumed lazily, by people unable to appreciate them. He had been moved by Veronelli's early love for the wines and trusted that Veronelli understood that they were still in their infancy: young, mostly from 1985—when the Prince stopped selling them—through 1995, when he razed his vineyards. Veronelli was to guarantee the Prince that these wines would not fall into the wrong hands. Veronelli, the Prince knew, did not go back on his word.

☙

"SO HERE WE ARE TODAY," Filippo said. The waiter set down a platter in front of each of us: a lightly fried whole egg, covered with a fondue of pecorino and local cheese. A few paper-thin slices of summer truffle sat atop delicately. I plunged my fork in and the bright orange yolk swirled out. The waiter gave us all our glasses of wine.

"That Malvasia is singing out of its glass," said Veronelli. *"Sentiamo i vini!"* Let's listen to the wines! He picked up his goblet, and we all followed suit.

Filippo presented the wines: six Malvasia di Candia—from '77, '79, '80, '82, '83, and '85—and six Sémillon—from '71, '73, '77, '80, '81, and '83. As he moved his hand across the lineup, I noticed something odd. Any old white I'd ever known had grown darker with age. Oxygen usually rusts wine over time. But these wines, pale yellow and glistening, appeared to have grown lighter with age. The oldest of them was brilliant; the youngest, dull. *Well, this is awkward,* I thought. *That was a nice story they told, but soon enough, they'll realize their mistake.*

"Are the oldest ones bright?" Veronelli asked Filippo. "Filippo, tell me what you see."

"The '71 is the brightest one I've ever seen," Filippo said. "The '83 is quite dark, though."

"Oh, it'll shine soon," said Veronelli. "They always do!"

We started to taste. I intended to smell all of the wines first, eliminate the inferior ones, and taste the superior ones. I pulled the first glass of Malvasia, the deepest and youngest, to my nose.

I inhaled and felt it: a twitch in my arm, a tightness in my throat. The wine was alive. Everything faded from the room—the background noise, the glasses clinking, the tones of conversation, all color and movement. We were served the *cappelletti in brodo,* delicate yellow pockets filled with veal, cheese, lemon, nutmeg, and cinnamon, closed by hand, and swimming in a clear broth. I picked up the next wine and pushed the inhale back out of my mouth, perplexed: I certainly hadn't expected that. I smelled, and knew it was there, that quality; then the next, and the next, and so on. When I reached the Sémillon, I took in the scent—the same experience, but a different smell.

No Malvasia has ever had such an effect on me, I thought. *And since when was Sémillon so gracious and well bred?* The Sémillon didn't remotely resemble a French wine, either; it was so obviously Italian, with the taste and smell of the Lazian earth within it.

"Where did you get these?" I asked Filippo.

"The Prince's cellar, every one of them," he said. "When Gino said we'd take them, we thought we were talking about a few hundred. But when we started going through the *cantina,* there were twelve thousand. I have a photo."

He showed me the picture. He had entered through a small

black door low in the ground, into the dusty stone basement, barely lit by a couple of dull lightbulbs. But the camera flash revealed the room: bottles piled atop one another in perfect pyramids, covered with a thick blanket of white mold. It looked like an ocean floor—cold, blurry. Lichen ran through the black cracks in the stone walls. The fermentation room contained big chestnut wood barrels, nearly invisible behind the inches of mold. Filippo and a team of five people had spent two years moving, cleaning, and rebottling the wines.

I went back to my wine and continued to smell it. I put my head back and eased the first gulp into my mouth. I could hear my heart beating and feel my skin tighten. The excitement got to me, again and again; each wine was distinct, strange, beautifully flawed.

"In the eighties, Gino wrote about these wines," said Polidori, pulling a pile of newspaper clippings from the envelope. He read: "I can only imagine that the '77 Malvasia will, in twenty years, be even more glorious than it is today. The '71 Sémillon will last more than twenty-five years. The '80 Malvasia is just beginning to show its inherent character; it will develop for the next thirty years."

I looked at Veronelli, his smiling face, his long nose taking in the fragrance of the Sémillon. He couldn't see me watching him, so I stared. Now I knew what this meant for him. This was his homecoming, the reunion of dear old friends; he was thirty years younger and in another town, with another person. And then he was happily here with us, too.

Filippo turned to me. "Can you describe these wines?" he asked.

I couldn't. The wines were the best I'd ever had, but there were no words for them. I wanted to grab them, jump in my car, drive them over to every winemaker I'd ever met, one by one, and scream, "Wake up, before it's too late! With all your consultants and machinery, you've never made anything close to this, disinfecting away the mold, filtering the life out of your wines, robbing from every modern consumer the chance to drink wines that are still growing!" I wanted to take off with the bottles down the mountain road and personally deliver them to every journalist who had ever implied that Italians didn't know how to make wine.

Of course, stealing, yelling, and speeding wildly away didn't seem to be the right approach. Instead I waited patiently, no longer checking my watch. Had we been brought here merely to taste these wines, or might we be allowed to buy some? Would Veronelli interview me? Might he deem me suitable for the task of placing these wines with the right people? I wanted the wines badly. I would have done anything for them. I felt like a child hoping to be picked for a team; I feared that I might literally drop dead of sorrow if I was rejected.

But Veronelli didn't want to interview me. He wanted to talk about my family. My wife was from Alaska? How hilarious! And how was my baby daughter? And my little son? When the hand-cut tagliatelle arrived, he ate contentedly, and told us more stories about the Prince and his wines.

"I remember that man in his cellar," he said. "He was a true alchemist, breaking it all apart. He was really down there, surrounded by that white mold and darkness, searching in his wine, in his fruit, for some spirit, some essence, for the purest element."

He finished every bite of his *filetto di Marchigiana,* made from a special regional cow, large and white, which fed only on local grass. At the end of the meal, Veronelli spent a half hour complimenting Filippo's aunt and mother. Then he shook hands with everyone, told us he hoped we could do it again sometime, and left, leaning on the young man's arm as he went.

"What did I tell you?" said Andrea, on our way back to Ancona. "Admit it, I was right all along."

"Are those wines for sale?" I asked. "Can we get them?"

"Probably not," he said. "But people are unpredictable. Tell me how much we can pay and where the wines will end up. I'll see."

❧

I DROVE BACK FROM ANCONA to Todi at night, through the winding Apennines in the pitch black, the rock lit only by the moon. All the while, I thought about those gorgeous wines, about the Prince, about Veronelli's intense devotion. At midnight, I pulled over to the side of the road, and, looking down at the black sea below, called Andrea and gave him an answer. Eight months later, a thousand bottles packed in brown cardboard boxes showed up at Andrea's doorstep; eleven thousand bottles arrived at mine.

The lunch was Veronelli's last business meeting. He died two months later.

I remembered him putting his spoon to the broth with almost childlike pleasure, and I thought of the moment, right at the start, when he cupped my hand in his, and held it tight for a while.

"Why didn't he ask me or Andrea anything about what we thought of the wines?" I said to Filippo. "Do you know?"

"What could you teach him about the wines?" Filippo said. "He knew all he needed to know about them; he was looking for something else. Gino was an empath. He didn't have to interview you to understand you. He may have been nearly blind, but he said to me the night before, 'I want to see them eat. I want to see the kind of faces they have. Then we'll decide.'"

EPILOGUE

TWO YEARS AFTER my Italian adventure, I flew to San Luis Obispo, California, with Stephany. Some organizers of a wine-and-charity event called the Central Coast Wine Classic had invited me to deliver a lecture, but more important, my friends Ed and Mary had promised me a barbecue on the range if I headed out west. For this, Stephany and I were making our way down a long, curving dirt road that cut through lush green meadows and dry yellow grain fields.

Ed and Mary were ranchers through and through, a duo that can be best described as "a good ol' boy and a good ol' girl." A smiling, tough-as-nails couple in work boots, they oversaw Rancho Sisquoc, a thirty-seven-thousand-acre combination cattle farm and vineyard. They were waiting for us at the end of the road in the midst of a smattering of white one-level houses. In the distance, cowboys on sweating quarter horses were herding hundreds of cows to pasture.

"You know, Sergio," Ed said, coming toward me, all 260 pounds of him, "I wouldn't be lying to you if I said you were the best Italian I ever met." He pulled me close and slapped my back. Mary, stout and apple-cheeked, gave Stephany a bear hug.

"The barbecue is all fired up," Mary said. "Come on back."

We followed them to their backyard and sat down as Ed laid five thick steaks on the grill.

"Say all you want about spaghetti, but for some serious beef, you'll never get better than these here beauties," said Ed.

Mary came out of the house with a bottle of Quintarelli Valpolicella in one hand and wine glasses in the other.

"This stuff just makes me weak," she said, uncorking the bottle and filling the glasses with deep red liquid. "It's so damn sexy I feel like I'm being seduced right in front of my husband! You Italians are *bad*!" She and Ed let out loud, whooping laughs.

Ed and Mary weren't likely Quintarelli fans, at first appearance. They were, after all, two native midwesterners who, back twenty years ago when Rancho Sisquoc was just a fledgling cattle ranch, lived on their own in the middle of the wilderness, driving their truck to the nearest town twice a year for provisions. But when they'd settled on the ranch, they'd found a vineyard that the previous manager had planted. Little by little, they began to study winemaking. They read about pruning and planting, about exposures, ventilation, growing, pressing, aging. They invited experts, they traveled to tastings, and, with time, they were introduced to all types of wines—Californian, French, Italian, Australian. These two once-novice Ohioans had discovered that they liked Quintarelli wines—those esoteric, complicated, magical drinks—the best of all. They always brought out a bottle when I dropped by.

As Mary was pouring the Quintarelli, the winemaker Steve Clifton, at whose wedding in Friuli Stephany and I had wept hysterically, arrived from the Central Coast Wine Classic auction. Steve was wearing a wide-brimmed leather hat and bearing some wines from his Palmina operation, an estate that grew only Italian varietals on the Santa Barbara hills.

"Sergio, you should have been there to see what happened to your donation," Steve said, setting down the bottles on the table. I had given a case of the Prince's wines to the charity auction. "That Malvasia you gave sold for more than any Italian white ever has at auction."

"That Malvasia made by that nutty prince?" said Ed. "Well, congratulations, Mr. Esposito. I myself would like to drink that wine one day." He began setting the grilled steaks on plates. Mary ran in for some roasted vegetables and doled them out, and we gathered around the picnic table on the patio and raised our glasses. Everyone looked at me expectantly.

"To my father, America, for providing me with opportunity and fortune, and a sense of what's right," I said. "And to my mother, Italy, for teaching me how to feel, and for always reminding me that there is nothing more valuable in life than being gathered around a table with my friends and family."

"*Salute!*" Steve said. We all clinked glasses, and then drank our wine, looking out at the long, flat range, dotted with cows and bordered by the gentle green hills far away.

If there was ever a time to have hope for Italian wine, this was it, I thought. These Americans—and the Americans at the Central Coast Wine Classic, and apparently legions of other Americans scattered around the country—had come to understand its value. They appreciated its diversity, its personality. It was a strong start to what I hoped could become a worldwide trend, a love for what is real and natural, for what is strange and true, for things made honestly, with a respect for the land, for imagination, for the beauty inherent in tradition.

By traditional wine, I don't mean wines made by a Luddite without a cell phone. I don't expect all producers to bury their juice in the ground or bottle by lunar cycle. Prince Alberico Boncompagni Ludovisi had made wine from grapes that didn't originally come from his region. He may not have used temperature control, but he did use tractors. He wasn't inflexible or lacking in initiative, and he was highly innovative. But he was traditional because the spirit in which he made wine was highly traditional. He believed that wine is alive, ever changing, a source of inspiration, a work of art. He always focused first on the *materia prima,* the material given to him by the earth, and last—or not at all—on cash, popularity, fame. He truly loved his work, and he felt a need to do it. And that was how he made one of the most soulful, life-altering wines that I have ever tasted. This was what Americans were learning to appreciate, and this was all I could ever hope for.

In the early twentieth century, Americans experienced Italy in the form of desperate, hungry southern immigrants flooding the country, begging for jobs. In the 1940s, Americans saw a fascist state they'd fought against, devastated by war. But today they've begun to explore and understand, maybe for the first time, everything that Italy has to offer. They've begun to connect to a sense of history that extends beyond that of America. They've begun to search for and find the Italian way—a way that derives its power and beauty from a rich history and an unwavering sense of the past—on a road in Piedmont, on a beach in Sicily, heading toward a farm in Tuscany, and now, even at a picnic table on a cattle ranch in the middle of sunny California, U.S.A.

ACKNOWLEDGMENTS

A heartfelt thank-you to my wife, Stephany, whose beauty will forever inspire me. I love you. To my gorgeous son, Sali Boy, and beautiful daughter, Lili Pie, for brightening each of my days; to my caring parents, Alma and Ciro, for leaving all they knew so we might know more; to my *fratelli* Salvatore, Anna, and Stefano, thank you for your love and protection; to Zia Maria, Sue, and Pino, for joining and supporting us; to all my wonderful nephews and nieces, Nicholas, Gabriella, Jennifer, Alessandro, Sabrina, Vincenzo, Gianluca, Isabella, and Sergio; to *le famiglie* Tschantret and Esposito, for all you've shared with me; to Margherita, Sandra, and Daniela Tschantret, for showing Justine Napoli's *anima e cuore;* to Paolo Rivelli, for your great insights into the south; to my best friends Maish Freedman, for bringing so much color into my world and always building up my confidence and then ripping it down for a good laugh, and Scott Conant, for filling the void when my brothers are far; to my dear New York family, Allison and Paolo Domeneghetti, Dino Tantawi, Isabel and Michael Volpe, tita Jaz and tita Joy; to my friend and partner, Perry Porricelli, without whose help I would never have had my business; to Gildardo Lopez, whom I love like a brother, for helping me build my dream; to Chris Deas, Julie Lee, and the rest of the gang at IWM, past and present, for your superb work and commitment; to my agent and friend Patricia van der Leun, who more than anyone is responsible for the existence of this book—you held me true to my wish, and for that I will always be thankful; to my cowriter, Justine van der Leun, the little sister I never wanted but am awfully glad I have, for putting on paper what only my heart knew; to my publisher and friend Steve Rubin, for believing in me; to my editor, Charles Conrad, for having the vision and for trusting in me; to my *fratello,* Carlo Maggi, for sharing your passions and emotions; to Tamar Davir Schulte, for helping me to literally find my soul; to the Federico family, for picking us up when we fell; and, lastly, to Franco Mancuso, for giving me a place to sleep when I most needed one. The love and generosity of each and every one of you have enriched my life and made this book possible.

© Tony Floyd

SERGIO ESPOSITO moved to the United States from Naples with his family at the age of six. After years of studying, tasting, and traveling through the great vineyards of Europe and the United States, Sergio realized that he most enjoyed the wines of his native land. Shortly thereafter, he decided to make Italian wine his specialty and conceptualized Italian Wine Merchants, a wineshop devoted exclusively to collectors and enthusiasts interested in obtaining and learning about Italy's best. Sergio lives in New York City with his wife, Stephany, their son, Salvatore, and their daughter, Liliana.

ABOUT THE TYPE

The text of this book is set in Legacy Serif, a typeface created by Ronald Arnholm and released in 1993 by ITC (International Typeface Corporation). ITC Legacy is a revival design inspired by the Venetian Old Style types by the fifteenth-century printer and publisher Nicolas Jensen. Named after the first roman typefaces that appeared in Venice in 1470, Venetian typefaces were initially designed to emulate the handwriting of Italian Renaissance scholars. Characterized by their clarity and legibility, these typefaces were created as book type and still serve that function well today.